RUN!

THE AMAZING RACE

DAVID S. PAYNE

RUN! THE AMAZING RACE
Copyright © 2012 by David S. Payne

Unless otherwise indicated, all Scripture quotations are taken from the Holy Bible, New Living Translation, copyright © 1996, 2004, 2007 by Tyndale House Foundation. Used by permission of Tyndale House Publishers, Inc., Carol Stream, Illinois 60188. All rights reserved.

ISBN:978-1-77069-738-6

Printed in Canada

Word Alive Press
131 Cordite Road, Winnipeg, MB R3W 1S1
www.wordalivepress.ca

WORD ALIVE PRESS
Just Write!

MIX
Paper from
responsible sources
FSC   FSC® C016245
www.fsc.org

Library and Archives Canada Cataloguing in Publication
Payne, David, 1950-
    Run! : the amazing race / David Payne.
ISBN 978-1-77069-738-6

    1. Self-actualization (Psychology)--Religious aspects--
Christianity. I. Title.
BV4598.2.P393 2012   248.4   C2012-905997-8

TABLE OF CONTENTS

INTRODUCTION

BUILT TO RUN

I HAVE LIVED MOST OF MY LIFE IN AN URBAN SETTING SURROUNDED by malls, driving on busy streets, waiting at stoplights, tuning in to traffic reports, and listening to sirens. People running in this direction. Racing in that direction. I have often wondered where everyone is going. The city is like a large magnet, drawing people from all over the world. Opportunity. A new beginning. Glamour. Excitement. Curiosity.

My roots are quite different. I was raised in a rural community. Farms. Maple sugar. Small school. Rural hospitality. And my spirit still draws from those roots. I grew up in Northern Ontario. I was drawn to the solitary places. The wilderness. I enjoyed walking and running along the isolated ridges of the Canadian Shield. Exploring a trail that led somewhere. Skirting a lonely lake, watching for whatever wildlife might make its silent exit from my intrusion into its terrain. Sitting on a beaver dam waiting for a moose to wander out from under the canopy of black spruce and cedars to stand and stare back at me from a marshy patch of water lilies. Paddling a canoe up a remote creek and portaging into some unexplored wetland. Sometimes I felt like I was living in the wrong period of time. It was not difficult for me to imagine the nomadic hunters of a time past wandering and running these same paths.

On clear, moonlit nights, my brothers and I would regularly decide to strap on the snowshoes and trek out into the woods, following the shadows illuminated only by the brightness above. Often, the night air was filled with the barking of a pack of young wolves as they played, unaware of our presence. They yapped for the pure joy of it, greeting one another in a ceremony much like a group hug. Then there was that moment when the silence was broken by the howl of a lone timber wolf. A long, evocative, lingering, plaintive howl. It would always rivet my attention. One could not listen without shuddering. It was a solemn moment.

The wolf has always captivated my mind. A most fascinating and magnificent creature. The keeper of the wild. Strong. Swift. An extraordinary sense of smell. Finely tuned ears. An amazing ability to communicate. But to see the wolf pack running across a snow-covered field is an image one never forgets. The wolf is built to run. It runs to survive.

I remember coming out of the barn one winter night after having completed the chores and bedded down the animals. As my friend and I stepped out into the frosty air, we heard the chilling howls of a pack of timber wolves just over the rise of a hill. We had spent that day at the slaughterhouse and had dumped the entrails of our work in the middle of the field, so we were not surprised at what we were now hearing. The wolves' sharp sense of smell had allured them to dinner. From miles away, their pad-cushioned paws carried them across the crusted snow to where their noses led them. It has been said that the wolf is kept fed by his feet.

We walked softly to the summit of the hill. The snow was deep but manageable. We crawled on our bellies over the crest, keeping our heads low so as not to be spotted. The full moon cast a blue hue across the snow, exposing the pack as it devoured the spoils. We watched in rapt attention. Transfixed. The larger wolves were gorging themselves drunk with meat. Others further down in the pecking order stood watching from the periphery, waiting their turn. Scouts circled the preoccupied pack looking out for any sign of intrusion.

Suddenly, we were detected. A sharp bark. A quick command. I don't know how it was understood, but the message was clear. Heads bolted upright. The entire pack began to run as one body. My mind took the photograph. I can still see it. The speed. The ease. The strength.

The agility. Their black silhouettes like ghosts running across the snow against the backdrop of a full moonlit night until they disappeared up into the shadowy hardwood hills.

Yes, the wolf is built to run. God has given it the anatomy to run. Its front legs hang close together, almost as if pressed into the animal's narrow chest. The knees turn inward and the paws turn outward so that the front feet swing in, breaking the path for the hind feet to follow exactly. When wolves are trotting, they leave a neat, single line of tracks, giving them an advantage when trekking over difficult terrain or through deep snow. Thanks to the way the Creator has built them, wolves can run with grace and efficiency at 60 to 70 kilometres per hour when need demands it. And they regularly cover an average of 15 to 25 kilometres each day. That's a half marathon every day.

There is a certain mystique about running. Wolves running across the tundra. Horses galloping around the track. A cheetah making a lightning dash across the open grasslands, pursuing its prey at 115 kph. It is another creature built for running. It can accelerate to 100 kph in just three seconds. Special pad paws. Large nostrils and lungs for quick air intake. A long agile body streamlined over light bones. A tail that functions as a rudder and a spine that performs like a spring for its powerful back legs. Cut the video down to slow motion and you see every muscle working. Straining. Pulsating. Rippling.

Man is also built to run. God has given us the anatomy to run. Especially to endure for long distances. Many creatures can run faster for a short distance. But ancient hunters recognized that, while they could not compete with the swiftness of the deer, they could outrun it, outdistance it. If the pursuer stayed on the trail of the deer long enough, he could overcome and eliminate its speedy advantage. By day's end, the hunter would be standing over his exhausted prey.

In centuries past, running was key to man's survival. Whether it was for the hunt or on the battlefield, for fight or flight, one's legs were as important a part of one's anatomy as the brain. Geronimo, the legendary Chiricahua warrior who led the last Indian resistance against American westward expansion, survived by the tactic of hit and run. Young Apache boys were taught to run and run and run. Running meant survival against odds much greater than themselves. It was Geronimo who said, "No one is your friend but your legs. Your legs are your friends." When General Nelson Miles was dispatched to pursue Geronimo's small band, the disparity was stunning. Miles commanded 9,000 American and Mexican soldiers to hunt and chase down 39 Apache fugitives. They did not succeed in capturing one. There were two primary reasons, other than Geronimo's brilliance. His two legs.

God has not only created us with a body that is designed to run, but, when it comes to living life, He has given us the spirit to run. There are numerous places in the Bible where we are commanded to run. Challenged to run. "...let us run with endurance the race God has set before us" (Hebrews 12:1). What motivated me to write this book is the sad reality that too many people run the race of life well below their potential. Too many begin well but fail to finish well. They have been given the wonderful gift of life to unwrap, but it sits like an unopened package on the shelf as time rolls by. I witness many runners slowing down. Settling for the mediocre. The uninspiring. The average. They feel the pain of the run but not the exhilaration of it. They become quickly discouraged. Slowly dismayed. Easily distracted. Gradually sidetracked. They live aimlessly and run on empty. But God did not put you here to simply exist. He put you here to flourish.

In this book, we are going to journey together and examine life's most amazing race. My desire is that this book will encourage, challenge, and inspire you to participate, endure, enjoy, thrive, and go the distance. Join me. Let's run!

ONE

HITTING THE WALL

THE BADWATER™ ULTRAMARATHON IS CONSIDERED BY MOST RUNNERS to be the most difficult, debilitating footrace in the world. The route treks through California's Death Valley, the lowest, driest, hottest piece of real estate in North America. The runners follow the centre white line along a scorching ribbon of asphalt for 217 kilometres (135 miles). They begin their endurance run 282 feet below sea level and climb 13,000 feet up Mount Whitney, which boasts the highest summit in the contiguous United States. Temperatures reach a withering 54 degrees Celsius (130°F).

Mingling at the starting line in 2005 were runners from all over the world. They had qualified to compete in Badwater. A dream come true. Standing somewhat aloof from the rest of the competitors was a young man, eyes focused forward, deep in thought, contemplating the outcome of the next 24 hours. He wore a white sun suit. His long hair was knotted inside a French Foreign Legion cap. Scott Jurek was considered to be the best ultramarathon runner in the world.

As a lad, Scott had always enjoyed running but had never had much success on the competitive level. His earliest memories on the cross-country trails were following in the dust of other runners, having to endure their taunting and harassment. He was known as the "Jerker," and the ultimate disaster was to ever be beat by the Jerker. He was always trying to catch up.

Life at home was difficult. He was the oldest of three children. His mother was diagnosed with multiple sclerosis when he was just a young boy. As a result, Scott's father had to work most of the time. Scott looked after his mother and two other siblings by cleaning the house, managing the home, and keeping the family together. As Scott got older, he longed to escape. To run as far away as possible. And that's where he found his escape. Running. And not just any running. Ultrarunning.

He became determined never to run in anyone's dust again. He developed the capability to push harder and harder through any intimidation that threatened him. "Scott stumbled upon the most advanced weapon in the ultrarunner's arsenal: instead of cringing from fatigue, you embrace it. You refuse to let it go. You get to know it so well, you're not afraid of it anymore."[1]

Early in the race, Scott seemed to lag. Two other runners were ahead of him and seemed to be increasing the distance between. By mile 72, the lead runner, Mike Sweeney, was running a full ten miles ahead of Ferg Hawke, running second. Scott Jurek was a distant third. The combination of heat and wind was like running into the blast of a jet engine. Scott dropped into a giant cooler filled with ice and lay there until his lungs could take it no longer. He got out and began to roast again.

At mile 60, Scott began to vomit and shake. At one point, he dropped to his knees on the pavement. Then he collapsed. His team gathered around him, but no one helped him. Everyone knew that Scott's inner voice was most persuasive. His mind began to taunt him: "You're not even halfway. There are two runners ahead of you. It's hopeless. You're done!" He had hit the wall. The voice persisted. "The only way you can win is to pretend you've just wakened from a good night's sleep and then run the next 80 miles faster than you have ever run them in your life."

Scott lay on the asphalt like a corpse for about ten minutes. The sun blazed down, defying him to get up. But he did. He dragged himself to his knees. He rose slowly onto one leg. Then the other. Like a resurrected body, he stood for a minute. One last opportunity to think things through. He began to walk. Then to shuffle. Then to run. He ran, and ran, and ran. The worse the wall looked, the harder he pushed. He embraced the fatigue and the pain. He ran through the wall, pressing forward with increasing strength, eventually passing the other two runners and shattering the Badwater record with a time of 24:36:08.

THE WALL

"Hitting the wall" is a running term. It identifies that moment in a long-distance run when the runner can go no further. Something hits the shutdown button in the brain. The left side of the brain screams, "Stop!" Some runners call it the "fire-breathing dragon." Others label it "the Beast." The runner is filled with an overwhelming sense of despair. There is an irresistible impulse to just turn one's back on a dream and walk away. The athlete's world has collapsed. Runners often become disoriented. Their reasoning powers are sometimes reduced to the level of a toddler. Focus blurs, strength withers and hope fades.

What causes the legs of a strong runner to turn to jelly, and then to a puddle of water on the road? Bottom line: the waste products and toxins in the body build up in the muscles faster than they can be eliminated. The muscles need food, and the body's preferred fuel is carbohydrate. That's why runners often fuel up the night before the race on a big plate of pasta. Then, during the run they snack on such things as carb gels, bread, fruit or candy. As the heart rate increases, the muscles begin to feel overwhelmed. The body burns away the carbs, breaking them down into sugar, or glycogen, producing energy. Carbs are like rocket fuel, good for short-range energy. But as the glycogen levels drop within the muscles, the toxins build, the mind fogs up, the eyes glass over, the skin pales, and the body begins to crash. One confronts the Beast.

A physiological shift begins in the body. At about the 30-kilometre mark, the body shifts from burning carbs to burning fat. Now, we all have an almost unlimited store of fat. Even the skinniest person stores about 600 miles of fat fuel. The fat fuel will get you through to the finish, but it burns slower than carbs. Less efficient. More like a furnace than a rocket. During this physiological shift from burning carbs to burning fat, the runner experiences no energy and complete despair. It triggers the wall. The challenge is to get through the wall.

3

Dehydration is the other factor. One needs water. But the runner needs more than water. Salt, potassium, and minerals called electrolytes are essential components that give a body vitality and strength. The further a runner goes, the more profusely the electrolytes are sweated out of the body. The body needs to be replenished continually. Runners will swallow salt tablets in water and gulp sports drinks methodically and consistently to give back to the body the nutrients it loses.

Gatorade* is a favourite. Named after the Florida Gators football team, the story is told that when researchers were searching for a drink that would give effective and potent replenishment to players' bodies, they dressed the Gator players in wet suits. After playing, the sweat was extracted from the suits and analyzed. From this analysis, they formulated a drink that contained the right amounts of potassium, chloride, sodium, and sugar to refresh the body and counter the wall. Sounds more like drinking sweat to me.

BREAKING AT THE WALL

A little while ago, I wrote a book entitled *Hitting the Wall: Finding Perspective When Life Stops Working*. Hitting the wall is as much a reality to the course of life as it is to the cross-country trail. The wall is an inevitable component of the race God has given us to run. A necessary ingredient in the journey of faith. It is not a pleasant time in your journey. It is a painful period in your life when you are immobilized by such unwelcome friends as brokenness, failure, and confusion. It is unavoidable and, yes, compulsory. A compulsory course in the school of spiritual growth.

God will allow you to hit the wall in order to bring you to the end of yourself. He allows you to arrive at the point of helplessness. You lie on the asphalt crippled by your infirmity or look in the mirror and come face to face with your humanity. Brokenness is the place where you are spilled out. It is the place where you let go. It is the moment of truth. A crisis of faith. Where is God? It is the moment of decision. Have my body, mind, and spirit reached the point of total drain and exhaustion? Is my tank empty? Do I have to stop? Can I go on? Do I want to go on?

Some of the Bible's best were exposed to the wall. People who encountered the Beast. Joseph hit the wall. A wall of betrayal, rejection, and injustice. Elijah hit the wall. A wall of overwhelming depression and dejection. John, the Immerser, hit the wall. Jesus said that John was the greatest of people who had ever lived. He introduced Christ to the world. Yet later, as he sat despondent behind the heavy iron door of King Herod's dungeon in the fortress of Machaerus, with death looming before him, he questioned whether Jesus was truly the Messiah they had been waiting for. The disciple Peter hit the wall. The same Peter who had witnessed the transfiguration of Jesus and saw Him in His glory. This was the same Peter who had confessed that Jesus was the Christ, the Son of the living God. Then, at the trial of Jesus, as Peter's world seemed to be imploding, he denied that he had ever known Jesus.

The apostle Paul wrote about the wall. *"We are pressed on every side by troubles, but we are not crushed. We are perplexed, but not driven to despair. We are hunted down, but never abandoned by God. We get knocked down, but we are not destroyed"* (2 Corinthians 4:8–9). Yes, the wall experience threatens to crush you. Something in your life today may be pressing you into a narrow, constrictive place. The perplexity, pain, and despair are intense and escalating.

FLOODWATERS

The Psalms often speak about the reality of the wall experience in the life of the believer. It is not the exception; it is the norm. In Psalm 124, David wrote about *"waters engulfing," "torrents overwhelming," "raging waters overwhelming our very lives."* He felt trapped by crushing odds. I remember at one time hiking in the Dead Sea escarpment on the east side. The Dead Sea is the lowest location on the face of the earth, sitting 1,300 feet below sea level. It is hot and dry. The parching dryness can lure the unsuspecting traveller into its suffocating stranglehold within hours. But there is another adversary, unforeseen and lethal, that awaits the unwary hiker. Floodwaters. More people are killed in the desert by drowning than all other causes put together.

Sudden heavy rains in the mountains become rivers that, within hours, transform the dry wadis into torrents of swirling water cascading down through the hardened gullies. The traveller can unexpectedly find himself trapped, confronting a wall of water and mud raging toward him that quickly envelops and drowns him. This is the picture in the Psalmist's mind when he writes that *"the waters would have engulfed us; a torrent would have overwhelmed us"* (Psalm 124:4). *"Save me, O God, for the floodwaters are up to my neck. Deeper and deeper I sink into the mire; I can't find a foothold"* (Psalm 69:1–2).

Sometimes you feel like you have been abandoned. The psalmist continued, *"I am exhausted from crying for help; my throat is parched. My eyes are swollen with weeping, waiting for my God to help me"* (Psalm 69:3). I believe that God waits because He wants you to understand that He is much more than One who merely comes when you call; He is there all the time. *"I waited patiently for the Lord to help me, and He turned to me and heard my cry. He lifted me out of the pit of despair, out of the mud and the mire. He set my feet on solid ground and steadied me as I walked along"* (Psalm 40:1–2). Life is not a sidewalk. It is a difficult path. Sometimes we think that if we pray enough, God will pave the path. But He doesn't. He has purpose in difficult paths. He has purpose in floodwaters. He has purpose in the walls of swirling water and mud that unexpectedly engulf you. He lifts you up. He breathes life into the powerless. His presence fills. His hold is firm. His peace overwhelms. His timing is perfect. His provision satisfies. His strength empowers. His life rejuvenates and restores.

Brokenness puts your heart in a better place. It is the place where you discover the reality of God in a whole new way. The place where you learn that God is more than a Helper; He is the Source of Life. J.E. Conant wrote, "Christian living is not our living with Christ's help, it is Christ living His life in us."[2] Brokenness is the place of surrender to Him. The place where He infuses life into His surrendered child. The place where God begins to put you back together. The point where you get up and begin to run again. This is the juncture that divides those who finish the race from those who don't.

Pushing Through the Wall

My friend Craig was running another marathon. He had notched many successful runs on his record. He felt fit and invincible. He had enjoyed a big pasta dinner the night before to fill up his energy tank with carbohydrate fuel. It was a Sunday morning and the run seemed easy. That is, until he hit the 36-kilometre point. He began to feel nauseous, like he was running in a tunnel. He had felt some pain earlier in his left knee. But now he suffered the excruciating pain of muscle spasms extending from his lower back down to his toes. His muscles contracted in the back and front of his legs, immobilizing him.

But even more immobilizing pain threatened his run. He had hit an unexpected mental wall of intense despair. An overwhelming sense of hopelessness. He dragged himself to the curb and sat down with his head in his hands. "I am never going to run again," he cried.

He sat by the side of the road for about fifteen minutes. People kept running past him. He could hear their feet hitting the pavement. Even seniors. He resented them running past. He hated himself for failing. No one cared about him. Craig didn't even care anymore. That was when he heard a voice. A woman had paused her own race and come over to him. He looked up. She smiled while Craig peered out at her through the bars of his fingers. "You're almost there," she encouraged. "Get up, and just put one foot in front of the other." It took nothing but a few seconds from her own race, but gave Craig everything for his. That's all it took. A word of inspiration. Those words gave him the fuel to push through the wall. The hopelessness evaporated. He got up slowly. He began to hobble. Then to jog. Then he broke into a slow but steady run. And he finished the race.

More than once, I have discovered the words of Isaiah 40:29–31 to be a source of inspiration. God has whispered in my ear:

He gives power to the weak and strength to the powerless. Even youths will become weak and tired, and young men will fall in exhaustion. But those who trust in the Lord will find new strength. They will soar high on wings like eagles. They will run and not grow weary. They will walk and not faint.

The wall unmasks our frailty. It reveals God's power. It discloses our limitations. It exhibits His infinitude. Our love, power, wisdom, knowledge, and strength are measured by degrees. We grow weak and tired, and fall with exhaustion. God's love, power, wisdom, knowledge, and strength have no bounds, no degrees. God's greatness never diminishes. He never grows too tired to stop, listen, and restore. He is life.

As you push through the wall, you discover fresh revelations of God. New heights of living in the life of the Spirit. A new depth of character and spiritual formation. New levels of faith. A new intensity of devotion. Scott Jurek said, "Beyond the very extreme of fatigue and distress, we may find amounts of ease and power we never dreamed ourselves to own; sources of strength never taxed at all because we never push through the obstruction."[3] This holds so true of the walls in our lives. We quit too quickly. We give up prematurely. Our goal is to relieve the pain. We devise a speedy exit. We fail to arrive at our full potential for God because we short-circuit the struggles God would use to take us to new and deeper levels of love, power, wisdom, knowledge, and strength. We need to push through the obstruction.

Don't give up. Embrace the wall. Discover the source of your life. I am going to examine this subject in more detail in the remainder of this book. Let's read on.

TWO

MORE THAN A RACE

EVERY SO OFTEN, SOMEONE COMES ALONG IN YOUR LIFE WHO IS AN inspiration. This happened to me a little while ago. I met Jim Willett in the local newspaper. The story was entitled, *Grueling Challenge Therapy for Cancer Survivor.* After reading, I felt compelled to get to know this man. So I made every effort to connect with Jim in person. Soon after, we were sitting at a local coffee shop getting acquainted over a hot banana chocolate drink. That was the beginning of a friendship.

Jim was a personal trainer. Always preparing for the next half-marathon. He felt incredibly healthy and optimistic about the New Year. But he had no idea what was looming on the horizon. Just a couple of weeks later his world was rocked. What he thought was a hernia turned out to be something far worse. The report from a colonoscopy contained the words "colon cancer." Jim was stunned. Staring at his own mortality. Over the next few weeks, his schedule filled with a dizzying number of appointments at the hospital for CT scans, MRIs, blood work, and ultrasounds. Jim was 36 years old.

Surgery was scheduled, resulting in the removal of a six-inch section of Jim's large intestine and a number of lymph nodes. After four and a half hours in surgery, he spent the next five days in a hospital bed. Short walks up and down the hall were like climbing a mountain. The recovery was the most humbling period in Jim's life. To this point, he had been independent, fit and active. Now he required assistance for everything. He couldn't even roll over in bed without help.

Jim returned home with a sizeable scar, a shorter intestine, and complete and utter weakness. Six weeks following surgery he received more unwelcome news. He learned that the cancer had spread to at least one lymph node, putting him at stage-three cancer. He would need chemotherapy. Six months of chemotherapy. Twelve cycles. By the second cycle, Jim was feeling debilitating nausea. Self-pity was beginning to set in.

He spent hours sitting in the cancer clinic, listening to the constant drip of the chemotherapy cocktail and the hum of the IV machine. He would watch, think, and write. He watched the faces of the other patients receiving treatment. There is an unspoken bond between people undergoing chemo. The mental battle may be more draining than the physical battle. He would try to read their faces and analyze their body language. What he mostly read was despair.

That was when Jim decided to do something about his situation. He refused to sit and feel despair and self-pity. He craved something to wake up for each morning. That something would be running. Running had saved his life before. Years earlier, Jim had been a wild teenager whose life was going nowhere. His father was an alcoholic. There was little family support and lots of time to get into trouble. But he loved sports, especially rugby. The problem was that Jim was not a big, tough guy. How could he play rugby? He decided to begin running. He would excel as a runner. During his first year playing rugby, he was merited as most improved player. At the end of his second year, he won the trophy for most valuable player on the team. By the fifth year, Jim was playing at the top level. How did he accelerate so successfully up the ranks? His fitness. His ability to run. His stamina. Eighty minutes into the game, when other players were beginning to fade, Jim was going strong. Running kept him off the streets. Running gave him purpose. Something to wake up to each morning. Running had saved his life. Maybe running would do that again. He would run through chemo.

Despite the objections of the staff at the cancer clinic, Jim began to run. Carrying his chemo pump in his pocket, he built himself up to 3.5 kilometres. He felt like an old man running, but it was empowering. He was physically weak but felt mentally strong. Visits to the oncologists were ongoing. The cancer clinic was his second home. But he kept running. Jim celebrated cycle nine of chemo with a nine-kilometre run. While Jim ran, he thought. One word dominated his thoughts. Life. He was just beginning to grasp its magnitude. Hitting the wall in your life tends to do that. He was running to counter thoughts of despair and self-pity. Cancer doesn't define who you are as a person. Seven-inch scars on your body don't speak to the type of character you possess. How you respond to adversity says everything about the real you. Jim's cancer and running was about something bigger. It was about life.

As Jim processed these thoughts, he made a decision to raise the bar. He would prepare to run the seven-day 250-kilometre race across China's Gobi Desert. The Gobi is one of the world's most forbidding deserts. The race through this remote location is one leg of the 4Deserts race coordinated through the RacingThePlanet organization. Jim had just six months to prepare. Every day, he could be seen running along the streets with a 20-pound backpack strapped to him. He would need to carry everything essential for survival up to 20 pounds on his back while running the Gobi. So he trained. And ran. And ran. Wind, rain, sun, snow, or sleet. It didn't discourage or deter him. He followed a strict schedule. And every day increased the distance a little.

Life, like running, is not about the things that happen to you; it's about the things you make happen. And Jim wanted to make a difference. Jim was well aware of the struggles he had encountered as a youth. He knew well what it was like to be going nowhere because you lacked a critical support system. So Jim linked up with an organization called Toronto Trails Youth Initiatives. Trails Youth Initiatives ministers to "at-risk" teens living in the inner-city of Toronto. Jim would run the "Gobi March" for himself and for Trails. He wanted vulnerable, troubled kids to be inspired by his example to have the courage to face what might appear to be impossible odds, and understand that anything is possible.

THE RACE OF YOUR LIFE

I'll come back to Jim later in the book. At this point, we need to understand something Jim came to appreciate. That running is about more than a race. It is about life. God has given all of us the wonderful gift of life. Every day you live is a gift. All of us who are breathing are living out this incredible gift. What you do with your life is your gift to God.

You begin your first day at the starting line. During the first mile you get your running legs as a toddler. For the first 16 miles, you run like an adolescent, with strength and confidence. Somewhere near this point in the journey, one often hits a wall. Getting through the teen years is a critical challenge for many. Crucial decisions. Significant hurdles. Dangerous mistakes. The wall, however, can loom into view and intimidate at any stage in the journey. At mile 20, one approaches adulthood. One often feels a new vigour for the run accompanied soon after with worrisome concerns about where the run is going. Do I have what it takes? What do I want to accomplish with my life? What difference am I making? A mid-run crisis generally follows. Questions regarding direction and purpose. Challenges to your values. Sometimes the wind is at your back; at other times it suddenly turns and drives into your face, thwarting your progress. At the 50-mile mark, one is cruising along with a kind of second wind for life. You look forward to the next unexpected adventure. You laugh and you cry. But when you least expect it, you find yourself falling headlong over a stony embankment. You crawl back up onto the trail. At 55 miles, thoughts of retirement are getting stronger. Every mile has its joys and sense of accomplishment. But every mile also brings new struggles, an added ache, another pain. Old injuries recur. Fresh injuries turn up. Mile 65 seems more like a steep incline. You are wondering where the illusive "all downhill from here" has disappeared. You see mile 80 just ahead. All one can think about is the massage table and a hot bath. Over any hill or around any bend is the finish line. The principal goal is to go the distance and to finish well.

Just to be alive is an enormous gift and an opportunity to participate in something grander than any one of us can fully comprehend. The sad thing is that many people run the race of life with no genuine appreciation for its grandeur. Without any true sense of a greater purpose, except what one can design for oneself. They run with no conception of destiny but what they can forge for themselves. They run as though the race goes nowhere, and what comes to pass is happenstance and luck. What is, is. And what will be, will be. They do not enjoy the wonderful security of knowing their lives are in the hands of a God who loves them. Many live without any understanding of moral accountability to anyone except themselves. There is no sense of a sovereign Creator who has a dream and plan for their lives. Ultimately, they run with little all-encompassing meaning for their lives. But there *is* more for you, far more than meets the eye.

THE AMAZING RACE

While everyone breathing is running the race of their lives, there are many paths that one can follow in life. The money trail. The career course. The pleasure path. The education track. None of these are wrong in themselves. Money is a necessity. A career is advantageous. Leisure and pleasure are beneficial. An education is valuable. But if your attention centres on these things as the priority, they will dictate the kind of race you will run. They will define you. You will be known as a wealthy person. A successful person. A pleasure-seeker. An educated person. In the end, you may discover that you've put a lot of energy into running along a path that leaves you empty and unfulfilled.

There is a path God has set for you to run in life that will raise the level of your living to the highest plane of quality, fulfillment, and significance. It is not an easy or painless run. It can be demanding and tough. The Bible says, *"Run with endurance the race God has set before us"* (Hebrews 12:1). God's race has an astounding eternal destination. But this book focuses on the *running*. The amazing journey of getting there. We often think the greatest races are reserved for the gods we read about in books and magazines, or watch in the movies, not for mere mortals like us. That isn't true. The most amazing race is reserved for everyday folk like you and me.

If you have watched or run a marathon, you know that when the starting pistol cracks, hundreds, sometimes thousands of runners break out and along the streets. But they don't run in thousands of different directions, wherever their hearts lead them. No, there is a course that has been predetermined and marked out. The route goes up one street and down another. Orange cones, flags, arrowed signs, ropes, and traffic officers mark the path. People line the curbs cheering the runners on. Stations at specific points along the way hand out water and sports drinks. The Bible teaches that God has a predetermined path marked out for your life. There's lots of room to engage freewill on the path. I believe that at some places the path is narrow and constricted; at other places it is broad and wide-ranging. But that is a subject for another day. My point is a sovereign, purposeful, loving God has set a course for your life. A path for you to run.

This path follows along the bedrock of an old, but true and proven pathway. Jeremiah wrote, *"Stop at the crossroads and look around. Ask for the old, godly way, and walk in it. Travel its path, and you will find rest for your souls"* (Jeremiah 6:16). I remember hiking through the Cumberland Gap in Kentucky. Early frontiersmen and pioneers followed this path through the Gap, giving them access to the other side of the mountains. As we walked along the historic road, I read a notice that said we were hiking on the bedrock of the ancient path. The path God has set for you is filled with obstacles, struggles, blisters, and bliss, but the path runs along the bedrock of God's absolute truth, principles, promises, values, proven faithfulness, and provision. Jeremiah urges you to stop at the crossroads, evaluate where your life is going, and choose the path God has set for you to travel. You will find rest and fulfillment.

The psalmist certainly grasped the truth that God has marked out a path for each of us to travel. *"He guides me along right paths"* (Psalm 23:3). *"Show me the right path, O Lord; point out the road for me to follow. … he shows the proper path to those who go astray. … He leads the humble in doing right, teaching them his way. … Who are those who fear the Lord? He will show them the path they should choose"* (Psalm 25:4, 8, 9, 12).

When you begin to run on the path God has set for you, you begin to live by a new script. In life, things happen to you. Bad things. Destructive things. Disarming things. Maybe you were raped. Bullied. Rejected. Betrayed. You were brainwashed as a child into believing you wouldn't amount to anything. And unfortunately, you are living up to that belief. Pain from your past has a way of writing a script for your life that you just live out without demur. You act out the script that has been handed to you. You run the race other people have set for you. But when you run the race God has set for you, you begin to live by the script that He has written for your life. This is both liberating and reviving.

Running the path God has set for you will also restore your passion for life. We live with tensions. The bondage of the past. Uncertainty about the future. The expectations of other people. The scourge of the urgent. The choice between the good and the best. How often does your life fill with the demands of good things that rob you of the best? The endless rabbit trails that lead nowhere but embezzle your time and energy and prevent you from getting to where you want or need to go. These things and countless more deflate enthusiasm for life.

Running on God's path hits the refresh button on your enthusiasm. God made you who you are. He built purpose and meaning into your life that embrace all of eternity. You are more than a temporary, insignificant blip on life's sonar screen, passing through and soon to disappear off the monitor. As you grasp a true sense of eternal purpose and destiny and align yourself to that, you become passionate about living again. Purpose spawns passion. You become less preoccupied with what has happened to you and more absorbed and engaged with what you can make happen. You become focused on what God will make happen through your life. More important than what you do well is what you are passionate about. There is a difference between a person who does well in life and a person who is passionate about life.

Eric Liddell, the great Scottish Olympian and the character behind the film "Chariots of Fire" is credited as saying that he believed God had made him for a purpose, and that He had made him fast. And when he ran, he felt God's pleasure. It is unclear whether or not Liddell actually spoke those words, but they are powerful and have been fixed to his name forever. Yes, Liddell was fast, but what gave him passion for running was not that he was swift on his feet. It was that "fast" was the way God had made him, and when he ran fast he brought God pleasure. When you believe you are doing what God made you to do, and that your life brings a smile to the face of God, you are passionate about life.

Dean Karnazes is one of the great ultrarunners in the world. He has become known as the Ultramarathon Man. In May 2011, Dean completed an amazing 3,000-mile run across America in just 75 days. But the story that most captivated my attention was when he ran the Western States 100-Mile Endurance Run for the first time, in June 1994. The Western States is a rugged, single-track mountain trail. The trail rises 38,000 feet over 100 miles. That's like ascending and descending the Toronto CN Tower, the third-tallest tower in the world, ten times, over a 100-mile distance.

When Dean talks about running, he finds himself philosophizing about life. He recognizes the juxtaposition that exists between running and life. Running 100 miles gave him something to live for. A goal to achieve. A sense of hope and aspiration. It furnished him with a dream that exceeded everything else. This quickly translated into his life. When he converses about his new passion for running, he finds himself talking about his passion for life. "My newfound love of running seemed to awaken a sense of hope. There was something in our future to look forward to; something, perhaps, grand and monumental. Attempting to run 100 miles was a spectacular aspiration, and the pursuit of this dream seemed to transcend career goals and other ambitions. … A flame has been ignited."[1]

The same is true for running the path God has set for you, but in greater, more monumental ways. You are a participant in the most amazing race ever run. A newfound love for Christ, a newly awakened passion and hope, and a new aspiration all merge to ignite a flame whereby the whole ambition of your life is to pursue the dream God has for you. To follow His path for you, wherever it takes you and whatever that means. For God … anything, anywhere, anytime. This pursuit transcends every other goal and ambition.

THE STARTING LINE

You arrive at the starting line for the amazing race by means of faith. It is in the context of running this race that we read, *"We do this by keeping our eyes on Jesus, the champion who initiates and perfects our faith"* (Hebrews 12:2). Romans 1:17 states that when you believe in Christ as your Saviour, you are made right with God. *"This is accomplished from* start *to* finish *by faith"* (emphasis added). It is a path of faith. Let me explain.

Sin placed all of us on the path to destruction. At some point on your journey through life you come to a crossroads. There is a signpost with two pointers. One reads "path to death"; the other, "path to life." The road to eternal death is wide and paved; the other pathway, to eternal life, is narrow and winding. It is the more difficult way. But it follows along the bedrock of that ancient, proven, godly path. To follow the road to death you need do nothing. Just keep going. To turn onto the path to life, you need to make some choices. There is a registration fee. But it is far greater than you can pay. The wages of sin is eternal death. Then you see that the fee has been paid for you … by Jesus. You need simply to put out your hand and receive the free pass. It's free to you, but at great cost to Him. He died upon the cross for you. He died in your place. The penalty for your sin was paid in full by Him. He loved you so much that He chose to give up His life for you rather than give up on you. This is called grace. So it's a grace race.

You need to make a decision. There stirs a fearful awareness and disparaging consciousness of sin's destructive deception and of one's own personal unworthiness before God. You feel a profound sorrow for your sin. This is contrasted by a growing knowledge and grasp of God's love and an unremitting aspiration to respond to that love. So you turn around from the course you have been travelling and cast your eyes back along the trail snaking up a winding hill in the other direction. That's repentance.

You walk through a gate and come to a wooden cross. It is empty. So is the tomb where Jesus' body was placed. Jesus has died and is risen. You fall on your knees and embrace the cross. You cry, "Lord Jesus, please forgive me! I believe. I believe that You died for me. I believe that You rose from the dead for me. I believe that You live for me. I believe! I surrender my life to You." That's faith. But it's only the beginning. The beginning of the most amazing journey that you will take with God. The race of faith.

As mentioned, "Chariots of Fire" is the story of gold-medal Olympian sprinter, Eric Liddell. Liddell was a man who would not surrender his convictions to man because he had surrendered his life to God. The movie closes where the real story begins. At one point in the story, Liddell says to a group of people who have gathered to hear him speak, "You came to see a race today. To see someone win. It happened to be me. But I want you to do more than watch a race. I want you to take part in it. I want to compare faith to running a race."[2]

TURNING POINT

What leads runners to reject the easy path and turn to the road less travelled? What motivates people to embrace the challenge of running against intimidating odds for incredible distances? For runners, it can be anything from the boredom of being a couch potato to getting high on endorphins. Losing weight. Boosting one's attitude and self-worth. Increasing blood circulation. Just feeling better. Escaping mediocrity. Experiencing the exhilaration of stretching oneself beyond one's perceived limits. For my friend, Jim Willett, it was to escape the debilitating feeling of self-pity because of what cancer was doing to him. He wanted to make a difference.

One day, a pizza-delivery guy asked Dean Karnazes why he ran such long distances. Was he possessed? Was he just crazy? Dean answered,

I run because it's my way of giving back to the world by doing the one thing I do best. ... I run to breathe the fresh air. I run to explore. I run to escape the ordinary. I run to honor my sister [who had passed away at a young age] and unite my family. I run because it keeps me humble. I run for the finish line and to savor the trip along the way. I run to help those who can't. ... I run because long after my footprints fade away, maybe I will have inspired a few to reject the easy path, hit the trails, put one foot in front of the other, and come to the same conclusion I did: I run because it always takes me where I want to go.[3]

There are numerous reasons that cause someone to reject the easy path and turn onto the narrow, less-travelled course God has marked out. There is a history behind every runner. Many times it is triggered by a loss. Loss of health. Loss of one's job. Loss of self-worth. Loss of a loved one. I have a friend, Joy, who has never been athletic or physically active. She is more of a bookworm, a student. She has a PhD in Political Science. But when she experienced the difficult loss of her mother to leukemia, she decided to take a pro-active approach to grief. She bought a pair of running shoes and some books on training for a marathon. On the first anniversary of her mother's death, Joy completed the Paris Marathon in memory of her mother.

Other runners begin because they are experiencing disillusionment. Disenchantment with wealth or the corporate ladder. World-weariness. An overwhelming dissatisfaction and sense that there has to be more to my life. It may be regret. It can even be a fear of hell. Or one may be drawn by the powerful, magnetic pull of God's love. Whatever it is, there is a story behind every runner, something that draws them irresistibly to the starting line. They bend their knees before the cross of Jesus. They place their feet into the starting blocks. The head is bowed in surrender. The eyes rise and fixate on a forward point. They reflect upon what they are leaving behind. They ponder the path ahead. There is no regret. The feet suddenly spring out of the blocks and they begin the amazing race of faith. What they will encounter is something bigger than they ever imagined.

THREE

THE AGONY OF THE RACE

MARATHON IS A SUNNY, WIND-SWEPT COASTAL PLAIN IN GREECE. IT was here that one of the most pivotal battles was fought in European history. The Battle of Marathon. It is now probably more famous as the inspiration for the Marathon race, and while the story is intertwined with historical fact and the stuff of legend, it has become, nonetheless, the inspiration for this increasingly popular athletic event.

In 546 BC, the powerful Persian Empire extended from Asia to Egypt, and up into Asia Minor, now Turkey. Greece, on the other hand, was just a scattering of independent city-states, called poleis. Athens and Sparta were the two most significant of the poleis. Athens was the largest and most affluent, built around democratic ideas and philosophy, while Sparta boasted a regimented, disciplined society, built around military training. Throughout history, both cities were like continually warring cousins.

By 490 BC, the Persians had turned their attention to Greece, intending to expand their empire into Europe. The outcome of this battle would determine the course of history. They landed a large force on the coast of Greece, on the plains of Marathon, within striking distance of Athens.

When news of the massive beachhead of Persians at Marathon arrived in Athens, it was immediately decided to send word to Sparta for help. While the two cities were barely on speaking terms, they were confronted with a common enemy that threatened their extermination. Time was short, so the Athenian generals chose a professional long-distance runner named Pheidippides to run the rugged mountainous course to Sparta with the news of the Persian threat and to request immediate assistance.

Professional long-distance runners were commonly used to communicate between cities and provinces. They were called hemerodromoi (all-day runners), experts in the art of endurance running, navigating the harsh landscape faster than horses could run it. Pheidippides ran the 240-kilometre distance in two days and delivered the urgent message.

The Spartans listened intently. The good news was that they agreed to respond. The bad news was that they were in the middle of a religious ritual and could not come for about ten days. Pheidippides retraced his steps across the rocky terrain to Athens, another 240 kilometres. Some 480 kilometres on foot in less than a week. The news was disappointing. Athens would have to fight the Persian army alone.

The Athenians were outnumbered 4 to 1. While to many it seemed suicidal, they had no option but to launch a surprise attack. The attack was unexpectedly successful. By day's end, 6,400 Persians lay dead on the battlefield, while the Athenians listed only 192 casualties. The surviving Persians retreated to their ships, but rather than returning home, they made the decision to circumvent the Athenian army and sail for Athens. Their intent was to counter with a surprise attack on the city while its army was absent.

Pheidippides was again called upon to run. He was ordered to run as quickly as possible the 40 kilometres to Athens with the news of the victory and a warning regarding the approaching Persian ships. Despite a recent 480-kilometre run to Sparta and back, and having fought all day in a grueling battle in heavy armour, Pheidippides pushed himself beyond human limits of endurance. He ran the most punishing, demanding race of his life, and arrived at the gates of Athens in about three hours. He delivered the now-famous word of victory, *Nike*, meaning: "We have won!" Athens was spared. But then the story takes one of those poignant turns of events so typical of a Greek tragedy. Pheidippides, the hero of the day, collapsed, exhausted, and died.

The modern Olympic Games were inaugurated in 1896 in Greece. At that time, the organizers of the games were looking for an event that would celebrate the ancient glory of Greece. The story of Pheidippides was recalled, and it was decided to run an event that would echo this legendary story. Michel Breal, famed French philologist, suggested to his friend and the founder of the modern Olympics, Pierre de Coubertin, that a "marathon" race should be added to the program of the 1896 Athens Olympic Games. The runners would run in the footsteps of Pheidippides, along the original 40-kilometre course from Marathon Bridge to the finish line at the newly constructed replica of the Athens ancient stadium.

The decision was made. Twenty-five runners gathered on Marathon Bridge. Thousands of spectators gathered at the stadium in Athens to witness who would cross the finish line first. The crowd was ecstatic when Spiridon Louis, a Greek postal worker, ran up into the stadium and crossed the finish line in 2 hours, 58 minutes, 50 seconds, a full seven minutes ahead of the pack. Nine runners finished the course, eight of them Greeks. The host nation was jubilant and the marathon was born.

The plans for North America's first marathon were discussed on the boat returning from Athens to the United States. The Boston Marathon was born just one year later, on April 19, 1897, the date selected to commemorate Paul Revere's legendary ride on that date in 1775. The marathon became an increasingly popular event and the test of agonizing endurance. It became the benchmark for the human spirit to endure against adversity and to overcome.

In 1908, at the Olympic Games in London, England, the marathon distance was lengthened to 42.2 kilometres (26.2 miles). The change was made to accommodate the wishes of the British monarchy. A distance of 2.2 kilometres was added so that the race could run from Windsor Castle to White City Stadium and finish in front of the royal family's viewing box. That year, the most recognized incident of the Games occurred at the finish line of the marathon. Some called it the greatest race of the century. A huge, cheering crowd, including Queen Alexandra, watched as the little Italian, Dorondo Pietri, in first place, staggered across the final 385 yards toward the finish line. He collapsed several times and even began running in the wrong direction at one point, disoriented and exhausted. Irish-American Johnny Hayes moved closer and closer. Two overzealous officials rushed out onto the track and hurled Pietri over the line. Of course, he was disqualified and Hayes was awarded the gold medal. Queen Alexandra, however, was so moved by the enduring spirit and plight of Pietri that the next day she presented him with a gilded silver cup.

ULTRARUNNING

Today the ultramarathon has taken endurance running to a new level. An ultramarathon is any event longer than the traditional marathon length. Runners have taken up the challenge to run incredible distances, marking hundreds of miles, endeavouring to go beyond the perceived human limits. They challenge any obstacle, inclement weather, extreme temperatures, elevation changes, and rugged terrain. They run along paved roads, dirt roads, mountain paths, desert wadis, frozen tundra, and ice trails.

Ultramarathons are now conducted all over the world and have become the ultimate test of the ability of the human spirit to persevere and prevail. Over 70,000 people complete ultramarathons every year. Among some of the biggest is the Spartathlon, considered one of the most difficult foot races in the world. It is a non-stop foot race covering 246 kilometres from Athens to Sparta. Germany's multiday Deutschlandlauf is 1,200 kilometres, and Badwater, 135 miles through Death Valley, California, takes place in 125-degree heat. The 4Deserts is a foot race series, each race 250 kilometres through the world's most forbidding landscapes and harshest climates: the Gobi March in China; the brutal Atacama Desert in Chile; the Sahara Race in Egypt; and the final and ultimate event in the series, the Antarctica.

I have met many long-distance runners. I have spoken to some of the greatest ultramarathoners in the world. People who have challenged the limits and overcome. I have discovered that they are more than runners; they are philosophers. They love to philosophize about life. Their running is a depiction of living. Long-distance running is about overcoming the odds. Confronting challenges. Facing fears. I have discovered from these remarkable people remarkable parallels between distance running and going the distance in life's run, particularly the race God has marked out for each of us.

COUNTING THE COST

The Bible describes the race God has set for us as an endurance run. It is not a quick sprint; it is an arduous ultramarathon, long and hard. It demands determination, resolve, and perseverance. *"Run with endurance the race God has set before us"* (Hebrews 12:1).

The exhortation from Hebrews 12 was written to Christian believers who struggled with the pressure of how to live a life of faith in a hostile world. Christians were commanded to throw a pinch of incense to an image of Caesar and declare, "Caesar is Lord," once a year. Then they could worship whomever and whatever they wanted for the rest of the year. But many could not in clear conscience do so even once. Only Jesus was Lord. Every day. All the time. For some, this decision resulted in death. For many others, ostracism from the family and community. Financial ruin. Unemployment. But they persevered despite severe persecution.

Others, however, reconsidered the cost of living a life of faith in Jesus. Was the cost too high? Should I quit? Many were dropping out of the race. Even today, in numerous places in the world, Christians endure the same consequences for following Jesus. Here in the west, we don't face the same kinds of pressures. However, there are many other unique pressures and reasons for people to ask, "Can I go on?" "Can my faith hold out?" The book of Hebrews is written to those of us, then and now, who would consider dropping out. The letter gives many reasons why we need to keep going.

In Hebrews 12:1–3, the writer accentuates the need to persevere. The word "race" is the Greek word "agon," from which we get our English word, "agony." The race is an agonizing long-distance ultramarathon. The course comprises steep inclines, numerous obstacles and challenges, and relentless temptations. Our strength is small. Our minds fill with confusion, doubt, and loneliness. You pray but God seems silent. You feel physical, emotional, mental, and spiritual exhaustion. The reality is that pain is an essential part of the journey. The Bible gives no unrealistic or deceptive propositions or illusions. Struggle is the reality of life with or without faith. You will encounter pain whether you are running on your own path in life, or on the path God has marked out for you. How much better to go the distance on God's path with a faith that holds you to Him.

When the apostle Paul began his race, he had no idea where the course would take him. Jesus did say, *"I will show him how much he must suffer for my name's sake"* (Acts 9:16). The course led him through unsafe and hostile territory often controlled by roving bands of bandits. Fever. Disease. Injury. Prison. Five times, he felt across his back the vicious 39 lashes from a cat o' nine tails, a nine-tailed whip with small pieces of sharp bone tied to the end of each lash to cut into the flesh and tear the back to shreds. Beaten with rods. Once stoned. Shipwrecked. Sleepless nights. Hunger. Thirst. Cold. Then, besides all this, the daily burden he carried for the needs and struggles of all the churches. But then at the end of his life, when he had completed his race, he said that it was worth it all. We'll examine the finish line later.

Incredible suffering. Genuine faith. Exceptional endurance. Superlative courage. Authentic commitment to the cause of Christ. Paul was a sterling example to all of us who are in need of spiritual vitality and encouragement to endure.

RUNNING HURT

Pain is a reality in life. An essential reality. It is a sign of life. In one sense, it's supposed to hurt. If it doesn't, you are not achieving at your fullest potential. A problem in our materialistic society is that we have confused comfort with happiness. The opposite is equally true, perhaps even more realistic. Disturbance and agitation are also sources of happiness because they arouse and stimulate the runner to push beyond the limits, to accomplish the unexpected and unfamiliar. Pain hurts, but it can be a good hurt. Pain is one of life's secret weapons.

Dean Karnazes writes that after running ten hours straight, the pain really sets in. But the pain ignites something within. It awakens everything in him and energizes him to persevere. "Never are my senses more engaged than when the pain sets in. There is magic in misery. Just ask any runner."[1] After running past Mile 99, with only one mile left to go, Dean was crawling along the road inch by inch. His legs were numb and useless, so he pulled himself along with his arms. A car stopped and a man and woman jumped out of their car and asked him if he was okay. He replied that he never felt better. The woman said they thought he had been hit by a car. Dean tried to explain what was going on. As the two stood staring at him, Dean got to his feet, let out an animal-like growl, and began to run. "Though it hurt like never before, I no longer just numbly accepted the pain for what it was. Now I went after it, sought it out, hunted it down. The pain radiated from every cell in my body, and my response was to push even harder. The tables were turned."[2]

There are many purposes for pain. I have discussed this more fully in my previous book, "Hitting the Wall," but I would like to give three more reasons for why pain is essential to the run of life. Three ultrarunners share three reasons why "running hurt" is essential to running a good race.

PAIN EMPOWERS

Ray Zahab is one of Canada's greatest runners. Ray has been known to challenge and conquer the most difficult courses in the world. He is an inspiration to read about and to talk to. A little while ago, I was speaking with Ray and we got talking about the issue of managing extreme pain when running such long distances. He told me a story. He had recently run the Atacama Desert in South America. The Atacama is a narrow, 1,000-kilometre strip of plateau running down the Pacific west coast, comprised mostly of salt basins, sand and volcanic rock. It is considered the driest desert in the world.

Ray was running alone. His goal was to run 1,200 kilometres in twenty days, carrying a 25-pound backpack. The terrain was unbelievably difficult. He had made a commitment to himself to just take each day as it came. On day 5, a tiny blister appeared on the side of his foot. Ray had never had a blister in that particular spot. It was small but very painful. That night he drained the blister and disinfected it with iodine.

The next day was a demanding 70-kilometre run through an active salt lake. It was like running on popcorn. The soreness in his foot persisted. That night, he examined the blister. The soreness was increasing but the wound didn't appear to be any deeper.

Day 7. Something didn't feel right. He ran for several miles, but the pain became unbearable. The blister had grown to the size of a tennis ball. His team took a look at the foot and discovered an abscess down inside the wound. Infection had set in. The abscess had been previously undetected because it had been covered by skin. But now the skin was hanging off, exposing the problem. When the medical attendant cut the excess skin from around the wound, the foot began to swell. They cleaned the wound with water and disinfected it again with iodine. Ray was advised to sit the day out to avoid severe infection. He did. The foot became so swollen that he was unable to fit his foot into its running shoe. He thought the expedition was over.

Ray faced two options: (a) the run is over, or (b) find a way to run. I think this is where, in life's run, many people quit too early. We give up because the going is too tough. The pain is too unbearable. We come to the crossroads. We choose comfort over pain. Ease over ache. Peace over perseverance. Calm over storm. We fall short of discovering our full potential. We fail to discover what might have been. We fail to learn one of life's secret weapons. Ray chose to find a way to run.

Day 8. The team treated the blister with antibiotics and bandaged the foot. Ray took some duct tape out of his backpack. What did men do before the discovery of duct tape? He cut the upper front half of the running shoe to allow his foot to slip into it. He then used the duct tape to piece the shoe together. He walked and ran for about 10 kilometres. The foot was insanely painful. He told himself not to panic, but to wait and see what happened over the next 30 kilometres. He made a mental commitment to himself. "I can manage the pain as long as the foot does not get worse. If the foot does not worsen, I can and will keep going."

At lunch, he checked the blister. It had not worsened. Mentally he knew that he could keep going. He began to run. He felt exhilaration. Every step was painful but strangely invigorating. He walked and ran for the next 45 kilometres. Every painful step gave him renewed confidence that he would overcome. There was strength in adversity. The more it hurt, the stronger he felt. The pain was actually empowering him.

Day 9. Ray ran 70 kilometres. He kept bandaging. Hurting. Persevering. Running. And he went on to finish running the Atacama. Yes, pain is one of life's secret weapons. It can actually empower you to keep going.

PAIN DRIVES EXCELLENCE

I've already introduced you to Dean Karnazes. He is a runner that exhibits sheer courage, determination, and stamina. He talks with admiration about the coach who taught him to push himself beyond the limits. He just called him "Coach." Coach was built like a tree trunk. He wasn't into the fancy running attire. Not when grey gym shorts and white T-shirts would do the job. But he was into hard work. Pushing oneself to the brink of exhaustion. The theory was simple: "Whoever was willing to run the hardest, train the longest, and suffer the most would earn the spoils of victory."[3] He who could endure the most pain would be the most rewarded.

One day, Dean ran a particular race as hard as he could and broke across the finish line in first place. As he stood doubled over trying to catch his wind, coaches and other runners were coming over to him and congratulating him. When everyone had left, Coach strolled up and also congratulated him, telling him he had run a good race. He then asked Dean how it felt. Dean replied, "It felt good." Coach looked down, kicked some dirt with his foot, and then looked back up at Dean, squinting. He answered slowly, "If it felt good, you didn't push hard enough. It's supposed to hurt."[4] Dean never forgot those words. If it comes easy, you're not pushing hard enough. A great life lesson for all of us.

Hard running hurts. But it gets you to your full potential. It drives excellence. I know that hockey coaches will tell their teams, just before they skate out onto the ice, that it's not the most talented team that will win, but the team that most wants to win! The team ready and willing to suffer the most will earn the spoils of war.

After watching a pack of Kenyan runners gliding silently but swiftly along a mountain trail, Toby Tanser could not help but appreciate how they ran the unpredictable path with the same stride as they lived life. He wrote, "Pain is the validation of accomplishment. Each one of this dozen or so runners renews their faith daily when they afflict the doubts and torment their limbs in a quest to be the very best they can, best beyond the mind's own pitiful limitations."[5]

Yes, pain drives excellence. It validates the accomplishment of becoming the best you can be. That you are willing to put the effort, suffering, and sweat into becoming everything God made you to be. That you want it bad enough.

PAIN DRIVES BEYOND THE ORDINARY

Rick Ball lives near the town of Orillia, Ontario. In 1986, he was involved in a serious motorcycle accident that resulted in the amputation of his left leg. He had been travelling one direction, and a pick-up truck another, resulting in Rick needing to choose a completely new direction for his life. The loss of his leg devastated him and self-pity overwhelmed him. That is, until one day, Rick's brother sat him in a wheelchair and wheeled him around the hospital ward. What he saw shook him. People with head injuries, disabilities much worse than his, challenges much tougher than he faced. The sights so disturbed him that he decided he would be thankful for his life and do something with it, something significant. Adversity could lead him down a road of self-pity or along a road to accomplish something significant. He would choose the latter.

Rick was released from hospital with a prosthetic leg. He found a new passion: running. Now, running didn't seem like a fitting passion for a man with one leg. But not only did he take up running, running became the means of Rick showing that adversity could be the catapult in a person's life to drive one beyond the ordinary to the extraordinary. He was soon running 100 to 120 kilometres per week. He discovered the benefit of wearing a carbon-fibre prosthesis, with a high-tech running blade. It looked like a C-shaped spring attached to his upper leg. He began competing with able-bodied runners and was finishing in the top 1 percent in races.

In April 2009, Rick ran in the Boston Marathon, contending with 26,000 other runners. He was the first and only amputee Canadian to qualify to run in the "able-bodied" category. He ran hard but felt himself fading with only one kilometre to go before the finish line. He lifted his arms into the air and called to the crowds lining the street: "Bring me in; bring me in!" They did. He amazed everyone by setting a world record for single-leg amputees, running the marathon in 3:01:50.

In May 2010, Rick ran in the Ottawa Marathon and became the first single-leg amputee to break the 3-hour mark in a marathon, running it in a time of 2:57:47. He was quoted saying: "The missing leg that once tormented me now fuels my hunger to accomplish more."[6] Rick has been an inspiration to so many who have been afflicted with adversity.

Someone once asked Rick if he could imagine how fast he could run if he had his real leg. He replied that he probably wouldn't be running at all. He would not have had the same drive. The injury and the pain he had endured were what drove him to go beyond the limits.

Pain is one of life's most powerful secret weapons. Pain is the great teacher of life's most essential, fundamental lessons, and can be the greatest motivator to change. Pain need not *define* you, but rather it will *refine* you. Pain is the tool of refinement. It prods and prompts the fallen to get back up. It inspires the mundane existence to morph into a life that makes a difference. Pain turns spectators into participants. Pain is the catalyst to move you beyond your perceived limits to becoming all that God intends for your life. God will use it to take you from the ordinary to the extraordinary.

We could call it the theology of pain. Theology is the study of God. God experiences pain when confronted with the sin and suffering of mankind. When He observed the extent of human wickedness in the days of Noah, we read, *"It broke his heart"* (Genesis 6:6). God endured Israel's desertion from Him and cried, *"My heart is torn within me"* (Hosea 11:8). Follow Jesus from the Mount of Olives, to Gethsemane, to Calvary, and you see and hear God's suffering in its intensity. You can bring grief and sorrow to God's Holy Spirit by the way you live (Ephesians 4:30).

God's creation is exposed to pain. Pain is mankind's constant companion. Pain seems to be omni-present. But pain draws your attention to God. Pain puts your heart in a better place, a place of surrender. Pain brings you to the end of yourself and leads you to God. God uses pain and adversity to teach you about Him, and yourself. Your need; His sufficiency. Your weakness; His strength. Your inadequacy; His adequacy. Your limitations; His infinitude. Pain teaches that you can do everything through Christ, who gives you strength (Philippians 4:13). Pain is the key to discovering that God *"is able, through his mighty power at work within us, to accomplish infinitely more than we might ask or think"* (Ephesians 3:20). The path may be long, hard, and painful, but God understands and identifies with you in your adversity. He walked where you walk. He ran the race you run. He is compassionate, all-sufficient, and more than enough for the journey.

FOUR

STADIUM OF CHAMPIONS

THE OLYMPIC GAMES ORIGINALLY CONSISTED OF A SINGLE EVENT: THE *stadion*. The stadion was a short race or sprint that measured approximately 200 metres. The word *stadium* is derived from the word *stadion*. Runners would sprint the length of the stadium. The length of Olympia's stadium became a general standard measure of distance. Today, one can visit the site of ancient Olympia where the Games originated back in 776 BC. You can still see the original ancient stone starting line known as the *balbis*. The *balbis* had double grooves carved into each stone block into which the contestants placed their toes. When the trumpet blew, the runners set off running naked down the packed-earth track.

You can still feel the thrill of planting your feet in the grooves of the starting blocks used by those ancient runners, the tips of your fingers touching the same points their fingers touched, and running the length of the stadium. As your feet hit the primeval path, you feel a strong connection to those early runners and, if you listen closely, you can hear the cries of the spectators cheering from the stands. You are running the ancient course and you feel inspired to run all day.

KAMARINY STADIUM

Kamariny Stadium is hallowed ground. You can easily drive past the site if not watching carefully. When you do spot it and stop to take a photo, you wonder whether or not you have arrived at the right place. You see a dilapidated 440-yard running track with cows strolling across it to graze in the centre field. The track is bordered on one side by old wooden stadium benches that give more splinters than support. A ramshackle roof covers some of the benches, with enough holes in it to give you the feeling of sitting under a sieve rather than an umbrella.

But this is Kenya's Stadium of Champions. The Holy Grail. This is where the gods have run. Kenya has produced some of the greatest distance runners in the world, and most Kenyan world champions have trained and run in the Kamariny Stadium. Champions like Daniel Komen, the first man to run 2 miles in under 8 minutes. Paul Tergat, the first Kenyan to break the world record in the marathon. Catherine Ndereba, the first Kenyan woman to win a gold medal in the marathon, and 4-time winner of the Boston Marathon. Lornah Kiplagat, one of Kenya's greatest female champions. Pamela Jelimo, the first Kenyan woman to win Olympic gold. And the list goes on and on.

Today, as young runners trek in the same steps as Kenya's greatest, they feel the thrill of the run. They jog along the identical timeworn track, steering clear of the gifts deposited by free-roaming cows, and experience a direct connection to those who have triumphed before them. Their feet run in the same grooves as the world's best and they are inspired to aspire to the same levels of greatness. They run where the gods have run. They imagine themselves cheered on by the crowd to give their best and run with honour. And something inside of each new, developing, emerging runner tells him or her that they can run with the same endurance, passion, and excellence as those who have gone before.

THE HALL OF FAITH

In Hebrews 12:1, we read that we are to *"run with endurance the race God has set before us."* The same verse begins, *"Therefore, since we are surrounded by such a huge crowd of witnesses…"* It is a metaphor of running in a stadium full of spectators. So, who are these spectators? Who makes up the "huge crowd of witnesses?" The word "therefore" points to what has come before. When you read the previous chapter, you discover the record of some of the Bible's greatest runners in the race of faith. Spiritual champions. Gold medalists.

If you were to enter the Runners' Hall of Fame, you would read the names and stories of the world's champions. Ferg Hawke ... husband and father, station attendant with Air Canada ... great Canadian ultramarathoner ... first person to complete three consecutive finishes at Badwater Ultramarathon, the world's toughest footrace, under 30 hours. Scott Jurek ... arguably the greatest ultramarathoner on the planet ... seven-time winner of the Western States 100-Mile, the most competitive trail run in the world ... a literal running machine! Pam Reed ... first person to run 300 miles without stopping. Ray Zahab ... Canadian world-class adventure runner. Monica Scholz ... Canada's top female ultrarunner ... placed 3rd at Badwater in 2004, finishing under 30 hours, only two weeks after clocking 22:06 at the Western States 100-Mile. Dean Karnazes ... the Ultramarathon Man ... holder of 11 Western States 100-Mile silver buckles for running under-24-hour finishes ... winner of Badwater. And this is just our generation. The string of names of champion runners goes back for centuries.

Hebrews 11 is the Bible's Hall of Faith. It records the names—and brief stories for some of them—of the Bible's spiritual champions. There are the better-known "greats" such as Noah, Abraham, Sarah, Moses, Joshua, and Gideon. And then there are many lesser-known runners. But they all ran the race God gave them to run. They followed the red path of grace all through the terrain of the Old Testament. And now, having completed their race, as the metaphor paints the picture, they sit up in the stands of the stadium and cheer us on as we continue the race down on the track. I don't believe that they literally look down on us as we run our race. Rather, they surround us by their encouraging testimonies to the life of faith as recorded for us in the Bible.

They are "witnesses to the life of faith." A witness is one who testifies to the truth of what one has seen and experienced, and knows. These witnesses testify to the agony of the run. They are witnesses, by the example of their own lives, to the incredible power and faithfulness of God to prevail over our personal limitations, weakness, woundedness, hurts and struggles. They testify to the amazing grace of God to be greater than all our sin and failure. They witness to the remarkable power of God to transform a wayward, strong-willed, rebellious human being into a humble, surrendered, obedient man or woman of faith. They give evidence to the astonishing ability of God to use ordinary people to do extraordinary things for His glory. They urge us to run with faith and endurance, to keep going and finish well.

Let's back up and take a look at the Hall of Faith. The chapter showcases 17 men and women who ran the race in their day. They encountered extraordinary and sometimes peculiar challenges, but they ran in faith. Abel, a shepherd, gave a sacrifice to God that flowed out of a righteous heart even though it cost him his life. God told Noah, a farmer, that He was going to destroy every living thing on the earth with a universal flood. Sounded outrageous. Unbelievable. Laughable. But Noah believed, and his faith went into action. He built a huge boat in his backyard to the exact specifications God gave him. To everyone passing by, Noah was a joke. To God, he was a man of faith.

Abraham, a businessman, picked up everything and moved to … well, he didn't know where. Wherever God told him to go. It takes faith to move out of the security of your comfort zone into the unknown and unfamiliar. But sometimes that is exactly what God calls us to do. Abraham gave up his permanent home to become a tent-dweller. His faith told him that true security rests in obedience to God.

And then there was Sarah, Abraham's wife. The first woman listed in the Hall of Faith. Sarah and Abraham had been promised a son. But they were both well beyond the years of childbearing. She was 65 years old and Abraham was 75 years. Sometimes our faith is weak, and Sarah's faith faltered. She had trouble believing God for this one. So she hatched a plan of her own. Like all of us, she tried to work out her problems on her own. She defaulted to a cultural practice of having a baby through a surrogate. She tried to push God's timetable ahead and allowed her husband to have a baby through her maid, Hagar. But that wasn't God's plan. And God responded to Sarah even in the midst of her failure. God renewed the promise to the elderly couple. By this time, Sarah was 89 years old and Abraham was 99. Sometimes God brings us to the point where what happens is clearly of God and not of us. God does what only He can do, and we are to live by faith. Then it happened. The unheard-of. Sarah gave birth to a son, Isaac. She was

90 years old. Abraham was 100 years old and adding a nursery to the tent.

Joseph was a slave who rose to become one of the most powerful leaders on earth. He believed that despite betrayal, injustice, slavery and imprisonment, God was present and had a plan for his life. God's plan extended far beyond his lifespan. He was faithful to God in his day and believed he had a part in the greater plan for God's people.

Moses was born into slavery but raised in Pharaoh's own household. He was raised in luxury and ease, with unlimited opportunity, educated in the best schools. But when faced with the choice of wealth, power, and pleasure over oppression and suffering, he chose the latter. He chose to give up the treasures and opportunities of the palace, and to step out in faith to confront Pharaoh's anger and pilot God's people into the unknown, knowing that's where God was leading. It is so easy for us to be charmed and misled by the temporary benefits of wealth, power, comfort, status, and success and be blinded to the long-term eternal reward of living according to the values and benefits of God's Kingdom. Moses gave up everything that is so important to man in this life because faith had given him strong confidence in the invisible God and a firm assurance that the best is yet to come. One will never be sorry for following the path God has set for you, despite the personal cost. The gain far offsets the loss. The reward far overshadows the cost.

It was by faith that the Israelites believed they could defeat Jericho, not with an attack, but with a walk-about around the walls. The defeat of Jericho was something God would indelibly print on their minds as a "God-thing."

Rahab was a prostitute living in Jericho. She had a bad reputation, but a good sense of judgment. She had just enough faith to believe that Israel's God was different and unique. She acted on the little faith she had and welcomed the Israelite spies who had been discovered in town into her home and protected them. God responded to her faith and rescued her and her family from the destruction of Jericho. A small act of faith can reap huge consequences.

Gideon, a farmer, more closely resembled the cowardly lion in the fictional Land of Oz who believed fear made him inadequate. God called him to rescue the Israelites from the hated Midianite occupiers who were swarming over the land like a plague of locusts. Gideon replied that he was inadequate for the job. Aren't we all? But then God changed this fearful, inadequate man into a man of faith. As you read on in the story, you witness God cutting Gideon's army from 32,000 warriors to an alarmingly anorexic-looking band of 300 men. They advanced on the enemy armed with what amounted to flashlights, ceramic jars, and party-blowers. This was like attacking a field of swarming locusts covering every blade of grass with a fly swatter. But this was faith in action. Faith is obedience to God in spite of the odds. Faith says that God is bigger and stronger. And God responded by doing what only He could do. A midnight Midianite massacre. God uses the ordinary to do the extraordinary. *"By faith ... their weakness was turned to strength. They became strong in battle and put whole armies to flight"* (Hebrews 11:33–34).

Jephthah was a young man rejected by his family. He became a misfit and rebel. He gathered a band of like-minded troublemakers around him and ran through the countryside like a gang of Hell's Angels causing havoc and fear. Then God got a hold on this young man and transformed him into a brilliant military strategist and man of faith.

And we can't overlook David, the young man after God's own heart. God grew David into a man of faith in the hidden valleys. It was while caring for flocks of sheep in and around the hills of Bethlehem that David learned to worship God and trust Him for everything. One day, David entered unknowingly into the public ring. There is an old saying: "Champions don't become champions in the ring—they are merely recognized there."[1] God had already prepared David for what came next.

The occasion was a military stalemate. The valley of Elah and a brook snaking its way up through the valley drew a line between the Philistine and Israelite armies. The Philistines stood behind Goliath, a soldier of gigantic and extraordinary size, who, while cursing God and His people, challenged someone to come and fight him. The winner would take all. R.S.V.P. No one replied. When David, however, heard the threats and blasphemy, he was offended that this should be allowed to go on. He offered to go out and defeat this fire-breathing behemoth. King Saul was relieved that finally someone was willing to go. He suited David up in his armour. But it was the wrong size, weighty and cumbersome. David looked out through the belt buckle of Saul's armour and said, "I don't think so." He would confront the giant dressed in his shepherd's clothes, holding a shepherd's staff in one hand and a sling in the other, and with a simple but powerful faith in the living God.

I have watched many Bedouin shepherds. They are often children. And I have noted that one of the things they do well is hurl stones. They do it with amazing accuracy. Usually the sheep will follow the voice of the shepherd or shepherdess, a strange clicking sound that comes from the vocal cords. I have also been fascinated by the way the sheep will follow the shepherd as he or she strolls along, playing a flute. I have watched several thousand sheep all quietly following one shepherd as one body while he walked along playing on his flute. But sometimes, a sheep will challenge the voice of the shepherd. That's when the shepherd will bend down, pick up a stone and throw it. The stone finds its intended target ... the butt end.

One day, we stopped to camp in the Wadi Rum, a beautiful red-sand desert in southern Jordan. We had no sooner set up camp when around the bend came a herd of sheep and goats. It looked more like a sheep stampede, coming straight for us. We felt relatively out of harm's way since we had set up camp on a small rocky plateau about eight feet off the desert floor. Until we remembered that these were goats and sheep. Eight feet is not a challenge; it's an opportunity. We were soon inundated by several hundred animals interested in our food, clothing, bedding, anything they could get into their mouths. Providentially, a young Bedouin shepherdess came running along after them and began to call them back to her. Peculiar clicking noises issued from her mouth, and the sheep seemed to understand what she was saying. Most returned to her. But there was the usual black sheep, not responding to her voice. She stooped and picked up a stone. She flung the stone, striking the animal in the butt end. It immediately scurried back to rejoin the flock. She continued with remarkable precision until every animal followed her command.

As I watched her, my mind fixed on David the day he walked toward Goliath. He stooped and reached his hand into the brook, picking up five smooth stones. He was prepared to do what he was equipped to do at any time on any given day. He was a young shepherd. He could hurl stones from a sling with remarkable accuracy. His life and the lives of his sheep depended on his accuracy with a sling. He would not try to be someone else. He would not try to fight in someone else's armour. He would just be himself and do what he did best. But he also understood the spiritual significance of what he was doing. He had another weapon that no one else seemed prepared to carry. He depended upon the living God to go with him and to direct the stone to its intended target. He carried the weapon of faith. Goliath sneered at David, this ruddy-faced boy. David retorted, *"You come to me with sword, spear, and javelin, but I come to you in the name of the LORD of Heaven's Armies. … This is the LORD's battle, and he will give you to us!"* (1 Samuel 17:45, 47). As Goliath moved closer to attack, David did not retreat. He actually ran quickly to meet him. He reached into his shepherd's bag and took out a stone. He then hurled the stone at the giant. There was only one small window of opportunity not covered by armour and God's hand directed the missile to its intended end, planting it in the unprotected forehead of Goliath. It is stirring to recognize what God can do through you when you give who you are and what you can do to Him in faith.

These are the kinds of champions recorded in the Hall of Faith. Common, ordinary, even undesirable characters. Failures. Cowards. Misfits. Deficient, defective, and inadequate. All of them sinners. Yet they qualified as men and women of faith. When you read their stories, you will find someone you can identify with. Ordinary people who faced many of the same kinds of challenges and trials that you do, but who lived extraordinary lives by faith. Their faith took them to some pretty incredible places and astonishing victories. By faith they ran, stumbled, fell, bled, got back up, persevered, overcame, and finished the race God gave them to run.

THE HALL OF THE ANONYMOUS

Hebrews 11:34 speaks of *others*. Who were these others? What were their names? We aren't told. But the Bible is filled with the stories of these others. We know who Gideon was. But who were the 300 men who advanced in the enemy with him? We know who David was. But who were his 600 mighty men who joined him and dared to identify with him? We know who Elijah was. But who were the other 7,000 who had not bowed the knee to Baal? We know the names of Jesus' 12 disciples. But what are the names of the other seventy who followed Jesus? We don't know. In Hebrews 11, we read the names of seventeen champions. But there were others. Their names are not recorded, but they were tortured, mocked, whipped, chained in prisons, stoned to death, sawed in half, killed with the sword, forced into a life of destitution and oppression, and driven from their homes to hide out in the wilderness in caves and holes in the ground.

When you walk into Westminster Abbey in London, England, you immediately find yourself strolling the halls of the famous. A pageant of the names and tombs of many of the greatest statesmen, leaders, kings, queens, poets, and heroes in British history. Two tombs, in particular, stand out to me. The first is the tomb of David Livingstone. Livingstone was not a statesman in the eyes of people. He grew up in obscurity as a youngster working fourteen hours a day in the hot, stuffy cotton mills near Glasgow. But he felt an inescapable call from God on his life to go to Africa, the Dark Continent. With the fortitude and courage of an explorer and the passion and heart of an evangelist, he travelled more than 40,000 miles and mapped vast areas in the heart of Africa, sharing the gospel and serving the despised, exploited, and oppressed everywhere he went. His name has been written in the history books as a great missionary and explorer. The second grave is the Tomb of the Unknown Soldier. By contrast, this tomb bears no name. Beneath the marker lies the body of a soldier. We don't know whose son lies there, but someone's son lies there. His grave is a monument to all the *others*. The unknown. The anonymous. Those who fought faithfully and bravely, and died in the line of duty, but were never identified.

Similarly, the Hall of Faith in Hebrews 11 includes the record of the exploits, struggles, obedience, endurance, and faithfulness of those who ran the race, but who are never identified. This is the monument to all the *others*, the unknown, the lesser known, like most of us, but whose names are indelibly imprinted in the mind and heart of God.

When I was a boy, my parents used to conduct Bible studies and children's meetings in the rural areas throughout the Muskoka region in central Ontario. My dad would drive his '56 Chevy past the homes and shanties along the gravel road, picking up anyone waiting at the end of their driveway. In those days of no seatbelts, it was not uncommon to load 25 people onto the springs of the vehicle. They jammed into the seats in multiple layers, sat on the car roof and stood on the bumper. My favourite place to ride was in the open trunk. I'm not sure which was worse, the BO or the dust. Those were the days.

There was one location where my father would stop, get out of the car and walk up to the house. This was a place where we would pick up a half dozen children. These kids lived a meager and pitiful life, but they loved to come to church. He would have to step over the body of the father dead-drunk in the doorway. The mother had died several years previous giving birth in the barn out back. My father would shout the "everyone ready?" call, and the kids would emerge, jumping over their drunken father and bounding into the Chevy. One of those children was a boy who listened intently every Sunday to the gospel of Jesus' love. One day, when he returned home after church, he sat looking out of the window in his bedroom and sang the chorus, "Into my heart, into my heart. Come into my heart, Lord Jesus. Come in today; come in to stay. Come into my heart, Lord Jesus." Poorly educated, he learned to read and write, and a few years later, attended a Bible college. He graduated and returned to the same neighbourhood where he had grown up and continued the ministry my dad had begun. He continued to pastor in several churches for many years. He is one of the *others*. I believe he is one of the *last* who one day shall be *first* at Jesus' judgment.

Our task is not to be famous, but faithful. Our joy is not to be known, but to make Christ known. Our need is not to be acknowledged by man, but to be acknowledged by Christ. The greatest joy will be to hear from the lips of Jesus Himself, *"Well done, my good and faithful servant. You have been faithful in handling this small amount, so now I will give you many more responsibilities"* (Matthew 25:21).

41

Several years ago, I was privileged to attend a Promise Keepers conference for pastors. We enjoyed a feast of great speakers. La crème de la crème. Well-known preachers representing widely publicized ministries. But the person who touched my life the most was another pastor. I don't remember his name. I couldn't pronounce his name if I could remember. I was standing behind him in a lineup to get lunch. He had long black hair down to his waist and dark brown skin. I decided it would be interesting to find out who he was and so opted to join him for lunch. I followed him outside the stadium and casually sat down beside him. He seemed uncertain about the packaged food and so I asked him if he knew what he was eating. He didn't. This opened a conversation. It turned out he was a Native American pastor from Alaska. He had never been outside his village. A businessman had underwritten his round-trip flight to Atlanta and provided for all his expenses. The businessman? Another one of the anonymous. This native pastor lived on a diet of moose and fish, and when not hunting, spent his time pastoring his small church. He is another of the anonymous. His name, challenges, suffering, and hardships are unknown to us, but fully known to God.

These are the true heroes, faithfully serving God and influencing people in the corner of somewhere. Men and women who are not in any public eye, but commit to God, "anything, anywhere, anytime," and live out that commitment despite the cost, and sometimes very alone.

The writer of Hebrews 11 comments, *"They were too good for this world, wandering over deserts and mountains, hiding in caves and holes in the ground"* (11:38). Many believers escaped raids and found refuge during times of persecution by hiding in underground cities. Cappadocia, Turkey, is home to many of these cities, originally dug for protection and religious purposes. Derinkuyu is one such city. I remember the day clearly when we explored its tunnels. The city reaches a depth of 85 metres, its winding passageways descending 11 floors. It could accommodate from 35,000 to 50,000 people with their livestock and food stores. It had wine and olive presses, stables, storage rooms, schools, and chapels. A 55-metre vertical ventilation shaft rose to the surface and was the source of oxygen and the conduit to the water supply. Large, heavy millstone doors weighing 200 to 500 kilograms were used to close the entrance. They were sometimes used to trap enemy soldiers inside tunnels, forbidding escape and ensuring certain death. Whole armies were known to march right over these underground cities, not knowing that thousands of people were living below.

But put yourself back in the sandals of those early Christians. Torches were not allowed because they ate up oxygen. Just darkness. Silence. Listening for enemies. Living like moles in the blackness of the earth. Every day, you have to make a conscious decision to walk the walk. Your children ask if you will ever get a normal job. Will they ever live in a normal house? Will they ever be able to play outside in the sunshine? Will they ever see the sun again? Will they ever not be afraid? You don't know. These Christians chose to live a life of risk rather than deny Jesus. Thousands of anonymous believers chose to live underground in poverty rather than aboveground in prosperity. These were Christians who knew sacrifice. They gave up everything for the sake of the Rabbi Jesus. Brave, faithful, and nameless. While their names have disappeared in history, they have passed their legacy of faith on to us. They challenge us with a faith question. What are you doing with what you have been handed? How far would you go to follow the Rabbi Jesus?

Sometimes the idea is floated that suffering is evidence of sin or lack of faith. Job's friends tried to counsel him in this direction. There may be times when this is true. But, in this case, quite the opposite is true. *"They were too good for this world"* (Hebrews 11:38). They are an example of the truth that *"it is impossible to please God without faith"* (Hebrews 11:6). They suffered because they were faithful. Their stories and often short-lived lives bring balance to what it means to live by faith. The reality is that, by faith, ordinary people not only achieved extraordinary accomplishments, but endured extraordinary suffering. Faith gives amazing grace and power to bear anything. It supplies the muscle to run the race with endurance. Not merely to survive, but to thrive.

Faith enables the David Livingstones and the William Wilberforces to become world-changers. Their names go down into the history books as people who had a strong faith in God and whom God used to bring good to humankind. For most of us, however, our names are forgotten. Faith provides a man with the wisdom and perseverance to overcome challenges and to build a successful business for the purposes and glory of God. Faith leads another to pick up stakes and move to a perilous region of the world or to move anonymously into a needy community to be the presence of Christ there. Faith empowers a single mother to support and raise her children in a godly environment against all the odds. Faith motivates the working guy, who parks his pickup outside Tim's and grabs a coffee, large double-double, to head off to work and be a witness for Jesus at an unreceptive, antagonistic job site. Faith enables another to believe God for a miraculous healing. The same faith enables yet another to endure the heart-wrenching devastation of losing of a child to leukemia. Faith supplies the grace to endure the incapacitating rejection of being deserted by a spouse for someone else. This is the truth to which the witnesses of Hebrews 11 testify. Their names hang in the Hall of Faith. They have run their race and now sit in the Stadium of Champions to encourage us to run ours. They cry, "Run! Run!"

Jim Willett gives an insightful comment in his blog, "The Journey Beyond Average." He remarks, "There's nothing inspiring about average. … What moves us are the people who overcome adversity; stare down and face their challenges—own them. It's the people who rise above and show strength of character who become our mentors, our motivators."[2] These are the people of Hebrews 11.

PASSING THE BATON

Now it is our turn to run. Hebrews 12:1 continues, *"Therefore … let us run."* You are running in a first-century stadium. Beads of perspiration glisten in the sunlight on your shoulders and run down your face. You look up and see the crowd. You hear the cheers. These are not just spectators who have paid to watch; these are past participants, running champions.

In my days of track and field, I used to enjoy running the relay race. The relay race is a team race. It is run by multiple runners. The first runner runs a fixed distance, holding a baton in his hand. The baton is a short, wooden, plastic, or metal stick. Tension builds as he approaches the second runner. The receiver holds his position with his hand fixed to his side but open and ready to receive the hand-off. When the runner

44

enters the space, the receiver, hand in position, begins to run. The baton is thrust into the hand of the receiver. The exchange completed, that runner runs his prescribed leg of the race with the same intensity and endurance as the preceding runner. Each runner runs his leg of the course until the race is completed.

Moses handed the baton of faith to Joshua. David passed the baton to Solomon. Elijah passed it to Elisha. John the Immerser passed the baton to Jesus. Jesus handed the baton off to His disciples and commanded His followers to pass the baton off to others. Paul handed the baton to Timothy. Each runner must be vigilant to receive the baton from those who have gone before. Each runner must run his or her own race. Each runner must be intentional to pass the baton to the next runner. John passed the baton to Jesus and exclaimed that He must increase and that John must decrease. That is true in a sense for all of us. When you have run your leg of the race, it is time for you to decrease and for the next runner to increase. You step aside and cry, "Run!"

Young Israeli soldiers are sworn to their duty today by being taken back to their roots. Every recruit is sworn in at one of three locations. The first location is the Western Wall, sometimes referred to as the Wailing Wall. This is the one piece of the original temple wall left standing when the Romans destroyed the Temple in 70 AD, and is perhaps the most hallowed place in Israel. The second is Masada, an isolated mountain plateau rising above the Dead Sea on the eastern edge of the Judean Wilderness. It is best known for the first-century siege by the Roman 10th Legion that led to the mass suicide of 960 Jewish Sicarii rebels. Israeli soldiers are reminded that never again will the nation be put in this state of affairs. The third location is an isolated site out in the Negev desert, the grave of Ben-Gurion. David Ben-Gurion was the first Prime Minister of Israel and the man responsible for creating the independent nation of Israel in 1948. He was really the first modern Israeli. It began with him. Israeli soldiers are taken back to their roots, to those who lived, led, fought, and ran the race before them. This is where they find inspiration.

They are then given the baton … a Bible in one hand and a gun in the other. The Bible takes them back to their faith. The gun is a poignant memory aid of the reality that they are in a battle for survival. The Romans held an old adage: if you want peace, prepare for war. Young Israeli soldiers understand and adhere to that same maxim, that to enjoy peace they must be stronger than their enemies. With Bible and gun in hand, and a keen sense of the example of those who have gone before, they tread down the road in military array, rededicated, galvanized, and motivated.

What a parallel to the race we are to run! It is a difficult, agonizing run. But we are inspired by the example and testimony of those who have gone before. They have thrust the baton into our hands. The baton of faith. We do well to remember that we are running warriors. We are in a battle against the world and the devil. We are in a battle for the souls of people. We are fighting to expand the Kingdom of God in the kingdom of this world. We are encouraged and spurred on by those who ran before, who by faith *"overthrew kingdoms. ... They became strong in battle and put whole armies to flight"* (Hebrews 11:33–34).

A CONTINUING RACE

The writer of Hebrews concluded the chapter on the Hall of Faith with a surprising comment: *"All these people earned a good reputation because of their faith, yet none of them received all that God had promised. For God had something better in mind for us, so that they would not reach perfection without us"* (Hebrews 11:39–40). The race of faith that these pioneers blazed and that we continue to run from generation to generation is not an individual exercise. It is a team activity. We all run as a community of faith. It is much like a relay race. They ran their leg of the race in their generation and now we run ours today. But the race is not over. It will not be over until the last runner has crossed the finish line. At that time, runners from every age and generation will mount the winner's podium together. Their faith and ours will be recognized as one complete whole to the glory of Christ.

FIVE

THE CALL TO RUN

FOR ULTRARUNNERS, IT'S NOT JUST SOMETHING TO DO. IT'S NOT JUST an aspiration. It's not simply a need. It's more than a reaction to a particular trial in one's life. It's more than a challenge to tackle. It's a way of life. A calling.

As mentioned earlier, Jim Willett confronted both cancer and the Gobi. For him, it was a call he felt stirring within while staring at a picture of a silhouetted runner treading wearily through a daunting desert landscape. The book he held in his hands was *Running for My Life,* written by ultrarunning adventurer Ray Zahab. At the time, Jim defined himself as a "cancer patient" and was bumbling his way through the seven steps of grief. A voice within urged him to pick up the phone and call Ray. That single inspiring phone call led him to connect with other top Canadian ultrarunners, Stephanie Case and Ferg Hawke.

None of these people were running prodigies when they began. Ray Zahab was a pack-a-day smoker. When Stephanie began running, she couldn't wait for the run to end. She ran for charity and each run was unbearable. Ferg began running after a doctor's visit. He was overweight—too much beer and wings after slow-pitch. His blood pressure was too high and he would need to begin taking medication. So he started running. But what caused each of them to go to the next level and become genuine ultrarunners was a growing sense of call—that, for various reasons, this was what they were put here to do.

Stephanie Case advised Jim, "Find a race that you think is out of your league and sign up before you have a chance to talk yourself out of it. Next, tell all your friends and family about it to make sure you won't back out!"[1] Jim signed up for the 250-kilometre Gobi Desert Run and told the entire iRunNation in an article, "Taking it to the next Level." There was no turning back. This was a life-changing moment. Jim began training under a strong sense of calling.

THE CALL

I recall a humourous depiction of a man out on the golf course. He was in full swing and his club had just connected with the ball. What really caught my attention was the comic's caption: *What appears to be a man driving a golf ball is really a golf ball driving a man.* The implication was poignant. There is always something that drives us. Something that motivates us. Something that compels and propels us. Something that shapes you. What drives me? What drives you?

The greatest call for anyone's life is discovered in Hebrews 12:1. *"Let us run with endurance the race God has set before us."* This race is not something you choose. It is something God chooses and sets before you. He has a plan and purpose for your life that He calls you to. At a time when Paul knew that the path before him would be severe, he wrote with determination, *"My life is worth nothing to me unless I use it for finishing the work assigned me by the Lord Jesus"* (Acts 20:24). Literally, he is using the metaphor of a race and his goal is to finish the course God has called him to run. That is the most imperative thing in his life. The Latin word *voco* means *to call.* Our word *vocation* is derived from this root. A vocation is a calling. It helps me to endure under trial when I know that what I do is something God has called me to. I know that what He calls me to, He will enable and equip me for. The call of God is the strongest motivator in my life.

Paul encouraged Timothy, *"Fully carry out the ministry God has given you"* (2 Timothy 4:5). God has given you a ministry to fulfill for Him. Focus on that. This is critically important to recognize because there are many opportunities, expectations, and challenges that fall into one's lap but were never intended by God for you to do. Somebody ... but not you. But you say it's hard to say *no*. A sense of divine calling gives you focus and helps you to say *yes* to things that line up with your calling and to say *no* to many other noble assignments that only detract from what you have been called to do with your life. Even Jesus didn't heal everyone or do everything people expected of Him. He focused on what His Father in heaven had called Him to do. *"I always do what pleases him"* (John 8:29). *"I have come down from heaven to do the will of God who sent me"* (John 6:38). He had a clear sense of His calling. And you need to clarify and follow God's calling on your life.

Today, we think more in terms of career than calling. John Ortberg draws a clear contrast between career and calling:

> A career is something I choose for myself; a calling is something I receive. A career is something I do for myself; a calling is something I do for God. A career promises status, money or power; a calling generally promises difficulty and even some suffering—and the opportunity to be used by God. ... A career may end with retirement ... a calling isn't over until the day you die. The rewards of a career may be quite visible, but they are temporary. The significance of a calling lasts for eternity.[2]

A career may be embedded inside a calling, but a calling is more inclusive and all-encompassing than a career.

A CALL STORY

Esther was a young Jewess living in exile in Persia. She was an orphan. She was also drop-dead gorgeous. She was trapped in an ancient cultural practice of being added to the king's harem. The king was infatuated with her beauty and made her his number one wife. Her career was to be a queen and to fulfill all the responsibilities that accompanied such a position. But it was not until a situation arose that threatened an ethnic cleansing of her entire Jewish generation that her calling in life materialized. She was the queen. She was also a Jew. If anyone could do something, she could. She hesitated. It could cost her life. Not even the queen was permitted to enter the presence of the king without being invited.

At this point, her cousin and closest confidant, Mordecai, stood in the gap and sent a message to Queen Esther. *"Don't think for a moment that because you're in the palace you will escape when all other Jews are killed. If you keep quiet at a time like this, deliverance and relief for the Jews will arise from some other place, but you and your relatives will die"* (Esther 4:13–14). Then immediately Mordecai asked a question that distinguishes the difference between career and calling. *"Who knows if perhaps you were made queen for just such a time as this?"* She may have been the queen, but her life-calling was to intercede for her people and represent them before the king. This was the race God had set for Esther to run. There was risk. There was a potentially high cost. But this was a divine calling. Esther recognized that this was God speaking and rose to the occasion. Her *"weakness was turned to strength"* (Hebrews 11:34). And God used her to make a difference in the existence of people and to bring glory to Him. You can read the rest of her intriguing story in the book titled after her name.

Everyone who is called has a "call story." Gordon MacDonald says, "A call story is a history of whispered words and events that capture the soul and make one aware that God is speaking."[3] As you live your life, God uses the history of your upbringing, particular people who have helped to influence your life, prayer, circumstances and events, successes and failures, the Scriptures, challenges, training, spiritual gifts, talents and anything He may choose, to shape your purpose, legacy, and life call. The Holy Spirit whispers in your ear. He stirs a passion in your heart. He tugs on your soul. There is a gravitational pull that cannot be suppressed. And when your sails catch the wind of where the Spirit is blowing in your life, you know this is what you were meant to be and do. You are in your sweet spot. MacDonald continues, "Let us be frank: men and women have obeyed God's call and become martyrs. Others have undertaken unspeakably difficult and discouraging tasks and barely survived. Many more have lived the relatively common life between home and job. They hammer nails, sell widgets, create software, or fix things. But in the process they make a difference in the existence of the people around them. And they, too, are called."[4]

IN THE DUST OF THE RABBI

I will talk about the Tarahumara Indians later in this book, but they are considered by many to be the world's greatest distance runners. Distance runner Christopher McDougall wrote a book entitled *Born to Run*, telling his experiences living amongst the Tarahumara, learning their secrets. He linked up with a mysterious loner, Micah True, who lived among them and went by the name of Caballo Blanco. Caballo became his friend and mentor. He could run the mountain trails faster than they could be run on horseback. McDougall wanted to learn how to become a runner like Caballo.

One day when they were running one of the canyon trails, Caballo gave him the keys to becoming a great runner. Four words: "Get right behind me." McDougall did exactly that. He ran right behind the master runner. He stuck with him. He tried to copy everything he did. He kept his eyes on Caballo's sandaled feet. You become a great runner by running in the footsteps of a master runner. And that's how you learn to live your life to its fullest and intended purpose, by running in the footsteps of the Master of life.

Jesus walked along the shores of the Sea of Galilee and called people to follow Him. It is noteworthy that He didn't go to cities like Scythopolis or Jerash, places of notoriety. Places that boasted theatres and colonnaded streets, power, wealth, and luxury. No, He walked through the villages of the Galilee. He called Matthew, a tax collector. Matthew was considered a traitor; one of their own who worked for Rome; one who was ostracized from the community. He called five young men— Peter, Andrew, James, John, and Philip—all from one small village. Can you imagine? They all grew up in Bethsaida, which means "fishing village," a village of only a few hundred people. Their trade was fishing. Their education was limited. Their social status was low. Their hopes and dreams for the future were shallow. Then one day the Rabbi Jesus showed up and called them to follow Him.

Matthew had a financial career. The other five had fishing careers. But this was different. Jesus saw Peter and Andrew throwing a net into the water. James and John were sitting in a boat a little farther up the shore, repairing nets. Jesus looked into their hearts and saw something of great value. He called out to them, *"Come, follow me and I will show you how to fish for people"* (Matthew 4:19). He was picking them for His team. Do you remember what it was like at school when the team captains were picking teams for baseball? And it got down to a few people left who had not been chosen? And you were one of them? Then the teacher would just quickly divide up the remnant. "You go here, and you go there." You got placed on a team because no one wanted to choose you. As you walked over to line up with your team, the captain screwed up his nose as if to say, "No, not you!" And then you were relegated to the backfield where no one could even remotely hit the ball, stationed to simply observe the game. Jesus looked at the ones who had not been picked for the team, and said, "I want you for my team."

Jesus was a rabbi. He was looking for *talmeid* for His team. *Talmeid* were disciples. *Talmeid* were called to leave family, job, and everything to join the rabbi. It was said of a disciple that he or she was to cover oneself in "the dust of the rabbi." They were to follow so close to the rabbi that the dust from the rabbi's sandals would settle on them. They got right beside him. They walked in his footsteps. They stuck to him 24/7. They listened to every word he spoke. They obeyed what he said and did what he did. They began to think how he thought, absorbing a new way of thinking. They studied the master and became like him. The *talmeid* followed the master for several years, learning and training under him until he commanded: "Now you go and make your own disciples."

ABSOLUTE LOVE

These men Jesus called understood the nature of the call. It meant to abandon everything and to walk in the dust of the rabbi. But they had no idea of the extent of the call. What would it mean for their lives? Where would it take them?

Jesus defined the call as embracing absolute love for Him. Jesus came to earth to die upon the cross for our sins because of His absolute love for us. To follow Him would require the same kind of love. Jesus stipulated, *"If you want to be my disciple, you must hate everyone else by comparison— your father and mother, wife and children, brothers and sisters—yes, even your own life. Otherwise, you cannot be my disciple"* (Luke 14:26). Jesus was not commanding us to hate our loved ones. He was using a typical rabbinic form of comparison to make a strong point. He selected the ones we love the most in this life. You know how much you love your father, mother, wife, and children. You know how much you love your own life. Well, this high-level intensity of love is to be *hate* compared to your love for Him. Your love for Christ must be at the highest level. Absolute! Unconditional! Unrivaled!

TOTAL SURRENDER

Jesus also defined the call as embracing a total surrender to Him. *"If any of you wants to be my follower, you must turn from your selfish ways, take up your cross, and follow me"* (Matthew 16:24). In Jesus' day, the cross was an instrument of torture and death. The Romans would line the roads with crosses from which hung the writhing, bloodied figures of poor wretches enduring their last agonizing breaths. The Galilean fishermen Jesus called had witnessed many times the long processions of prisoners on death row being led to the places of execution. Each prisoner was forced to carry the cross-bar, the horizontal beam, of their cross tied to their shoulders. Carrying one's cross to one's own execution is a poignant, powerful picture of what it means to follow Jesus. But what does it mean?

It means the death of the self-life. Selflessness. The abandonment of every selfish way. The total surrender of self. You go to your own funeral and bury your selfish ways and will. But when the self-life dies, then the Spirit's life can take control. Your will has absolutely no power to do God's will on its own, but when it dies, then the life of the Holy Spirit takes control and empowers you to do the will of God.

Romans 12:1–2 gives another potent image of surrender. Paul begins, *"Give your bodies to God because of all he has done for you."* God gave His best for you. He gave His Son, Jesus, to die as a sacrifice on the altar of the cross. On the basis of what God, through Christ, has given for you, is it too much to ask you to give everything to Him? *"Let [your bodies] be a living and holy sacrifice—the kind he will find acceptable. This is truly the way to worship him"* (Romans 12:1). The last phrase can be translated, "This is your reasonable service." The word *reasonable* or *logical* is the Greek word *logikos*. *Logikos* is not an emotional, irrational, foolish response or impulse, but rather an intelligent, rational, responsible decision about what to do with your life, based upon what Christ has done for you. Christ gave His life as a sacrifice for you; it is only reasonable and logical that you give your life as a sacrifice to Him.

Paul sketches the picture of a sacrifice lying on an altar. A sacrifice is another depiction of death to the self-life. Death is a total, absolute surrender. You cannot be half dead. You are either dead or alive. Note, however, that this is not a dead sacrifice, but a living sacrifice. But just because you are living does not mean the surrender is any less absolute. You are to surrender your will, failures, struggles, challenges, future, ambitions, rights, the cottage, the career, money, possessions, family, fears, hurts, weaknesses, body, life—everything—to God. A living sacrifice is total and unconditional. Someone said to me many years ago that the challenge of laying your life on the altar as a *living* sacrifice is that it keeps crawling off the altar. There needs to be a daily surrender. This surrender results in transformation (I will examine this later), and transformation results in experiencing God's perfect will for your life (Romans 12:2).

I think the greatest fear of surrender is that if I surrender everything to God, He is going to take everything from me and send me to a swamp somewhere at the ends of the earth to live on a log and eat bugs. God is going to "take me down!" Well, first of all, God doesn't need to wait for you to pray a prayer of surrender to take you down. He can do that anytime. Secondly, if the swamp is where God wanted you, the life of surrender would make you, the swamp-dweller, the most fulfilled person on earth because you are where God wants you. Joy and fulfillment have nothing to do with comfort; they have everything to do with living where God wants you to live, doing what God wants you to do and being who you were meant to be. The swamp would be your sweet spot. Thirdly, Jesus said He came to give the abundant life, not a lousy life. The issue is not what you give up but what you gain. Everything you give to God is an investment in His kingdom and in the life He meant you to live.

ANYTHING, ANYWHERE, ANYTIME

If you are going to give someone absolute love and surrender, you had better know who that person is. The Gospel of Luke gives a fuller, more detailed picture of what happened that day when Jesus called the fishermen from Bethsaida to follow Him. He noticed two empty boats at the water's edge, so Jesus asked Peter, the owner of one of them, to push out into the water. Jesus then stood in his boat and used it as a platform from which to teach the people crowding in on Him on the shore.

When Jesus had finished speaking, He said to Peter, *"Now go out where it is deeper, and let down your nets to catch some fish"* (Luke 5:4). Peter protested a little. It made no sense. He had fished all night, as was the practice, and had had no success. Then came one of those significant statements that every so often came from the lips of Peter, like honey from a rock. *"But if you say so, I'll let the nets down again"* (Luke 5:5). I will trust You, Jesus, even when it doesn't make sense. At that point, Peter's little bit of faith intersected with Jesus' infinite power. The nets suddenly filled so full of fish that they began to tear. Peter called to another boat for help, and soon both boats were so full that they were on the verge of sinking.

When Peter saw what happened, he was awestruck. His response was immediate. He fell to his knees before Jesus and acknowledged, "Oh, Lord, please leave me—I'm too much of a sinner to be around you" (Luke 5:8). What had just happened in Peter's head and heart? He had been in the fishing boat with Jesus for the last hour. So, why this unusual response now? Why was there this sudden sense of personal unworthiness? Well, Jesus had just displayed His power and authority. Peter had simply thrown out a net in obedience to Jesus' command, and Jesus brought the fish miraculously into the net. What a partnership! It was so miraculous that Peter was no longer thinking about the fish; he was thinking about Jesus.

Miracles were Jesus' credentials for who He was. They manifested His person, power, and authority. This was just the beginning of a journey of learning that Jesus had power and authority over fish, wind, storms, disease, demons, death, all things … because He was the Son of

RUN! THE AMAZING RACE

God, the Almighty God, the Creator of all things, the Omni-everything. Peter was getting the point. And that changed everything for Peter.

When you recognize that you are in the presence of God, you feel like one of those fish out of water. When you recognize who Jesus is, you feel the dismay of who you are. When you stand in His presence, you become overwhelmed with the presence of sin in your life. But that's good. Because your sin is why Jesus came to the earth. Until you acknowledge your sin and unworthiness, you will never acknowledge Him as your Saviour and Master, or give up everything to follow Him.

When Peter dropped to his knees in Jesus' presence, he was conceding surrender. When the general of an army surrenders to another, he is acknowledging the superior power and authority of the other. I lay down my rights, agenda, goals, plans, and priorities. Surrender is summed up in three words you declare to Jesus as your Master ... *anything, anywhere, anytime.* Surrender is the critical response in answering the call to becoming everything God made you for. To running the race God has set before you.

A New Identity

Jesus said, *"Follow me."* From that point on, these fishermen would no longer fly the banner "Bethsaida Fisheries," but would be known as *talmeid* of the Rabbi Jesus. They were chosen for Jesus' team. Whenever a particular team drafts a new player, his new coach and manager stand beside the player for a photo as he proudly shows off his new jersey. When one is selected to play with the Toronto Maple Leafs hockey club, one wears the blue and white jersey with the big maple leaf with pride. When a player is selected to play on Team Canada, he has been chosen for one of Canada's highest honours and wears the sweater like royalty. The jersey symbolizes pride, excellence, belonging, and identity.

Jesus commanded us to go and make disciples and to baptize them (Matthew 28:19). The act of receiving Christ as one's Saviour through faith brings one into God's family. This can be done in the secrecy of one's own home. It is the decision of the heart. Immersion in water is like visibly putting on the jersey of Christ. One is openly identifying oneself as a "Christ-follower" or "Christian." A *talmeid* of the Rabbi

56

Jesus. One wears the jersey with a sense of distinction but also with a sense of humility. It is humbling to have been chosen to play on Jesus' team. Jeremiah stated it another way, as wearing the name of the Lord God of Heaven's Armies (Jeremiah 15:16). Jesus said to the victorious in the church in Philadelphia that He would write on them the name of God (Revelation 3:12). How humbling! What an identity!

COMPLETE TRANSFORMATION

More than anything, to follow in the dust of the Rabbi meant to become like Him. Following Christ can be summed up in two words: death and resurrection. Just prior to Jesus being led away to be crucified, He said, *"Anyone who wants to be my disciple must follow me"* (John 12:26). He was looking death in the face. Follow Him? In the same passage and context, He said these words: *"Unless a kernel of wheat is planted in the soil and dies, it remains alone. But its death will produce many new kernels—a plentiful harvest of new lives"* (John 12:24). The kernel of wheat is no longer high on the stalk, but is dropped into the cold, damp earth. The darkness rots the shiny, golden skin of the kernel. The coat disintegrates and falls off. The seed shrivels and dies. Then something wonderful occurs. There is a sign of life. The dead kernel generates a tiny green shoot. The shoot becomes a plant. And the plant produces fruit that carries many more wheat seeds. Death is followed by resurrection, and resurrection produces the fruit of life. Jesus was drawing attention to His own approaching experience of death and resurrection and identifying the nature of His call upon us.

Jesus said, *"If any of you wants to be my follower, you must turn from your selfish ways, take up your cross, and follow me"* (Matthew 16:24). When Jesus summoned His disciples to follow Him and to run the race He set for them, it was essentially a call to abandon one's life to His life. To die to self and be transformed into His likeness. The word *metamorphosis* is a Greek word and means to *change form,* or to *transform.* It describes the process of change that a worm undergoes when it wraps itself inside a cocoon and emerges as a beautiful moth or butterfly. The change is astonishing. And so is the transformation a man or woman undergoes when becoming like Jesus. You die to self and emerge from the tomb, the cocoon, a new person … like Jesus. It's like a resurrection. Paul stated it succinctly: *"My old self has been crucified with Christ. It is no longer I who live, but Christ lives in me"* (Galatians 2:20). When Jesus died, your sins were nailed to the cross with Him. But that's not all. Your old self was crucified with Him. Life is now a process of dying to the control of self so that the resurrection life of Christ can rule within and produce the fruit of a transformed life.

It will be wonderful to go to heaven one day. But following Jesus is about more than going to heaven, as critically important as that is. By faith in Christ, your destination is secure. You have a perfect standing before God as His son or daughter. This is your position in Christ. But as you make your way toward your final destination, there should be a progressive transformation in your daily condition to becoming more and more like Jesus in nature, character, attitudes, appetites, and actions. In other words, every day you live you should become a little more like Jesus. Read the Sermon on the Mount in Matthew chapters 5 to 7 to discover the characteristics of a life lived in His likeness.

Faith is not a blast that rockets you into heaven. It is not instant gratification. It is the beginning of a journey of spiritual formation in which the Holy Spirit daily conforms you into the likeness of Christ. *"And the Lord—who is the Spirit—makes us more and more like him [Christ] as we are changed into his glorious image"* (2 Corinthians 3:18). Most often, the Spirit uses crises and pain in our lives to cultivate that growth. Again, pain is the strongest motivator to change. He also uses the routine of life, however—the mundane, times of rest and waiting, and even the periods of abundance. Sometimes spiritual growth is noticeable; at other times it seems like nothing is happening. It's like looking in the mirror each day. You see no apparent change in your appearance from day to day. But when you compare a photo of yourself taken this year to one taken last year, the change is quite noticeable.

It is noteworthy that when Jesus called the fishermen to follow Him, He said to them, *"I will show you how to fish for people"* (Matthew 4:19). I can envisage Peter peering down into the water over the side of the boat and saying, "There's people down there too?" Peter had no idea of the extent of what this call entailed. Peter, like all of us, was a huge work project for Jesus. There were lots of flaws. We all carry emotional baggage, insecurities, weakness, chemical imbalances, anger, fears, and failures. We are not fine; we are on a journey. We are omni-nothings surrendering to Christ, the Omni-everything, to become everything He wants us to be, for His glory.

Paul urged the Philippians, *"Work hard to show the results of your salvation, obeying God with deep reverence and fear. For God is working in you, giving you the desire and the power to do what pleases him"* (Philippians 2:12–13). Do you see the balance between human responsibility and divine power? You work at surrendering and obeying, and He will give you the desire and power to live a transformed life. *"We are God's masterpiece"* (Ephesians 2:10). You are the painting; He is the divine Artist.

Terry Wardle writes:

> Spiritual development is not my job; it is God's. My role is simply to surrender, over and again, to what He is doing. Formation is not about my performance or striving. It is about Christ's performance and my ongoing death to self-centredness and control. All this is to say that spiritual formation is a process of being conformed, not conforming. You and I are the ones being shaped, and the Lord is the one doing the shaping.[5]

During art class at school, a little girl was drawing a picture. The teacher was having difficulty deciphering what the little girl was drawing, so she asked her to interpret the meaning of the picture. The little girl said it was a picture of God. To this, the teacher replied that no one knows what God looks like. The young girl quickly countered, "They will when I get through." Such is the Spirit's objective for spiritual formation. Such is the purpose of following in the dust of the Rabbi. When people look at your life, they will know what Christ looks like.

Simon Cowell is the highly successful owner of a record company, a talent scout, and one of the original creators of *American Idol*. He has a mind like a sponge that absorbs what is going on around him. He is better known for being someone who speaks his mind. Cowell attributes his success to Peter Walterman, an eccentric but brilliant music producer.

When Cowell was just starting out in his career, he recognized that if he wanted to succeed in the music business, he needed to follow a master in the business. So Cowell shadowed Walterman everywhere like a dog for two years. He would sit at the back of his music studio and just watch him. After about one and a half years of being followed, Walterman finally asked, "Simon, are you following me?" "Yes," replied Simon in typical "Simon" fashion, "Do you have a problem with that?" "No, just curious," responded Peter. Simon always had a feeling that Peter would change his life. And he did. He gave him the skills and showed him the course to follow. He taught him such principles as the necessity of a great song ... that no matter how good the artist, the song has to be incredible. That is the relationship between the master and the disciple that leads to transformation and success.

Paul emphasized the essential requirement of discipleship when he said:

> *Give your bodies to God because of all he has done for you. Let them be a living and holy sacrifice. ... Don't copy the behavior and customs of this world, but let God transform you into a new person by changing the way you think. Then you will learn to know God's will for you, which is good and pleasing and perfect* (Romans 12:1–2).

R.S.V.P.

Dean Karnazes, the Ultramarathon Man, describes his call to distance running in his book, *Ultramarathon Man: Confessions of an All-Night Runner.* It began with the sudden, tragic death of his sister on the eve of her eighteenth birthday. Pary was killed in an automobile accident. The one who had always encouraged Dean to follow his heart was gone, and her death left an agonizing void in his heart. As the years rolled by, the stresses of the job became unbearable. Holding an MBA and pulling in six figures a year didn't bring any satisfaction. There was a growing, nagging emptiness. His life was moving at a whirlwind pace of important meetings, expensive lunches, lucrative deals, and the demands of corporate life. But an inner passion for life eluded him. When he looked thirty years down the road, he feared he'd be in the same spot plus wrinkled, bald, fat, and bitter.

One night, after being propositioned by a beautiful woman at a bar, he excused himself to run to the washroom. He kept running. And running. And running. After running for three hours straight, he was exhausted, his feet were badly swollen and he had a massive blood blister on his left big toe. He sat by the curb for a few moments and then continued to run again. He ran down into the valleys and up over the peaks and steep, hilly inclines of the San Francisco peninsula. At times he felt delirious. It was cold and foggy. At one point, Dean seemed to be running forever up a brutally steep hill. The pain was excruciating, but he ignored the pain. He finally punched through the fog and found himself standing on top of the clouds, viewing the spectacle of a still, black, star-studded sky. He was exhausted, half-naked and in the middle of nowhere, but he had an overwhelming sense that this was where he was meant to be.

That night, he ran for seven hours and covered thirty miles. In the early morning he found a pay phone and placed a collect call home to his wife, Julie. "Where are you?" she asked anxiously. He informed her that he was at a place called Half Moon Bay, about thirty miles away and needed a ride home. Startled, she asked him how he got there? "I ran," he replied. "You what?" she countered. "I ran," he replied again. She inquired if he was okay. "I think so," Dean answered. "I've lost control of my leg muscles, and my feet are swollen stuck in my shoes. I'm standing here in my underwear. But other than that, I'm doing pretty well. Actually, I feel strangely alive."[6]

He writes, "In the course of a single night I had been transformed from a drunken yuppie fool into a reborn athlete. During a period of great emptiness in my life, I turned to running for strength. I heard the calling, and I went to the light."[7]

I see some amazing parallels to the call of Christ on our lives. As noted earlier in the chapter, God will use one's upbringing, tragedy, success, or failure as a means of speaking into one's life. He will utilize the barrenness of having everything right down to the trauma of losing everything, to create a gravitational pull that cannot be suppressed. He calls you to something of far greater meaning and consequence for your life. This is the call of Christ to run the race He has set for you.

The call from Christ demands a response. The Galilean fishermen had no idea what lay on the other side of the decision. The cost. The gain. But their response is amazing. *"They left their nets at once and followed him"* (Matthew 4:20). *"They left everything and followed Jesus"* (Luke 5:11).

It reminds me of the story of an ad that appeared in 1914 in a newspaper in London, England. It had been placed by Ernest Shackleton, the famous explorer to Antarctica. "Men wanted for hazardous journey, small wages, bitter cold, long months of complete darkness, constant danger, safe return doubtful." While no copies of the ad have ever been found in any archives, the content of the ad described the reality of the call. For men willing to sacrifice their lives for a cause. Shackleton was looking for 27 crewmen to man his ship, the Endurance, bound for Antarctica. His goal was to be the first to cross the continent from sea to sea via the pole. The response was overwhelming. More than 5,000 applications arrived on Shackleton's desk.

The story adequately illustrates the call Jesus extends to follow Him. To deny your rights, comforts, family, friends, possessions, anything and everything, to take up your cross, the symbol of death to the self-life, and follow Him. Countless numbers have responded to that call down through the centuries. They have gladly surrendered everything and followed Him, regardless of the cost. Following Jesus isn't for cowards. Surrendered people are willing to give up anything, endure anything, and to follow Him anywhere, anytime, if it pleases Him and brings Him glory. Surrendered people walk in the dust of the Rabbi, who gave up everything and endured everything on the cross for them. The cost may be great, but so is the glory. Now is the time to respond. You don't want to look back on your life one day and wonder what might have been.

MY CHRISTIAN COMMITMENT

One day, a young African pastor was martyred for Christ. Soon after, a written commitment was found tacked on the wall of his house. The commitment embodies what it means to follow Jesus. What it means to walk in the dust of the Rabbi. What it means to run the race. I have the commitment sitting on my library shelf. I encourage you to make his commitment, your commitment.

I'm part of the fellowship of the unashamed. I have Holy Spirit power. The die has been cast. I have stepped over the line. The decision has been made. I'm a disciple of Jesus Christ. I won't look back, let up, slow down, back away, or be still.

My past is redeemed, my present makes sense, my future is secure.

I'm finished with low living, sight walking, small planning, smooth knees, colorless dreams, tamed visions, mundane talking, cheap living, and dwarfed goals.

I no longer need pre-eminence, prosperity, position, promotions, plaudits or popularity. I don't have to be right, first, tops, recognized, praised, regarded or rewarded. I now live by faith, lean on His presence, walk by patience, am uplifted by prayer, and labor by power.

My face is set, my gait is fast, my goal is heaven, my road is narrow, my way rough, my companions few, my guide reliable, my mission clear. I cannot be bought, compromised, detoured, lured away, turned back, deluded or delayed. I will not flinch in the face of sacrifice, hesitate in the presence of the adversary, negotiate at the table of the enemy, pander at the pool of popularity, or meander in the maze of mediocrity.

I won't give up, shut up, let up, until I have stayed up, stored up, prayed up, paid up, and preached up for the cause of Christ. I am a disciple of Jesus. I must go till He comes, give till I drop, preach till all know, and work till He stops me. And when He comes for His own, He will have no problems recognizing me—my banner will be clear![8]

SIX

TRAINING FOR THE RUN

THE CHILL OF THE NIGHT AIR DISSIPATES AND THE HEAVY FOG LYING IN
the Rift Valley begins to dissolve as the sun rises over the huts of Iten,
a high-altitude training camp. A small group of Kenyans slips into
their running shoes, stained a dark russet shade from the red dirt of the
mountain trails and roads. The smell of burning charcoal wafts in the air
as villagers light their fires for the day's cooking. The runners wear tights
and loose-fitting running jackets. They stand at the side of the road and
begin the usual stretching warm-ups. Their arms reach up while arching
their backs. They stretch their hamstring muscles and bend their legs up
behind the buttocks. Others run on the spot, lifting their knees almost
to their jaws.

In Kenya, long-distance runners train in camps. These camps are
nothing like Western training centres. They are much more Spartan in
nature, tough, no-nonsense, and meager. Training camps are usually
rough wood huts furnished with the bare necessities. The bare provisions
are sometimes no more than wooden bed frames and, sometimes,
mattresses. Food is scarce and often rationed. There is no electricity. No
running water. No distractions. And no complaining. One does what it
takes to become one of the best.

Iten is one of the better-known training camps. Runners come to Iten
from all over Kenya. There is a sense of something magical running on
the roads of Iten. Often, a camp is associated with a particular champion

runner. Every day the pack will train and run with this successful athlete. This person becomes a mentor to his or her disciples. Kenyans believe, "When you run with champions in training, then you know you too can be a champion."[1] The runners form strong bonds with each other and their leader.

The roads of Iten are comparable to cow trails. They are scarred with deep potholes and easily reduced to gummy mud trails after a downpour. But the Kenyans believe that training on these roads builds strength and endurance. The belief is that if they can train to run well on these Kenyan trails, they will fly around the tracks of America.

Lornah Kiplagat is a world-champion distance runner. Most of her life, she has run uphill against an oppressive, male-oriented society. But her dominance in the sport has made her a role model and inspiration to hundreds of young girls in Kenya. She and her husband, Pieter Langerhorst, fund a training camp in Iten dedicated to supporting young female athletes. Lornah, nicknamed "the Simba," can often be seen running the trails with a group of about a dozen runners. They glide silently along the road like a pride of lions. They run with a balance of strength and grace, their thin, strong legs moving in unison while their feet barely seem to touch the ground. Their posture has little core movement. Their lean bodies remain upright, elbows at right angles, hands relaxed and heads steady and horizontal. They seem to run effortlessly while watching to dodge small piles of garbage or clods of ploughed earth that litter the trail. The stride accelerates as runners push the pace, each one sharing a spell at the front of the pack, and always without a word being spoken.

There are varieties of training. Tapering. Tempo training—runs between 45 and 70 minutes. The runners begin at a steady, moderate pace but then end up running the last half of the distance at top speed. Long runs. Hill work. The Kenyans place great confidence in the effectiveness of hill work. Thin air, extreme heat, and a long hill combine to create a demanding challenge, but produce great reward. A pack of runners will run up and back down a 200-metre dirt hill a number of times in succession. Sometimes 25 times. Training also includes running a hill that can be up to 25 kilometres long. Such runs are followed by sufficient periods of rest and recovery. Hard work and extensive rest are closely associated. At day's end, exhausted bodies are strewn all around the grounds of the training camp. An early night to bed, however, refreshes and revives them to do it all again the next morning.

Training is hard work. There's no easier way to say it. But the results are rewarding. Kenyans should know. Look at their success. Ponder the following quotes from some of Kenya's best.

Moses Kiptanui: "If you are not sweating, you are not training."[2]

Daniel Komen: "Have patience: it takes years of hard training to get good results."[3]

Peter Rono: "Aim high, and then higher. Training hard—that is all."[4]

John Litei: "Training is sacred; just a little training does not win the race. Training is a repetition and very hard, not like a race where you just go out once. You must put it in your mind that training is everything."[5]

Christopher Kangogo Cheboiboch: "When I train hard then I win easy."[6]

Benjamin Limo: "Don't bother going to your race unless you have dragged your body to the last inch of survival in the training runs."[7]

John Ngugi: "Discipline, hard discipline is the answer to all running success."[8]

Paul Tergat: "You may have the talent, but without hard training you will never arrive."[9]

When you consider these quotes, you recognize remarkable parallels to training for the most amazing race God has called you to. There are hundreds of ways to lose, but just one way to win. Train hard! Your commitment to training will enlighten you as to how serious you are about your commitment to following Christ.

STRIPPING DOWN

"Let us strip off every weight that slows us down, especially the sin that so easily trips us up" (Hebrews 12:1). Jim Willett trained every week for the Gobi Run. He ran with a backpack, beginning with it empty and working up to 20 pounds. He needed to get used to eating new kinds

of food, such as freeze-dried cuisine. You can't carry a buffet on your back when running through the desert. He worked up to running 125 kilometres each week. He faithfully followed a daily routine of stretching exercises. He ran and trained on a treadmill in a sauna to acclimatize himself to running in such extreme temperatures as 50-degrees Celsius. One day, I was speaking on the phone with ultrarunner Ray Zahab. He seemed to be panting profusely, and I asked him if he was all right. He replied that he was training for a run in the Arctic, where he would be pulling a sled. To train, he was running in the Gatineaus, even as we spoke, pulling a tire.

The first-century runners trained with weights strapped to their arms and legs. This would build strength and endurance. But when it came to race day, they would strip off the weights. I can't imagine a runner running a marathon, coming over the hill at the three-mile mark, neck muscles straining, sweat pouring down his face, with weights still strapped to his arms and legs. The spectators would be screaming, "Take off the weights!" I can't imagine Ray Zahab running on race day dragging a tire. That's for training. On race day, you cut the weights loose.

Paul Bitok, Kenyan Olympian, trains in extremely hot conditions wearing two complete tracksuits on top of a long-sleeved T-shirt. You might look at him and think he is mad. He smiles and says, "Don't think I am cold, my friend. This is the Kenyan way, so we sweat and it is hard for training. I am suffering in all these clothes! And then when the race comes, you throw off the heavy suits and you fly."[10] In the first century, runners took off all of their clothes and ran naked. The word *gymnasium* is derived from the Greek word for *naked*, a reminder of days past when runners ran naked. Change is good! Although the spandex tights worn today aren't too dissimilar. A few decades ago, runners competed in cotton clothes. In thirty minutes your shirt would weigh a gazillion pounds. Today, clothing is made from tiny microfibers that gather your sweat and shoot it from your body like tiny catapults. Your shirt never gets heavy.

The Kenyans go even further in their training. They love to get on the trails after a good rain. The red clumps of honey-like clay cling to their shoes, making them very heavy. They believe that this builds up their leg strength and mental mettle and makes them unbeatable on smooth surfaces. Kenyan Joseph Nzau trained in size-13 shoes, four sizes too big for his feet. Then on race day, he slipped into his own race shoes and ran with a feeling of running on air.

The most expensive running shoes are not necessarily the best. In fact, some studies show that the construction of the best running shoes give so much support that they alter the natural movement of the feet. This can cause foot problems such as chronic planter fasciitis and increase the risk of injury. When you walk or run, your foot absorbs the shock by naturally landing on the outside of the heel and rolling quickly inward to a stable position before rolling forward onto the toe. This is called pronation. It has to do with the alignment of the structure of the leg and foot bones and tendons. When your bodyweight presses down on a support structure such as a running shoe that is out of alignment with your body, injury can occur. Jeff Galloway gives some *don'ts* of shoe selection. Don't wear a shoe because it has worked well for someone else. Don't select the shoe that best matches your outfit. Don't buy a shoe only because it's the most expensive. Don't get locked into specific models or brands.[11] Buy a shoe that allows your foot to function with the elasticity of being barefoot. First-century runners actually discarded their shoes and ran barefoot. This would have made sense, if even for reasons of style and fashion. Even in ancient days, it probably wasn't a pretty picture to imagine someone running naked wearing only running shoes. It certainly would have done nothing for aesthetic appreciation. But let's not go there.

In preparation for the race, hard sacrificial training is everything. No more junk food, saturated fat, refined sugar, or candy. Less sitting around like a couch potato, and more exercise. When race day arrives, strip off the gummy mud and clay sticking to your runners, the size-13 shoes, the heavy clothing, the old tire you've been dragging, the training weights that slow your pace. Strip off any spiritual fat or any parasitic sins that encumber the pace of your progress in the life of faith. Cut loose anything that drains your emotional and spiritual health and energy. Sever anything that robs you of the joy of running.

LOSING WEIGHTS

The writer of Hebrews 12 differentiates between weights and sins. Weights are things not necessarily rated as sins. But they can be anything that hinders spiritual progress. Past woundedness. Indifference. Procrastination. Impatience. Laziness. Busyness. Insensitivity. Oversensitivity. Wrong friends. Possessions. Money. Video games. Television. Some of us are trying to run today while still dragging an emotional tire. There is a whopping flat-screen TV strapped to your back. A crowd of bad relationships in tow. A list of worldly responsibilities that entangle you in their grip. A ton of unfulfilled overdue obligations that have been irresponsibly deferred and now break you under their load. Financial debt that paralyses you. Past hurts that weigh heavier and heavier. Habits that put a stranglehold around you. Fear that devours your passion. Anxieties and burdens that consume your energy. And the list of weights goes on.

Some weights are subtler. You may experience a hurtful co-dependency with your children. You do everything to prevent them from failing. You protect them from the harsh realities of life. You give your child everything he or she wants for fear of losing their love or losing their sense of need for you. You shower your child with favours just because he or she is your son or daughter. Soon, a sense of entitlement replaces the spirit of thanksgiving that you crave from your child. Gratitude is swallowed up by demands and expectations placed upon you. Failure to rescue them from their foolish choices results in blame directed at you. You then carry the burden of guilt. Sometimes you fail to construct healthy boundaries from those who hurt you.

Weights are often difficult to identify or classify. We don't recognize or acknowledge them as weights. Sometimes, we just carry them without questioning the need of their existence. I don't stop to ask why I have encumbered myself with this burden. We even become attached to the baggage. In some sort of misleading way, it plays a part in my sense of self-worth, my longing to be needed or hunger for attention. The subtlety of many weights is that we rationalize that they are a necessary part of life. We think we need them.

In 1845, Sir John Franklin set sail from England with a crew of 128 men to navigate and chart the elusive Northwest Passage through the

Canadian Arctic. They packed the necessities: food, clothing, weapons, coal. Plus a lot of other things: a 1,200-volume library, fine china, crystal goblets, and sterling silverware for all officers with his initials engraved on the handles. Astonishingly, they packed only a 12-day supply of coal for the ships' auxiliary steam engines. The ships became trapped in the Arctic ice, and the inevitability of death set in. The men decided to trek over the treacherous ice in small groups to safety. None survived. All died of starvation, hypothermia, tuberculosis, lead poisoning, or scurvy. Years later, the bodies of two officers were found with a large sled 65 miles from the ship. When rescuers looked into the sled, they discovered it filled with boxes of table silverware.

"Outrageous! Laughable! Absurd!" you say. But maybe the story sheds light on the way so many people live their lives. Maybe it hits closer to home than one might want to admit. Maybe what is outrageous are the weights people carry in their lives that are not only unnecessary but are life-sapping. This is the baggage that slows us down and keeps us from running the race God calls us to run.

DISCARDING SIN

Sin is not only a weight but it is something God hates. Psalm 32 lists four varieties of sin. The first is called *pesha*, and means "disobedience" against a rightful authority. God says "do" and we don't; God says "don't" but we do. It includes the idea of trespassing. What do you think when you see a sign posted, "NO TRESPASSING"? To many, it is an invitation to enter. Maybe there is something in there that I would like to see or would benefit from; something someone is withholding from me. So, over the fence you go. God told Adam and Eve they could eat from every tree in the garden except one. So what did Adam and Eve do? They reached for the fruit of that tree. God gave the Ten Commandments for the purpose of setting limits for our own good, security and order, and to teach us to obey Him. When we go against what God says, that is sin.

The second word for sin is *hata*. This word denotes "missing the mark." Whereas *pesha* means to do something you shouldn't, *hata* means to fail to do something that you should. Every morning, I go out with a quiver full of arrows. The arrows have names etched into their shafts, such as love, forgiveness, purity, and integrity. Throughout the day, I pull the arrows out of the quiver and place them against the bowstring; I aim at God's target or standard, and shoot. At the end of the day I go to retrieve the arrows. To my disappointment, I find none in the bull's-eye. In fact, I find none in the target board. I pick them up along the trail. All of them have fallen short. I have missed the mark. Sinned.

The third word for sin is *aon*. It means, "to get off the path." I am following along in the path God has set when I see another path that looks so much easier, so much more interesting. So I wander down that path to discover where it leads. Even in running a race, you follow the marked path or you are disqualified. Other paths are wrong paths. That is a picture of sin.

The fourth word is *remiyya*. It signifies "deceit." Giving an appearance of one thing, but being another. Like the lady who lived in a neighbourhood where crime was increasing, garbage was blowing in the wind, drugs were everywhere and gangs roamed the streets. She decided to do something about it. She wanted to make a difference. So she mobilized the good citizens of her community, called neighbourhood meetings, enlisted the support of churches and developed a plan to raise money. Within a year, she had raised $400,000. She took the money and moved to another neighbourhood. Such deceit is sin.

Theatrical performers on the Greek and Roman stage spoke and acted from behind masks. They were called *hypocrites* or *pretenders*. That's okay when acting on the stage of a theatre, but not when performing on the stage of life. A hypocrite is one who pretends to possess virtues or principles that, in fact, one does not actually possess. You say things to God that you do not mean. You make a promise that you do not intend to fulfill. You promote a particular image of yourself for others to see and believe, but behind closed doors and in your heart you are not that person. You wear a mask. You are an actor. A pretender. What people see is not what you are. When this characterizes your life, this is sin.

Susanna Wesley was the remarkable mother of 19 children, including John and Charles Wesley. She defined sin to her children in the following way:

Whatever weakens your reasoning, impairs the tenderness of your conscience, obscures your sense of God, or takes away your relish for spiritual things; in short, if anything increases the authority and power of the flesh over the Spirit, then that to you becomes sin, however good it is in itself.[12]

Sin greatly impacts the kind of race you will run for God. It *"easily trips us up"* (Hebrews 12:1), sending us sprawling head over heels down the embankment, causing injury and harm. That is why we are told to "strip off" the sin in our lives. We do this through the regular daily discipline of confession. The word *confession* means to *say the same thing as God.* It means to come clean with God. Being honest about your sin. The discipline of confession is the key to cutting the sin loose.

David, the Psalmist, writes, *"Finally, I confessed all my sins to you [the Lord]. ... And you forgave me"* (Psalm 32:5). Forgiveness means to be rid of the sin, to have the sin stripped off. *"If we confess our sins to him [God], he is faithful and just to forgive us our sins and to cleanse us from all wickedness"* (1 John 1:9).

You were dead because of your sins and because your sinful nature was not yet cut away. Then God made you alive with Christ, for he forgave all our sins. He canceled the record of the charges against us and took it away by nailing it to the cross (Colossians 2:13–14).

Everything about sin and forgiveness gets back to the cross of Jesus. The keys of faith and confession open the door to forgiveness and freedom solely because Jesus died on the cross and shed His blood as the payment and penalty for all of our sins. The keys of faith and confession turn a spiritual possibility into a spiritual reality. Your sins are pictured as nailed to the cross. But your sinful nature is also nailed to the cross. When Jesus died on the cross for you, He handed you the keys of faith and confession, making it possible for you to strip off the sin in your life and to snatch freedom from its power and control over you.

The word *cancel* means "to wash out." In Paul's day, the ink was basically soot mixed with gum and diluted with water. The pen applied it to papyrus, the paper of their day. The ink retained its colour for a long time. But the ink was water-soluble and the papyrus could be washed clean by wiping a wet sponge over the ink. In this way, the record was erased. When your life is washed clean of the stain of sin by the cleansing of Jesus' blood, you are free to run unhindered and unimpeded by its power and weight.

DISCIPLINE

Stripping off weights and sin is inseparably linked to the discipline of training. Webster defines *discipline* as "training that corrects, molds or perfects the mental faculties or moral character." It perfects learning and living. It advances what you know, how you live and who you are. Discipline embraces instruction, correction, refinement, order, practice, drills, and even punishment. It is designed to lead the beneficiary to the place of subjecting one's thinking and behaviour to a system of rules or habits that will result in success.

Back when I went to elementary school, discipline was a fundamental part of education. The disciplines of reading, writing, and arithmetic were subject to the discipline of supplementary homework if one did not perform up to one's potential. On the other hand, there was reward for excelling. A gold star. Extra time at recess. When the bell rang to end recess, we had to line up in a *straight* line with no talking. Failure to do so could result in forfeiture of the next recess period. Bad behaviour, offensive speech, disobedience, rudeness, and disrespect were not tolerated. For this, the strap hung behind the boardroom door, ready for employment at any time. Now, I had never seen the strap. But I had heard about it. It was six feet long, one foot wide, and one inch thick, and had nasty barbs on its end that would rip the flesh from your hands. Many times, while sitting in class, doors open to the hallway, I heard the terrifying sound of the crack of the strap and the wails of the latest casualty echoing through the corridors.

School was serious business. I must admit that we had fun, too, but it was more than apparent that we were there to learn. And learn we did! Yes, there could have been a much better balance between learning and laughing, facts and fun, chiding and cheer, punishment and praise. It was not as enjoyable as it could have been. But I did learn the three R's. I understood authority and respect. And I learned to appreciate the value of pushing oneself to the limits of one's potential.

Rigid discipline is essential for soldiers to be successful on the battleground. This was especially evident in battlefield strategy several centuries ago. The old muzzle-loading muskets were slow to load and inaccurate at best. They were effective only when fired in volleys and at close range by regimented masses of men. Thin columns of men would take position along the front line, staring eye to eye at their foe. They would march to within eighty paces of the enemy. At eighty paces a few murderous musket volleys could decimate a column to shreds. But the soldiers would stand motionless, exposed to artillery fire, cavalry charge, cannon ball and enemy musket volleys, seeking no cover and awaiting their commander's order to fire. No one must break position. On the field, discipline was what usually made the difference between defeat and victory.

Discipline meant everything; and discipline depended not on bravery but on habit. It took five years to train a recruit into a professional soldier. Five years of iron discipline, painstaking practice, and rigorous routine drill until a soldier's immediate unquestioned obedience to his officer's command prevailed over his fear, timidity, hesitancy, or rational self-interest on the battlefield.

Discipline is the decisive factor in becoming a winning team in the world of sports. I know that when it comes to the NHL playoffs, the combination of a disciplined team with a great goalie is the most likely squad to lift the Stanley Cup into the air. A disciplined team is the one that does not take retaliatory penalties. It is not intimidated by the behaviour of the opposing team. There is no mean-mouthing and no slashing behind the legs after the whistle has been blown. The players keep their positions, stick with the plan, listen to the coach and stay focused on getting the puck in the net.

THE PROOF OF LOVE

Hebrews 12 encourages one to run the race of faith with endurance. It is notable, however, that verses 5 to 12 are all about discipline in training. The point is unmistakable. Discipline is of paramount importance to success. The discipline of God our heavenly Father is contrasted with the discipline of our earthly fathers. In the days of the New Testament, the father was responsible for the correction, molding, and perfecting of the child's mental faculties and moral character. There was reward for good behaviour and punishment and correction for wrong behaviour. It was the proof of a father's love that he took the time, care, and initiative to do everything he could to help his child walk the right path. He loved his children the way they were, but he loved them too much to just stand back and watch them stay that way. He wanted them to mature, succeed, and flourish in life. He wanted the very best for their lives. That's the way our heavenly Father loves us. *"The Lord disciplines those he loves, and he punishes each one he accepts as his child"* (Hebrews 12:6).

Our earthly fathers discipline us as best they can. They aren't perfect. *"But God's discipline is always good for us"* (Hebrews 12:10). Even while His discipline can be painful, it is good for you. Whether He is instructing, correcting, refining, or punishing His child, it is rooted in a love so deep and intense you cannot fathom it. It is the expression of a deep-seated, passionate longing to see your life flourish for His glory. It is not the action of a demanding father paying you back, but the plea of a loving Father to bring you back.

May we never forget that in all of the Father's dealings with us, it is against the backdrop of the greatest love ever shown to us. He loved us so much that He gave His Son, Jesus, to die upon the cross for our sins. And God's Son, Jesus, loved us so much that He willingly surrendered His life for us. I was so bad that He had to die for me, and I was so loved that He was glad to die for me. Amazing!

THE SURRENDER OF THE WILL

Hebrews 12:11 states, *"No discipline is enjoyable while it is happening—it's painful!"* That's because, while it is good for us, it runs against our natural grain. It rubs us the wrong way. There is a collision of wills.

The psalmist, David, reminded us of God's aspiration: *"I will guide you along the best pathway for your life. I will advise you and watch over you"* (Psalm 32:8). The image is of God, your Shepherd, guiding you with His watchful eye. His perfect will and the best pathway for your life are the same thing. He longs for you to submit to His will and follow Him as your compassionate, tenderhearted and wise Shepherd. Unfortunately, that's not how it often plays out. Rather than sheep following a loving shepherd, we are more like a horse needing to be broken in by a cowboy.

The Shepherd urges us, *"Do not be like a senseless horse or mule that needs a bit and bridle to keep it under control"* (Psalm 32:9). The bridle is the gear over a horse's head used to control it. The bit is the steel part of the bridle inserted in the mouth of the horse. This tackle is attached by the reins to the hand of the rider, who controls the horse.

I have ridden horses. But it is not one of my passions. One winter, I went horseback-riding with some friends. Usually the horses used for trail-riding are on their way to the glue factory. At least, that's what I thought. The stable foreman asked me if I had ever ridden a horse before. I answered yes. First mistake. The truth was I had spent a little time around horses, but had never met one I trusted. Anyway, he led me to a big black horse named … you guessed it … Big Black. I didn't like black horses. I didn't like the name Big Black. It may as well have been named Black Fury, or Black Devil. I preferred a horse called Pokey, or Little Dawdler, or Dilly Dally, or Mr. Ed. I wanted a mare that looked down at me with sad eyes, pleading with me to mount carefully because of her sore back.

Big Black had attitude. He seemed to be staring down at me with the white in his eyes and saying, "Jump up, coward!" He brought to mind one of the four horses of the apocalypse. I sheepishly asked the foreman if he was sure Big Black was "okay" to ride. He replied, "I think you'll be okay." It was the *think* part that bothered me. After I had mounted, the foreman instructed me to hold the reins tight. Sounded more like a warning to me. The comment was on par with a dentist telling you to "sit tight." As we exited the corral, the foreman took hold of Big Black's bridle. Why, I wondered? I was beginning to feel more like a sheep being led to the slaughter. I noted that Big Black didn't walk straight and orderly, nose to tail, like the other horses. He strutted sideways, like he was going to the races.

When we arrived at the road, the foreman released his bridle, and that was when Big Black made his move. He bolted like he was coming out of the gates. Faster than lightning. Quicker than a speeding bullet. I pulled back hard on the reins, which meant nothing. He ran for about a quarter of a mile at a dead heat. The word *dead* still sticks in my mind. My whole life passed in front of me. I looked ahead and could see the Pearly Gates looming up in front of me. Then I realized that the "gates" were really a seven-foot snow bank moving ominously closer as the road took a sharp left turn. I braced myself to hit the wall at break-neck speed. But we didn't even touch the wall of snow. Big Black leaped completely over the snow bank, landing in waist-deep snow on the other side. His front hoofs sank into the snow and his hind legs went up and over like a gymnast catapulting over a vault. And me? Well, I found myself flying head-first through the air and landing on my back in the soft snow, uncertain at first whether I was stretched out on snow or floating on clouds. The foreman's voice awakened me. He clambered over the snow bank and waded through the deep snow toward me, inquiring with trepidation as to my welfare. When we ascertained that injuries were minimal, he told me he would return Big Black to the corral, and offered his horse to me. I declined.

He mounted Big Black. Only, this time, it was different. The reins were in the hands of an expert. He took immediate control. The animal tried to bolt. It was a battle of wills. But it soon became clear who was in charge. All the way back to the stable, the expert rider fought with the will of the horse, forcing it to yield. That's the kind of forceful discipline God will exact with us to conform us to His will, if He has to. It is necessary to understand that God's bit and bridle are not meant to keep you at a distance, but designed to bring you near and to keep you near. The psalmist adds this reminder: *"Unfailing love surrounds those who trust the Lord"* (Psalm 32:10).

Jesus blessed those who are humble and meek (Matthew 5:5). Meekness is not weak-willed acceptance of life or a doormat mentality. It means to voluntarily surrender your strength and will to His control. Like a powerful horse, seven or eight times the weight of a man, submitting itself to the master's control. A disciplined horse races, jumps, circles, prances and stands motionless at the rider's slightest command. That's strength under perfect control. That's the picture of meekness. A meek person is one who has learned to surrender his or her willpower to God's perfect will and authority and, hence, experiences His power living in and through them. Jesus said that's a blessed person.

Paul wrote, *"All athletes are disciplined in their training"* (1 Corinthians 9:25). A true athlete is one who willingly submits his or her body to the discipline of training. In the literal sense, an athlete exercises strict self-control in all things. He trains his body and abstains from anything, either food or habits, that will put his physical condition at risk. He will also devote himself to anything ... nutritious food, rigorous exercise, sufficient sleep ... if it will benefit his advancement and welfare.

Paul continued, *"I discipline my body like an athlete, training it to do what it should"* (1 Corinthians 9:27). Literally, "he gives himself a black eye." Paul stays with the context of sports but directs his attention to the boxing ring ... with a twist. He finds himself fixing a defiant stare at his opponent. And the opponent is *himself.* He delivers a self-inflicted knockout punch. Paul is addressing the real enemy. The self-life. The self-will. The comic strip character, Pogo, said, after returning from the swamp to do battle with the enemy, "We have found the enemy, and it is us."

The self-life wants you to believe it knows what is best for you. It tries to convince you that it knows what will make you happy and fulfilled. But it will prevent you from successfully running the race God has set for you. The self-will will challenge you at every step. It will protest any change that threatens its comfort and security. You know how your body feels when you begin a new program of exercise. The muscles scream, "No more! I hate this!" Then the will joins in, "Good! It's raining! No jogging today. I'll go back to bed." Rather, you need to take control of your will. You say, "Good! It's raining! Today, I get to exercise my body as well as my willpower." You must pummel the self-will into submission so that it cannot assert control, but will, rather, serve your goal of surrendering to the perfect and good will of God.

Today, we hear a lot about the power of self. Self-awareness. Self-fulfillment. Self-satisfaction. Self-sufficiency. Self-help. We hear much less about self-discipline, self-denial, or self-control. The latter embraces surrender to something or someone else. That can be good or bad, depending on what that something or someone is. For the person running the race of faith, self-denial and self-discipline mean to surrender to the will and authority of the Holy Spirit, who gives you the power to say *no* to anything that will compromise your physical, moral, or spiritual health, vitality and well-being. Conversely, He gives you the power to say *yes* to the good, pleasing, and perfect will of God.

CORE STRENGTH

The discipline of training gives you the core strength to keep going. Hebrews 12 begins with the exhortation to *"run with endurance."* Endurance is critical to a good run. The Tarahumara Indians of the Copper Canyon are more than great runners. They are great athletes. They are ready for any obstacle that challenges them on the trail because they confront the same obstacles in daily life. They climb steep slippery canyon trails, leap in and out of ditches, lunge into rivers, chase dinner, haul firewood, and kick a wooden ball over jumbles of jagged rocks. "Before the Tarahumara run long, they get strong."[13] The challenges of everyday survival ignite and strengthen countless ancillary muscles that would normally remain inactive and unproductive. Most runners don't live that lifestyle, so, to compete with the Tarahumara, one would need to duplicate their way of life with a stringent training routine of hill running, pushups, jump squats, and strength drills, many of them on a fitness ball to improve balance as well as strength. The training would be tough but the outcome would be sweet. You could run on the most rugged trails from sunrise to sunset and do it with a sense of ease and exhilaration.

David was a great king, warrior, and songwriter. After God had given him victory over all of his enemies, he wrote a song of celebration. In the song he wrote, *"He makes me as surefooted as a deer, enabling me to stand on the mountain heights"* (2 Samuel 22:34). The deer to which he referred is probably the ibex, a wild goat with long, curved horns. I have watched ibex leaping over the rocks with amazing bound and surefootedness as though they sport spring-loaded hooves. God has given the ibex feet to run and scale the most rugged mountain paths. David did not rejoice that God had eliminated the stones from the path and made life easy. He hadn't. But David celebrated that God had given him the feet and legs, the strength and agility, to run the most craggy, rocky paths.

And God will give you the feet and legs to do the same. He gives the grace, energy, skill, and core strength to run along the mountain heights. But this is more than a prayer request that you offer. While God gives you the grace and strength, you must devote yourself to becoming a spiritual athlete committed to a stringent training routine of rigorous exercise. That is how you become one who has what it takes to endure. That is what it takes to run a strong race. But more on that in the next chapter.

PRACTICE MAKES PERFECT

The apostle Paul often used the word *perfection*. So, what does perfection mean for you and me? In the Bible, the word *perfection* usually refers to spiritual *maturity* or *completeness*. *"Solid food is for those who are mature, who through training have the skill to recognize the difference between right and wrong"* (Hebrews 5:14). This verse is preceded by the picture of an infant who lives on milk and lacks the skill, experience, and maturity to make good, wise decisions. In contrast, solid food is for the mature adult.

Paul expressed his goal as pressing on *"to possess that perfection for which Christ Jesus first possessed me"* (Philippians 3:12). Another good word for perfection is *wholeness*. Christ wants you to be spiritually whole, and the more you become like Him, the more whole you become. What does it mean to be whole? It can mean many things. It means to come to the place in your life where you are spiritually sound and healthy. The character of Christ saturates everything. You know your limits and you know your Source of strength. You are able to forgive yourself. Accept yourself. Love yourself. Love your enemies. Face your fears. In the words of the Serenity Prayer, you accept the things you cannot change, possess the courage to change the things you can, and have the wisdom to know the difference. When you feel the pain of God's perfecting, you feel the security of the Father's overwhelming love. When you are judged and criticized by others, your self-image is not threatened because your identity is rooted in the Father's love and acceptance of you in Christ. You are content with living, and ready to die.

In Hebrews 5:14, the writer is using the metaphor of human development from infancy to adulthood to describe the development of spiritual maturity or wholeness. The image of athletics is also woven into the picture. The mature person is one who has *trained*. The word "trained" is derived from the Greek word *gumnazo,* from which comes our word *gymnasium,* the place where people train and exercise. The literal translation of verse 14 is "who through practice have their senses trained to discern good and evil."[14] Staying with the image of athletics, the athlete begins a program of rigourous, habitual, painstaking conditioning. In a true sense, one submits to God's rigourous training program for one's life. It is the practice that makes perfect.

When Ferg Hawke was preparing to run the Badwater race in Death Valley, he knew he would be running in extreme heat. He recognized that the only way to endure was to rigorously train for extreme heat conditions. He ran every day. But he didn't just run; he ran on a treadmill in a sauna to condition his body to running in extreme heat. He spent one week camping on location in Death Valley for the same reason. The heat climbed to 120 degrees Fahrenheit during the day and cooled off to 90 degrees at night. He was thankful for that conditioning when it came to race day and the temperature soared to 126 degrees.

Training is something you do over and over again until you are conditioned to successfully encounter the environment you will be running in. Similarly, in the spiritual race of faith, you submerse yourself in the spiritual disciplines day after day so that you are conditioned to successfully encounter the hostile environment of an ungodly, sinful world in a Christlike way. *"Physical training is good, but training for godliness is much better, promising benefits in this life and in the life to come"* (1 Timothy 4:8). You practice the spiritual disciplines until your spiritual perception is exercised to be able to discern right from wrong, good from best, and you have the wisdom and courage to choose the right and best pathway for your life. You have what it takes to follow that path through a hostile, rugged terrain, no matter how adverse it is.

That's maturity. That's wholeness. You are preparing for heaven and the life to come. Practice makes perfect.

It must be reemphasized that God's primary tool for change and transformation is pain. Hebrews 12:10–11 emphasizes, *"God's discipline is always good for us, so that we might share in his holiness. No discipline is enjoyable while it is happening—it's painful!"* It's what? Painful! But as you endure the painful process of training, you advance toward wholeness and character transformation. *"Afterward there will be a peaceful harvest of right living for those who are trained in this way."* The word *afterward* implies a time delay. *Harvest* indicates a long-term process of growth until you reap the fruit of Christ's character in you. *Training* embraces a commitment to a prolonged program of rigourous, habitual exercise. Over time, the Holy Spirit of God changes the centre and source of your life from self to Christ (2 Corinthians 4:8–11). You run the race, but, in fact, He runs the race in you.

SEVEN

THE "TO FINISH" PROGRAM

NO ONE WANTS TO WEAR THE DNF (DID NOT FINISH) LABEL. FOR MOST people, the marathon is not so much a race to win within a specific time as much as an endurance event to finish. They want to be able to say, "I did it!"

Training is critical. Training programs are designed to build endurance by incremental steps without subjecting the body to exhaustion or injury. More advanced programs are intended for performance-oriented distance runners who want to better a personal best finishing time, win a race or smash a record. The "To finish" program, however, is a more critical, basic program for runners who are not as much interested in performance as they are in participating. Enjoying the experience. Having fun. Just finishing.

Jeff Galloway is an Olympic athlete and a foremost proponent of the "To finish" program. Thousands of average people have followed his training programs to achieve the delight and experience the adventure of running and finishing a marathon. He believes anyone can run, and that with persistence and moderation, anyone can finish the marathon. Running should be fun. One should feel good about running for the thrill and fulfillment of it. It's okay to run for the sheer joy of staying healthy. Galloway's programs can be adjusted to your personal level of conditioning and cover training drills, motivation, choosing performance goals, nutrition, training to your heart rate, breathing, and even selecting appropriate shoes and clothing. Programs highlight the benefit of cross-training (other activities such as swimming and cycling) to improve one's overall fitness. Galloway emphasizes the major value of walk breaks during the long run. Runners learn to maximize the run-walk-run-walk technique. Over a period of six months, the "to finish" program pilots each runner to the place where he or she can finish a marathon successfully and safely.

TRYING VERSUS TRAINING

Many runners begin well but give up early. I think the problem for many DNFs is that they *try* to be something without *training* to be something. You might dream about running a marathon. You might put the date of the marathon on your calendar. You might write it on your bucket list. You might yet wake up one morning and go out and try to run a marathon. You might even pray hard to be successful in completing a marathon. But if you are merely trying without training, you are setting yourself up for failure. What if you sincerely and earnestly tried … really, really hard? You would still fail.

We have learned that God's overriding will for our lives is to become like Jesus. The problem is that many of us merely try hard to be like Him. You may catch yourself saying, "I've got to try harder to be like Him." But the trying proves futile and ineffective. You will become frustrated and eventually give up trying. Trying alone will not make you an athlete. Trying alone will not make you a long-distance runner. Trying alone will not make you Christ-like. Trying alone will not give you success in running the race God has set for you. You must train.

A PERSONAL COMMITMENT

In one sense, spiritual formation is God's work. *"We are God's masterpiece"* (Ephesians 2:10). From beginning to end, God's powerful, masterful work is mightily engaged within us to accomplish more than we might ask or think (Ephesians 3:20). But as I introduced in the previous chapter, there is the principle of human responsibility and cooperation with Him. It is hollow to ask God to grow a seed into a plant that bears delicious fruit if you are not prepared to plant and water the seed and do the hard work of cultivating the soil. It is foolish to ask God to help you to become a star player in the NHL if you never take the effort to learn to skate. It is pretentious to ask God to strengthen you to endure during a time of adversity if you have not been personally responsible to build up your spiritual strength and deepen your faith.

We need to maintain balance in our approach. Think of it this way. Three groups of people desire to cross an ocean. The first group is comprised of stalwart believers in human effort and responsibility. This group jumps into a rowboat and begins rowing hard. Their oars chop the water like a frenzied woodcutter chopping wood. Their boat disappears out of sight. Exhaustion sets in. Soon, success vanishes even as they vanish over the horizon. The second group believes in just "letting go and letting God." They believe that the way to cross the ocean is to just rely entirely on the power and wisdom of God to get them to the other side. So they hop on a raft and drift. They do nothing but hang on and hope God brings the right current along. Drifters on an open sea. If you aim at nothing, you're sure to hit it.

But then there's a third group who see themselves as sailors navigating a sailboat. They work hard trimming the sails to catch the force of the wind and manning the rudder to steer their craft. They exert energy tacking, jibing, reefing, and heeling. But with all of their skill and strenuous effort, there is something they are absolutely dependent upon. They need the wind. They can't control the wind, but a good sailor discerns where the wind is blowing and trims the sails for the wind to fill and power the craft forward.

It is necessary to expand your mind. Seek wise advice. Sharpen your skills. Work hard to become everything you were made to be. But keep the scales of your life balanced. Understand your absolute need of God to fill your life at the deepest level. There is a supernatural element to living that comes only when you catch the gentle breeze of the Spirit of God in your sails. Take adequate quiet time to listen carefully to the whisper and prompting of the Spirit. Allow Him to fill the sails of your life with the courage to obey Him, the assurance to run by faith, the power to overcome, the joy to sustain you, the humility to experience His blessing, the discernment to know when to adjust the sails and the guts to endure whenever the breeze becomes a gale. Yes, the Spirit of God can be blowing in the storm.

Paul encouraged Timothy, *"Be strong through the grace that God gives"* (2 Timothy 2:1). God gives you the grace to be strong in the midst of your need. That is God's part. But he also exhorted Timothy to *"endure suffering … as a good soldier of Christ Jesus"* (2 Timothy 2:3). Here is a personal challenge laid squarely on your lap. A personal responsibility. An individual commitment. Paul compared one's capacity to endure suffering to the example of a soldier, an athlete, and a farmer. Each person mentioned must make a personal sacrifice to attain the desired outcome. A soldier must forfeit the pleasures and responsibilities of civilian life and submit to the strict discipline of military life in order to please his commander and be strong in battle. An athlete must train hard and follow the rules to win the gold medal. The farmer must work exceedingly hard, forfeiting leisure and recreation during the summer months, if he is to be gratified with getting the hay into the barn on time and reaping a rich harvest. If you are going to endure the agony of the race God has set for you, and to endure it with a sense of exhilaration, fulfillment, and anticipation, you will need to train hard.

In Canada, the event of the year for many is hockey's Stanley Cup Playoffs. Ultimately, two teams get down to the final game of the playoff season. It is thrilling to watch the skills, puck-handling, speed, endurance, strength, and agility of the players as they battle for Lord Stanley's Cup. But they didn't just arrive unexpectedly or unpredictably at this point. This didn't just happen. Behind the scenes and off the ice are years of dedicated training and preparation. Hours of workouts. For anyone to become anything remotely like these athletes, one must espouse the disciplined life of an athlete long before the game.

Before you will ever be ready to run a strong, durable race, you will need to espouse the disciplined life of spiritual formation. You must embrace spiritual disciplines to grant God the space to work in your life. Exercises that are channels of His grace in your life. Hard work, personal sacrifice, and commitment to these disciplines will be the means of pummeling the self to death and making space for Christ to live fully in and through your being, making you a strong runner.

TRAINING LEVELS

One caution. When it comes to practicing the spiritual disciplines, guilt can subtly become the driving motive. Most of us cannot be monks living our lives in the monastery and dedicating every minute to silence, prayer, and study. Nor should we. Neither should you feel shame when you compare yourself to the person who boasts of getting up at the break of dawn to pray and read the Bible. I knew a person who used to brag in front of me that he would get up every morning at 4am to pray and study. He would then ask me when I did my "morning devotions?" I always wanted to tell him that I never slept; that I prayed all night. If one is not careful, it can become a subject that lends itself to good old Christian bragging. Christian Phariseeism. It is not about the hour of day or night or length of time. It is not a performance. It is about spending valuable time with God and growing strong in your faith. Most of us have kids to dress and feed, dishes to wash, the dog to walk, emergencies to attend to, and a growing list of tasks, duties, and responsibilities to tackle. I get it! That's reality. But I urge you to understand why you need to exercise spiritually, and carve out the time to do it.

The level of training will not be the same for everyone. Levels will vary depending on genes, life circumstances, seasons of life, time, or resources for training. The life situation for a working single mother is poles apart from the lifestyle of a healthy empty nester. Levels will vary depending on whether one is a beginner or experienced. As I stated earlier, you cannot just wake up one morning and decide to run a full marathon. You need to build endurance at a gradual, incremental rate so as not to subject your body to strain or injury. You'll start off with more walk breaks and rest periods. You will need to cross-train with alternate kinds of exercise, such as swimming or cycling, to develop different muscles. Levels will vary depending on maturity. Parents don't train and discipline a two-year-old child the same as they do a 16-year-old. Discipline changes as the age and maturity of the child increases. Schools don't teach the same disciplines to seven-year-olds as to 18-year-olds. You wouldn't teach trigonometry or calculus to a young child. Maturity and mental development dictate this.

So it is with practicing the spiritual disciplines. The level of training and intensity of the exercise will depend on age, life circumstance, and maturity. Paul recognized the difference between a young, inexperienced believer in Christ and one who has been a believer for a long time. He contrasted the former to an infant needing milk and the second to a mature adult requiring solid food. Then he added that training and maturity are closely associated (Hebrews 5:11–14).

THE "TO FINISH" PROGRAM

Kenyan champion Benjamin Limo said, "My philosophy in training is to stick with the schedule that has been given to me by the coach without making an alteration to it. That is what all running is about—following instructions."[1] God has given us a set of disciplines to follow that are key to successfully running the race of faith with endurance and placing a strong finish. The disciplines I list here are not an exhaustive inventory, but, collectively, they will energize those ancillary spiritual muscles that would normally remain inactive and unproductive. They will build your spiritual strength, health, and endurance. Your personal commitment to sticking with these disciplines will help you to understand how serious you are about running a strong race of faith.

Disciplines can fall under two categories. Some fall into the category of *exercise* while others fall into the category of *abstinence*. *Exercise* is associated with a daily workout. An athlete will exert energy doing push-ups, pull-ups, and sit-ups to develop or improve fitness. On the other hand, a *bstinence* is an act of self-denial. It means to go without; to refrain from certain practices to develop or improve fitness. An athlete will abstain from certain foods and activities that risk impairment to the body. Two very distinctive disciplines with the same goal. Similarly, the spiritual disciplines will relate more to one category or the other.

STUDY OF GOD'S WORD

I begin with the discipline of studying God's Word and will accentuate it because of its foundational nature. It is the nutrition for the growth and health of your soul. It feeds the new nature and starves the old. Every athlete knows that one needs a good, balanced diet of complex carbohydrates, some protein, and a little fat. Lornah Kiplagat, one of Kenya's greatest athletes, says, "Nutrition plays a very important role in my program. ... We designed a diet with a right mix of carbohydrates, proteins, and fats. I eat a lot of fresh vegetables, and of course fruits."[2] A successful eating plan gives you the nutrients essential for energy and strength. However, you need to follow the plan—not for a month or so, but as a lifestyle.

Our culture today places much emphasis on health and nutrition. And so it should. Health and nutrition are vital to quality of life. Conversations quickly get around to organic food versus non-organic. Food supplements. People read the ingredients on every package of food. They want to know the calorie count, the carbohydrate and fat content. They carefully measure their caloric balance, calculating their calorie intake with the number of calories their body burns off. They get advice from nutritional practitioners, dietitians, naturopaths, and homeopaths. There is the conventional and the non-conventional. The genuine and the hokey. There are more diverse diets than varieties of food. Low carb. High protein. Low fat. High residue. Low sodium. Fruit. Calorie counting. Raw food. Cabbage soup. And the list goes on. Food reports come out every week and are modified just as often. The whole nutrition fixation has become big business. People take this kind of thing very seriously. If only they took their spiritual welfare as seriously as they do their physical and emotional welfare.

The Bible is often referred to as food. *"How sweet your words taste to me; they are sweeter than honey"* (Psalm 119:103). Psalm 119 is both the longest psalm and the longest chapter in the Bible. And notably, almost every verse mentions something about God's Word. The point of the psalm cannot go unnoticed. God's Word is absolutely essential to living a healthy, fulfilling life. Jeremiah wrote, *"When I discovered your words, I devoured them. They are my joy and my heart's delight"* (Jeremiah 15:16). The writer of Hebrews contrasted an immature believer who needs to drink in the basics of God's Word to a mature believer who feeds on the solid meat of more advanced truth.

God led the Israelites out of Egypt and through the wilderness for 40 years in order to test their character and obedience. He even let them go hungry to see how they would respond. Only one month out of Egypt, they turned on Moses and complained against God. So God rained down bread from heaven on them. Not fire ... bread! They had no idea what the white stuff was, so they asked, "What is it?" The Hebrew question was, "Manna?" And that's the name that stuck. But the reason God sent manna is significant. *"He did it to teach you that people do not live by bread alone; rather, we live by every word that comes from the mouth of the Lord"* (Deuteronomy 8:3). In the same way broccoli and beans nourish your physical body, feeding on the words that God speaks is essential for spiritual health, vitality, and welfare. If your spiritual well-being is failing and weak, check your diet.

Before you read on, take some time to reflect on Psalm 119. As you read, you will be struck with the truth that God's Word is the foundation for your entire life. It is your source of joy in a despairing world, purity in a contaminated environment, the one right path in a maze of misleading pathways, the one true map in a pile of pseudo-maps. It is your source of comfort, encouragement, peace, wisdom, discernment, guidance, and faith.

"The very essence of your words is truth; all your just regulations will stand forever" (Psalm 119:160). The Word of God embodies truth that will stand forever. This means it is totally trustworthy, unerring, unchanging, and reliable. It is the anvil upon which everything is tested. The light to which everything living must bend. Solar time. It is the absolute upon which the principles of life are built. A principle is not situational, but a foundational rule with universal application. It stands true for everyone all the time. Direction, perception, culture, philosophy ... you name it ... all must bend to absolute principle. It is law. You can't break an absolute law; on the contrary, you will be broken if you collide with it. Principles embrace such absolutes as human dignity, integrity, justice, honesty, truth, and excellence. The late Steven Covey writes,

> The reality of such principles or natural laws becomes obvious to anyone who thinks deeply and examines the cycles of social history. These principles surface time and time again, and the degree to which people in a society recognize and live in

SaH

harmony with them moves them toward either survival and stability or disintegration and destruction.[3]

A factory foreman was responsible to blow the noon-hour whistle every day. On his way to work each morning, he would walk past a small clock shop and set his watch to the old grandfather clock in the window. That way the whistle would blow at exactly the same time each noon hour. One day, the clock shopkeeper stepped outside to chat with the man who stopped every morning outside his shop. As any good shopkeeper would, he asked, "Can I help you?" The factory foreman explained to him what he did each morning to ensure an exact time for blowing the noon-hour whistle. The shopkeeper smiled and replied, "That's interesting. I set the time on the old grandfather clock each day by the 12-noon whistle." That's how we often live. Our values, beliefs, and behaviours shift slowly but surely over time according to the changing cultural values, societal norms, and ideologies of man. But God's Word is solar time. Absolute. Authoritative. Unerring. Trustworthy. Orient your life-compass to it. Build your life-foundation on it. Live it.

When Joshua was called by God to take up the leadership of Israel after the death of Moses, God emphasized to him that the key to his success as Israel's leader rested in the priority he placed on the Word of God. *"Study this Book of Instruction continually. Meditate on it day and night so you will be sure to obey everything written in it. Only then will you prosper and succeed in all you do"* (Joshua 1:8). The word *meditate* describes the cooing of a mourning dove or the low growling of a lion that has trapped its prey. The word embraces the idea of pondering or musing over something. How does this apply to God's Word? Ponder it. Think about what it is saying. Memorize it. Give it time to sink into your mind and begin to transform your thinking. Let it take root and grow in your heart. Assimilate it into your life. You may not be successful in the world's eyes, but you will run the race God has set for you with endurance. And at the end of the day, that's what counts.

God gave the same instructions to Israel's kings. Every king was to write out by hand a copy of the Torah for himself. He was to carry that copy with him wherever he went and read it daily for his entire life. His knowledge and obedience to the Scriptures would guarantee a successful reign (Deuteronomy 17:18–20). You cannot overexpose yourself to the Scriptures. They must become the central core of the principles by which you live. The axis of your convictions, values, and conduct. Carried not only in your pocket but in your heart. God promises success to those who will study and meditate upon them. The responsibility to discipline oneself to doing so lies with us.

PRAYER

Prayer is a discipline that exercises the mind and heart to experience God at the deepest level. *"Be still, and know that I am God"* (Psalm 46:10). Prayer is separating oneself from the busyness of life to just *be* in God's presence. It is one of the paramount ways to get close to God. Prayer is not just speaking; it is being still and listening. It is connecting to the mind and heart of God. This is really the essence of prayer.

But prayer is not just spending time in some heavenly, sterile, serene spot. It can be a battle. It is also an occasion to hang out all the dirty laundry for God to see. He sees it anyway. Life throws a lot of frustration, disappointment, and hurt. We sustain wounds. Sometimes it appears that evil rules. The Psalms are both songs and prayers that vent powerful emotions. In Psalm 69, David prayed that God would go after his neighbour. Blind him. Break his legs. Burn his house down. Send him straight to hell. David was not having a good day. He was up to his ears with evil getting its way. But God can handle these kinds of potent feelings. In fact, the whole book of Psalms gives us permission to be honest and authentic with Him. That's real prayer. God prefers our outbursts over theological correctness and spiritually polite, anemic monologues. He wants to engage your heart and passion, not just your brains. Passion gives suction to your prayers.

Something else that gives suction to your prayers is need. Life's perplexities are birthed out of need. They have the potential to suck you down into the mire of disillusionment or suck you up into the presence of God. After Job had climbed out of his pit of despair, he announced to God, *"I had only heard about you before, but now I have seen you with my own eyes"* (Job 42:5). Need is God's way of connecting you to Him who is more ready to provide than we are to ask.

Prayer is worship. Like the Psalmist, while you may not understand the perplexities of life, prayer cultivates a deeper, fuller relationship with your sovereign, wise, loving heavenly Father. He understands. And He is in control. God may not respond to your need in the way you had hoped, but prayer is a process whereby you begin to love God not for what you get from Him or what He does for you, but for who He is. Prayer is the process of anchoring your hope, not in the answer to your specific request, but in your Father's heart, and worshipping Him.

WORSHIP

The heart of worship is expressing to God His supreme worth. The words *worship* and *worth* are derived from the same root. This discipline is essential to running a strong race. It is an exercise that engages the heart, mind, soul, and body. The most fundamental act of worship is one Jesus gave to us, that we call the Lord's Supper or Communion. While my purpose is not to give a detailed study of the meaning of *the Table*, this exercise of worship centres our whole being on the sacrifice of Christ and symbolizes the temple of our bodies receiving Him in His fullness. Jesus' sacrifice is at the core of the believer's new identity as a Christian, who we are and why we are. Think of it as a spiritual fitness exercise. The worshipper reaches back in remembrance of Christ's body broken and His blood shed for us. We reach forward to His coming again as we anticipate where we are going because of what He has done on the cross. We reach inward and examine our heart's condition before God. We reach out to one another who eat at His table, for it is His blood that breaks down walls that separate and binds us all together as one.

SERVICE

Another aspect of worship is service. Paul tells us that, on the basis of Jesus' sacrifice for you, you should offer yourself to Him *"a living and holy sacrifice"* (Romans 12:1). Then he adds, *"This is truly the way to worship him."* The word for *worship* is also the word for *service*. Worship

93

is not only an attitude of the heart; it is getting your life into gear to serve Him. Worship is responding to God's supreme worth and His indescribable gift of Jesus by giving your body to roll up your sleeves and give out.

God has given each of us lives, resources, abilities, and spiritual gifts, not to keep to ourselves, but with which to serve others. Jesus gave us an astonishing example of what He wanted us to do with our lives. At His last supper with His disciples, He took a towel and basin and began to wash their feet. This was a Middle Eastern practice to refresh one's guests after walking about the dirty, dusty streets in sandaled shoes. But Jesus' disciples were shocked! Shocked, because that was the duty of a slave or entrance-level servant, and something none of them were prepared to do. So Jesus did it. He then turned to them and said, *"I have given you an example to follow. Do as I have done to you"* (John 13:15).

Jesus was not saying we should go around looking for feet to wash. Rather, follow His example. Do whatever it takes to serve the needs of another. Serve the needs of your wife with the attitude of giving your life for her. Serve your children. Serve whomever God brings into your life. Don't wait for someone to serve you. You look for someone to serve, and God will fill your heart. You will discover that the discipline of serving is an exercise that will enrich your socks off. It will give your life momentum. It will energize you to run longer and harder.

THANKSGIVING

Many people experience a huge energy drain because they expend so much vigour complaining. It would seem that the more we have, the less we appreciate what we have. This is not only sin; it is debilitating. As you run the race of life, thank God for who He is and for all He has provided. The strength to run. The freedom to run. The view as you run. The beauty of His creation. The joy of the run. When something goes wrong, the spirit of thanksgiving will change your perspective. For example, a thief steals your wallet. Thank God that you were the one who lost your wallet and not the thief who stole it. Thanksgiving will prevent dynamism drain and enthuse you for living.

COMMUNITY

God never intended you to do it alone. When God created everything, He said that it was all good except for one thing. It was not good that the man was alone. So God gave him a woman. A person of different gender from him, but someone his equal with whom to relate and commune.

The early church enjoyed an amazing sense of community.

All the believers met together in one place and shared everything they had. ... They worshipped together at the Temple each day, met in homes for the Lord's Supper, and shared their meals with great joy and generosity—all the while praising God and enjoying the goodwill of all the people (Acts 2:44–47).

Incredible! There is synergy and energy in community. The writer of Hebrews called the believers to persevere in their life of faith and urged, *"Let us think of ways to motivate one another to acts of love and good works. And let us not neglect our meeting together, as some people do, but encourage one another"* (Hebrews 10:24–25).

The fact is we need each other. The discipline of community cannot be overrated. We motivate and encourage each other. There is so much on the journey to dishearten and discourage us. We need people who will speak courage, comfort, strength, and affirmation into our lives. Keep company with friends who have a positive, healthy outlook on life. Connect with people who will hold you accountable and prepare you for the challenges and setbacks in life. Integrate with a healthy, spiritual community that demonstrates love and assists you in growing your faith. I will devote a whole chapter to this in the book, so more on this essential discipline later.

FASTING

Let's look for a moment at a few disciplines of abstinence. Fasting is giving up something important for a period of time for the sake of something of greater importance. One might give up television, a hobby, or some other activity for an interval and give that time to God. It's like an intermission in a game or an interlude at a concert. Fasting is usually used in the context of food. One gives up the time taken to eat breakfast, lunch or dinner for the purpose of praying or communing with God. The idea of this discipline is to lessen the grasp of physical need and to focus on the greater spiritual need. To minimize the control of the lesser and maximize the import of the greater. Fasting opens the way to experience God in a greater way.

Solitude

Solitude is choosing to separate yourself from people, noise, clamour, distractions, disruptions, busyness, and responsibilities. On several occasions, Jesus took His disciples away from the pressing of the crowds and the pressures of challenges. Sometimes you need to *come apart before you come apart*. It is an empowering discipline to withdraw from your daily activities and to be alone with God. God encourages you to *"Be still, and know that I am God"* (Psalm 46:10). This discipline is essential to set your inner compass. It can be exercised for long periods of time or daily for just a few moments. Even a few minutes a day will do wonders to renew your strength and help you focus on what is truly important. I will write more about this in a later chapter.

Silence

While solitude is a discipline exercised in seclusion or isolation, silence can be exercised in community. It is a choice to say nothing to anyone except God and to listen to no one except God. There are some who enter the cloister and make a vow of silence for a lifetime. For the rest of us, this discipline is exercised for much shorter periods of time. Whatever length of time you give to this discipline, it is a time to draw near to God and listen to His whispers. It is a time to practice the presence of Christ in the midst of everything else happening around you. And it is soul-enriching.

There is a second reason for the discipline of silence. It is practice in countering the impact of one of our most cunning, malicious nemeses. The tongue. The tongue inflicts vengeance and undermines. It breaks hearts and ruins lives. James warns us that the tongue is a tiny flame that can set your whole life on fire. *"People can tame all kinds of animals, birds, reptiles, and fish, but no one can tame the tongue. It is restless and evil, full of deadly poison"* (James 3:7–8). He says, *"If we could control our tongues, we would be perfect and could also control ourselves in every other way"* (James 3:2). Hence, silence is an exercise in practicing control over the uncontrollable. Taming the untamable. More so, it is an exercise in practicing control over ourselves in every other way.

GENEROSITY

All the wealth we have comes from God. But it is not an end in itself. God blesses us so that we may be a channel of blessing to others. When one stops the flow of blessing and channels the flow into one's own pocket, that is a disease called hoarding. And you can't run the race of faith dragging a pile of stuff or a vault full of money. Everything God blesses you with is for the purpose of blessing the lives of others, especially those in need. The first-century Christians were a wonderful example of generosity. *"They felt that what they owned was not their own, so they shared everything they owned. ... There were no needy people among them"* (Acts 4:32, 34). That's hard to believe. But the record tells the story. Paul reminded us not to trust in our money because that is so unreliable. Rather, we should trust God and generously share our resources with those in need. Generosity means giving your best to those in need, and is the path of blessing for your own life.

Generosity and giving are joined at the hip. Giving is a sign of maturity. When I was a child, I would sit by the Christmas tree and count the number of gifts under the tree with my name on them. I would calculate the number of days to come before I could open my gifts. I would take each gift from under the tree, feel it, squeeze it, shake it, weigh it, and hold it up to the light. But as I grew older, I became far more excited about giving gifts than receiving them. I take greatest delight in watching the anticipation and joy in the eyes of those who are opening a gift I am giving. That's maturity. Maturity is understanding that it is not about me; it is about others. Maturity is recognizing that it is more blessed to give than to receive. Giving and generosity are sure signs that you are maturing as a runner on the path of life. It is also the discovery of a discipline that will both energize and bring you more joy than almost anything else.

Sacrifice sits at the deepest level of generosity. Sacrifice is a response to God's indescribable gift of His Son, Jesus. It is a response to Jesus' gift of His life on the cross for you. Sacrifice is giving your best to Him. It is giving beyond your limits, relying on God to supply your needs. Going over the top. Giving until it hurts. It is complete selflessness. Totally trusting in God to look after the outcome. It is the way to run with a full sense of freedom from the weights of this life.

SECRECY

Jesus said we should give to those in need, but that we should do it privately. Whatever you do, do it without calling attention to yourself. You will get your reward from your Father in heaven who sees everything (Matthew 6:1–4). *"When you pray, go away by yourself, shut the door behind you, and pray to your Father secretly. Then your Father, who sees everything, will reward you"* (Matthew 6:6). When you fast, don't dishevel your hair and apply white makeup to your face to look pale and appear to have fasted for 40 days and nights so that others are mesmerized by your spirituality. *"But when you fast, comb your hair and wash your face. Then no one will suspect you are fasting, except your Father, who knows what you do in secret. And your Father, who sees everything, will reward you"* (Matthew 6:17–18). Doing good things secretly is a discipline that deepens intimacy with God. The discipline of secrecy breaks the power and bondage of running to please people. It liberates you to live beyond the approving or disapproving gaze of people, to fix your eyes on Jesus and run to please God.

Often someone will hand me a gift of money to give to another person in need. They give the gift to me as a middleman because they don't want the recipient to know who is giving the gift. They want the beneficiary to receive the money as a provision from God. He is the Giver. He is the Blesser. As the man in the middle, I witness two things. Deep appreciation on the countenance of the one receiving the gift as from the Lord. But what always moves me most profoundly is the radiant, overwhelming joy in the eyes of the one doing the giving. It is something they are doing for God, and God alone. This simple, personal discipline of secrecy is an exercise that connects you to the heart of God like few other activities. From time to time, practice the discipline of doing something good, something extraordinary, something sacrificial, without anyone knowing except God. Do it purely for Him, and Him alone.

FRUGALITY

Frugality is choosing to deny oneself the luxuries and wants that envelop us. Or should I say, besiege us. We go to the mall and are confronted with things we were content without until we saw them in the store. We watch television and are inundated with stuff we are persuaded we need in order to live a fulfilled life. We see the brand-name clothes and shoes people are wearing and believe we need them. We tie self-image, self-worth, and self-importance to material things. Materialism has really messed with our heads.

Some ascetics choose to deny self by making a lifelong vow of frugality. They move to a monastery and live a life of austerity in a room flanked by four cement walls with a bed, chair, and table. For the rest of us, the choice is much less severe. It is a choice to say no to excess. A choice to deny the pull of opulence, extravagance, and wants and to focus on God as our satisfaction. This discipline breaks the control of the world and frees us to run the race of faith without the drag of excess stuff.

CONFESSION

Confession cleanses the inner person. A runner can look durable on the outside, but if the inner person is cluttered and weighed down with sin, the inner strength is slowly drained and the once-strong legs begin to falter. The soul becomes exhausted. You don't have what it takes to persevere over the long haul.

Confession means to *say the same thing as God does* about your sin and inward condition. When you confess your sin to God, He will forgive you. This discipline of confession releases the weight of the burden. Your steps feel lighter and you are rejuvenated to run with a newfound agility and restored joy for life. The discipline of confessing your sins to one another is also a healthy exercise. When you open your broken heart to another trusted person, you will experience mutual strength and support.

REST

One cannot overrate the importance of the discipline of rest in a runner's training. Rest is of paramount priority in the Kenyan training programs. "Kenyans are excellent at realizing that the most scientific, effective, superb form of resting the body is to do absolutely zilch. After a series of races, the Kenyan then stops running completely. It can be from two to three weeks, to one month or more, but … during this time the athlete does virtually no training."[4] The Kenyan system follows the cycle of resting the body, intense training and building up the body, racing on the circuit, and resting again. Taking time to recharge the batteries is an integral part of training to ensure longevity in running. The resting can embrace putting on a little weight, catching up with family life, taking a family vacation, just relaxing or getting back into one's career or business. For Kenyans, training is so intense that rest is essential to restoring energy. In fact, most Kenyan athletes take Sunday as a weekly day of rest. They go to church, read the newspaper, write a letter, or take a stroll.

Rest is an essential part of God's "To Finish" program. In the Old Testament He established a day of rest for His people every week. No one was allowed to do any work. He determined a year of rest for the land, one year in seven. The land was to sit idle for the entire year. The principle is clear: productivity is fixed to rest. Even your heart follows a cycle of beat, then rest … beat, then rest. If it was all one big beat, it would explode; if it stopped on the rest, it would implode. Efficiency and output stems from the steadiness of beat and rest. Work and taking a break. Running and resting.

INTENTIONAL REINFORCEMENT

The question you may be asking is what disciplines you should be focusing attention on and for how long? I would answer that it's like training for a marathon. Centre your attention where your greatest need is. Ask yourself some personal questions and then answer them honestly. Where is your strength failing? Where is your spiritual health deteriorating? Where are you allowing any sin to acquire jurisdiction in your life? Where are you giving the Devil a toehold? What spiritual discipline will best address this need and disarm wrong behaviour while reinforcing right behaviour?

If gossip is a problem, practice the discipline of silence. When everything in you wants to speak … don't! Rather, determine that every time the tongue and ears are tempted to become engaged in a juicy conversation that will hang some poor victim out to dry or undermines someone's reputation, you will remain silent until you can say something positive about that person. That will probably end the conversation immediately. Most importantly, each time you respond in this way, you intentionally reinforce right behaviour.

If stealing is a problem, or if you harbour a spirit of greed, practice the discipline of generosity. Work hard to earn what you have and then give things away to others in need. Generosity will break the enticement to steal or the influence of a greedy spirit.

If you are a complainer or are consumed by a spirit of ungratefulness, focus on the disciplines of worship and thanksgiving. Make a list of every blessing you can think of and turn complaint and ingratitude into praise and thanksgiving. Celebrate God, life, creation, friends, health, and the multitude of things you enjoy from morning to morning. If you lack joy, arrange your life around opportunities to serve. Help out a neighbour with a meal when they are sick. Do some yard work for an elderly person. Bring a homeless person a coffee. When you feel self-pity setting in, visit someone who is dying of cancer in a hospital. Exercise the discipline of serving someone else. When you give joy away, you receive joy back. Always! These are the kinds of disciplines the Holy Spirit uses to counter failing strength and increase your spiritual health and fitness.

Training is very practical. Often when struggling with a particular weakness, you will need to intentionally place yourself in the line of fire. By that, I mean if you contend with impatience, subject yourself to situations that will reinforce patience. Intentionally drive your vehicle in the slowest lane. Stand in the slowest line at the grocery store. And as

101

you purposely contend with impatience, give patience the time to grow. If you battle the addiction of pornography, discipline yourself to some rules. Locate the computer in a public room. Commit to not turning the computer on when you are alone. You will need to integrate yourself into a healthy, spiritual community, a person or small group that will hold you accountable, love you, and stir your faith and strength. Some battles cannot be won alone. You may be led by the Holy Spirit to submit yourself to the disciplines of solitude, fasting, and prayer for a period of time without computer or smartphone at your disposal.

Spiritual conflicts are commonly won or lost in the mind. That is where the battle rages. What you see, hear, and experience, both bad and good, is imprinted on your mind. If sin is ignored or denied, it will grow and begin to take jurisdiction over that part of your mind like a tumour stretching its roots in the brain. Good seed and bad seed germinate. And both produce fruit. Bad seed is like bad food. Chow that fills but does not feed. It slowly weakens your metabolism, diminishes fitness, and exposes you to injury. Successful athletes are those who are faithful to a good nutrition and fitness program, manage to stay strong and healthy, and escape injury over the long haul. Many other athletes who have equally great potential and skill are denied that success because of injury.

Imagine two dogs that are always fighting. Which dog wins? The dog you feed the most. Similarly, you need to feed your mind and spirit with nutritious food to build spiritual health and strength. We pray that God will grant us victory over our weaknesses, but then we give Him nothing to work with. That is where personal discipline comes in. Exercise is your responsibility. Feed your spirit. Fill your mind with Scripture. Read books and biographies that nourish your mind with what God has taught and done in the lives of others. Listen to music that enriches and reinforces truth. What you put into your head will seriously determine what you become. The spiritual disciplines will shield you from the destructive, caustic toxins that war against your soul and fortify you to run the race of faith with endurance. Get on a training program.

EIGHT

THE FOCUS OF THE RUN

SAMMY KIPKETER, KENYAN DISTANCE RUNNER, SAID, "DO NOT GIVE UP. You can make it as long as you are healthy and well-focused."[1] He emphasizes two keys to success. First, staying healthy. That was the subject of the previous two chapters. And secondly, focus. The writer of Hebrews emphasized the same critical point when he urged his readers not to quit the race of faith. *"Run with endurance the race God has set before us. We do this by keeping our eyes on Jesus, the champion who initiates and perfects our faith"* (Hebrews 12:1–2). There are many obstacles and distractions in the race of faith. The key to endurance is focus. Stay focused on Jesus.

If you were watching the tall, 6'2", 143-lb., slender frame of Robert Cheruiyot running through the streets of Boston in 2006, on his way to setting a course record for the Boston Marathon, what you would not have seen is the distance the runner had already travelled in the race of life. He had overcome severe adversity. Prevailed over many distractions, any one of which could have led him over the edge of despair. Like many children in Kenya, he was born into extreme poverty and merely followed the path fate seemed to have chosen for him.

Friends and family called him "Mwafrica." When Mwafrica was only four years old, he and his brother were abandoned by their parents. To add to his misery, he was torn from his six-year-old brother and sent to live with a cousin. This new home was a tough, demanding existence for the young lad who worked hard going to school and returning home to an endless list of household chores demanded of him in order to pay his way. Food was meager, living on a diet of tea, ugali (cornmeal porridge), milk, or kale.

When Mwafrica finished his schooling, he was kicked out of the house. He had nothing to do, no sense of purpose. Penniless, hungry, and homeless, he wandered about town, sleeping without a roof over his head. He survived on cornmeal and roadside kale. He recalled, "It was at this time I thought to end it all. Why live, nobody was together and I was all alone. I was very close to suicide."[2]

At this point, Mwafrica's life seemed to take a turn for the better. He had some apparent skill and talent as a runner and was a hard worker, and so received an invitation to attend one of Kenya's training camps, Moses Tanui's Kaptagat Camp. Moses Tanui, a champion marathon runner and owner of the camp, saw great potential in the lad. Life at the camp was hard, living on a single meal of maize and bread per day. But young Cheruiyot trained hard and ran well.

One day, something happened that would change Mwafrica's life forever. Paul Tergat, the first Kenyan runner to break the world record in the marathon in 2003, visited the camp. Mwafrica was captivated by the idea of sitting in the presence of one of the legendary gods. At the Kaptagat Camp, portraits and posters of the great runners hung on the walls. That night, Mwafrica stood beneath a large picture of Paul Tergat and focused for a long, long time on the face of the man who had visited the camp that day. The image was imprinted on his mind. He determined that night to become a great distance runner … just like Paul Tergat.

The next day, quite unexpectedly, Tergat returned to the camp. He interacted with the athletes and even ran with them. Mwafrica could barely contain himself, however, when Tergat called the barefoot youth aside and sat down with him one-on-one. Mwafrica would never forget those next few minutes. The champion looked into his eyes and inspired him to persevere with his running. He then did something that impacted the young athlete to his core. Tergat handed him his own running shoes. He told him to wear those shoes and train hard. But he reminded Mwafrica that success would not come without hard, hard training.

The words were like those of an angel sent from heaven to speak into the life of a poor mortal. And they reached their intended objective. Armed with his new shoes and inspired by the words and image of his champion, Mwafrica felt the shackles of his upbringing fall from his arms and legs. He trained harder, ran faster, and endured longer than all the other runners. He ran his next race, a 10-kilometre, in the fastest time ever over Kenyan roads. He won a purse of 1,000 shillings, a fortune for this Kenyan. He went out and purchased his first mobile phone, a new pair of shoes, a shirt and trousers, and some food.

Mwafrica had now been "discovered" by sporting scouts and was flown to Italy to compete in a series of road races. He won race after race. Winning the Boston Marathon in 2003 and setting a course record gave him an international profile. International success brought prosperity and Mwafrica used his newfound wealth to do many good things including bringing his parents back together. Unfortunately, success and wealth enticed other, unwelcome, unscrupulous intruders into his life, and he soon found himself running with the wrong crowd and living an undisciplined and unmanageable life. His life began to quickly unravel.

Mwafrica was wise enough, however, to come to his senses before it was too late. Like the prodigal son in the pigpen swallowing the corn husks the swine were eating, he made a decision to get up out of his mess and return to the success he had enjoyed (Luke 15:11–32). He reconnected with his friend and the person who had so amazingly inspired him in the first place, Paul Tergat. He asked Tergat to coach him and promised to surrender himself to the rigid training of the one man whom he knew could enthuse and prepare him to run again like a champion. Tergat agreed and welcomed him back. Since that turning point, the two runners have run together for at least 32 kilometres daily. Tergat uses this time to encourage, mentor, and build discipline back into his life. And Mwafrica has kept his eyes fixed on Tergat. He says of Tergat: "He gives you a heart like a lion."[3] And the young Mwafrica has gone on to become a truly legendary distance runner … just like Paul Tergat.

When my children were growing up, they enjoyed competing in track and field. My son, Jeremy, was an excellent jumper. He excelled in both the triple and long jumps. I would have to attribute his success to me. Just joking! But I became his self-acclaimed coach. I would position myself at the far end of the sand pit and instruct him to sprint down the runway and keep his eyes fixed on me. When he hit the board, he should stay focused on me, spring into the air, extend his legs and arms forward and try to reach and knock me down at the far end. It was the same with my daughter, Becky. She loved to run. I would station myself at the finish line. I drilled her that she was to keep her eyes focused on me at the far end. When the starting pistol went off, she was to run as fast as she could to me. I can assure you that I yelled and hollered, cheered, and waved my arms enough to seize her attention and, if nothing else, alert her to where the finish line was. I just hope I was a stimulus and not a distraction. And the reason for all of this? Focus. It's an essential key to success.

BLURRED VISION

The enemy of focus is distraction. You know how it goes. You decide to clean the garage. On your way to the garage, you notice the mail on the table. First, you'll go through the mail. You discard the junk mail and see that the trash can is full. On your way to take out the trash, you pass the refrigerator and get the urge to grab a cold drink. You take a sip and set the can down on the table. That's when you notice that the flowers on the table need some water. You go to get a jug to fill with water and see your glasses on the windowsill. *That's* where I placed them! You retrieve your glasses and put them on. And there ... is the TV remote! You were looking for it yesterday. Whoever put it down in the kitchen? You know that tonight when you want to watch TV you'll never think to look in the kitchen, so you put it back in the family room where it belongs. The word *garage* is stuck in your mind so you walk down the hall to the garage. You stand in the garage for several minutes trying hard to remember why you came out here anyway. By the end of the day, the mail is still on the table, the trash can is still full beside the refrigerator, there is a can half full of pop sitting beside the mail on the table, the flowers are dead, your glasses are missing again along with the TV remote, and the garage is still a mess. You are baffled, because nothing seemed to get done, and you were busy all day long! What happened? You have lost the battle of distraction.

Jesus drew our attention to the danger of distraction in Matthew 6:22–23:

> *Your eye is a lamp that provides light for your body. When your eye is good, your whole body is full of light. But when your eye is bad, your whole body is filled with darkness. And if the light you think you have is actually darkness, how deep that darkness is!*

What is He talking about? Well, the eye is the channel of light to the mind. All light that enters your mind and body enters through the eye. A good eye provides a healthy, single image of an object. It focuses clearly on one image. A bad eye, on the other hand, has difficulty focusing on a single object, but blends diverse objects. We call it having double or blurred vision, or being cross-eyed. Jesus contrasts seeing one image clearly (good sight) with seeing different images blended (poor eyesight). He equates that condition with darkness, or blindness.

To understand what Jesus is saying, we need to look at the context. He has just commanded, *"Don't store up treasure here on earth, where moths eat them and rust destroys them, and where thieves break in and steal"* (Matthew 6:19). There were three sources of wealth in Jesus' day. Clothing, grain-filled barns, and all the money and possessions contained within the walls of one's house. The hazard for clothing was moths. The menace for grain was rust. The word *rust* means, "to eat away," a reference not to rust as we know it, but to worms, rats, and mice eating away at the corn and grain. The threat to wealth and goods within the walls of one's home was thieves. The walls of most homes were constructed of baked clay. Burglars would dig through the mud-baked wall, and so were called mud-diggers. In other words, be very careful where you set your focus. The things of earth are temporary, and are going to vanish in some way, some day. It is a poor investment to devote your attention to assets that will all evaporate within a lifespan.

While they promise much short-term, they deliver nothing long-term. You never see a hearse pulling a U-Haul.

Money can ease financial stress, but doesn't ease a broken heart. Cash procures stuff, but doesn't secure satisfaction. Riches buy gifts, but don't remove guilt. Wealth provides passing pleasures, but not permanent peace. Now, Jesus is not condemning the proper acquisition or use of money and wealth. We need money to live. Money and possessions can be used to meet numerous needs and bless lives. He is warning against money and wealth becoming the centre of your attention. Why? *"Wherever your treasure is, there the desires of your heart will also be"* (Matthew 6:21). When anything that is of a temporary nature occupies your thoughts, time, and efforts, it controls the focus of your heart. It puts your heart in the wrong place.

That's when Jesus spoke about blurred vision. You claim to be devoted to God, but your focus is on temporal riches and possessions. You are cross-eyed! Distracted! You profess to be a devoted follower of Christ, but you focus on earthly distractions. And distractions soon control. *"[You cannot] serve two masters ... . You cannot serve both God and money"* (Matthew 6:24). The word for money is *mammon*. Mammon was wealth that one man entrusted to another man to keep safe. But it came to mean *wealth in which a man places his trust*. It was capitalized and regarded as nothing less than a god. You cannot serve two gods or masters. Exclusive devotion cannot go in two directions. You must choose one over the other.

I remember my days working on a pig farm. When slaughter day arrived, we had to go into a pen of perhaps 50 pigs and catch the ones chosen for dinner. As soon as I stepped into the sty, chaos ensued. Fifty distractions! Fifty pigs squealing and running everywhere. It was like hunting 50 moving targets at once. The trick was to ignore the 49 and devote your attention to the one pig needing to be cornered. If you failed to do this, you may as well give up the pursuit. Focus was essential to success.

Several years ago, Diane and I spent a wedding anniversary in a charming cottage on a quiet little lake tucked away in the Haliburton Hills of central Ontario. The owner had informed me that they had had a bat problem at the cottage, so some pest controllers would be around that day to get rid of them. No problem. The "bat busters" arrived and spent several hours sealing off every escape crack under the eaves. They then improvised two escape routes for the vermin. Two two-inch plastic pipes jutting out from the gables and sloping downward. The idea was that when dusk fell and the bat hordes deserted the attic to assault the mosquito-filled atmosphere (bats eat bugs), they would find their way out but not be able to get back in. What we had not counted on, however, was that while most found their way outside, many would also find their way inside.

We had just put our heads on the pillows when it happened. A scratching on the wall ... just behind us. We lay motionless, listening, speculating on the possibilities. Suddenly, we felt a whisk of air as something swooped just over our foreheads. I sat bolt upright and Diane slipped under the covers. More scratching. I switched on the bedroom light and immediately spotted four or five of the small black-caped creatures staring down at me. Thus began our night from hell! Diane sank deeper under the protection of the bedcovers while I went to do battle with the barbarian hordes. I opened the bedroom door, switched on the main living room light, and peered out. My nightmare came to life before my eyes. The pine walls were bleeding bats from every notch. My weapon of choice was a badminton racquet. I quickly turned it into a "batminton" racquet. In fact, two racquets, one for each hand. My racquets sliced the air while swing after swing failed to connect with anything but space. Initially, my efforts proved useless because I had too many targets diving and darting from too many directions.

It became apparent that I would need to change my battle strategy. (I had a new appreciation for the word "bat-tle"). My potential defeat lay at the hands of distraction. I would need to devote my whole attention to one bat at a time. My secret weapon was ... focus. As soon as I applied the new strategy to my predicament, the battle began to turn in my favour. I smacked one bat after the other out of the air as they swooped and dived here and there, up and down. My racquet became a lethal weapon and my swings became head-on collisions. Focus made the difference. Many made their retreat to the lofts of the ceiling, so I dropped my racquet in exchange for a stepladder and a ski. I climbed to the heights with ski in hand. Awkward. But one by one I dropped them from the peaks above to the floor beneath. The wounded lay hissing at me with disdain. I ceased their hissing with one whack. In the end, I stood back, like an ancient gladiator, racquet in one hand and ski in the other, and viewed the bloody wall-to-wall carnage. And with a sense of accomplishment, I began the job of collecting the dead from the floor of the battlefield.

In the race of faith, there are many distractions. For instance, other runners. If you keep glancing around at other competitors, you will lose valuable seconds that could have a significant impact on how you run your race. There are always runners who are slower than you, and you can easily pick up the weight of condescending pride and self-confidence. Like the race between the hare and the tortoise. The hare became so preoccupied with how fast it could run compared to how slowly the tortoise was running that it lost its focus and its edge. In fact, it stopped running and took a break! More so, it fell asleep!

The tortoise, on the other hand, kept plodding along at its own pace against all the odds. Fortunately, it didn't set its mind on the hare and its distinct advantages. There are always others who are better and faster runners. If it had, it would have become disheartened and quit in the first few minutes. Rather, the tortoise set its mind on the goal and didn't allow itself to become discouraged. Everyone knows that, in a race, a hare can outrun a tortoise. Well, don't be so sure. There is a difference between running faster and outrunning. You know the rest of the story.

The same is true of the run of faith. One morning, Jesus went for a stroll with His disciple, Peter, along the shore of the Sea of Galilee. It was a planned occasion for a heart-to-heart chat with Peter. Jesus challenged and encouraged Peter's commitment to Him, and informed him that he would die a martyr's death if he chose to serve and obey Him. Jesus then commanded Peter to follow Him. What would you do? Well, as scripture and history bear witness, Peter was prepared to follow Jesus, whatever the cost. But Peter's response is so typical and human. He looked around at his fellow disciple, John, who was following along just a short distance behind them, and asked Jesus what would happen to

THE FOCUS OF THE RUN

him? Jesus immediately recognized the distraction and answered, *"What is that to you? As for you, follow me"* (John 21:22). Your primary concern must be the race *you* are running, not someone else's. Where is *your* life going? What is *your* purpose? Are you giving *your* best? What or who are *you* following? Where are *your* eyes focused?

Do *your* personal best and do not be distracted by the success or failure of others. On the one hand, one needs to be careful not to become critical of those who are struggling, or feel a sense of pride at how well you are doing compared to someone else. On the other hand, it is easy to feel discouraged by those who are superior runners. Even jealous or envious. These feelings deplete your energy and suck the joy of running out of you. It is crucial that you run your *own* race.

Your most sinister diversion is yourself. Self-interest. Self-ambition. Self-pity. Self-sufficiency. Self-satisfaction. Self-gratification. Not long ago, a friend of mine walked out on his wife, children, and friends. When I tried to challenge him on his decision, his reply was, "It's time for me to be happy." So that's what life is about? As I stated earlier, the enemy is within.

It is effortless to become distracted by the things of this world. Demas was one such example. Demas had been one of Paul's valued co-workers in ministry. But sadly, one of the apostle Paul's last written comments was, *"Demas has deserted me because he loves the things of this life"* (2 Timothy 4:10). Demas fell in love with worldly values and pleasures—possibly wealth, career, power, pleasure, friends or a myriad of other attractions, or should I say distractions—and out of love with Jesus. Here was a man who at one time had a clear focus, but something happened to blur his vision. His spiritual eyes began to blend diverse interests and it was just a matter of time before darkness set in and he walked away from his faith.

A frequent distraction is the difficulty of the pathway. We notice how stony and steep the path is, and it becomes all we can see. This distraction is common to all. It descended upon some of the Bible's most well-known and esteemed characters. Think of Elijah. Elijah was a strong runner. The most unlikely person to be sitting alone under a tree in the desert and wanting to die. But there he was. And then there is a lesser-known person in the New Testament, John Mark, who started out with Paul and Barnabas on their first missionary journey. Before they were too far into the venture, John Mark packed it in and went home. We are not told the reason, but difficulty, exertion, fear, and discouragement are good candidates.

I love Joshua's challenge near the end of his life. He had spent his lifetime serving God. He was a military genius who had led the Israelites into Canaan to defeat the inhabitants and occupy the land. He was a spiritual giant and man of faith. But note his parting words. After recalling everything God had done for His people, he said, *"So be very careful to follow everything Moses wrote in the Book of Instruction. Do not deviate from it, turning either to the right or to the left. … Be very careful to love the Lord your God"* (Joshua 23:6–11). His words were a warning about distractions and a challenge to keep their eyes and hearts singly focused on the Lord their God. The one is the pathway of darkness; the other the pathway of light. He retold the story with a more detailed account of God's faithful provision and then reiterated, *"So fear the Lord and serve him wholeheartedly. … Serve the Lord alone"* (Joshua 24:14).

Joshua then made the challenge very personal. *"Choose today whom you will serve. Would you prefer the gods your ancestors served … or will it be the gods of the Amorites in whose land you now live? But as for me and my family, we will serve the Lord"* (Joshua 24:15). That's the critical challenge for us today. Will the eye of your heart blend diverse objects and interests that compete for your heart's devotion? Will you consider the myriad of gods, voices, allurements, and enticements that scream for your attention? Or will you set your whole affection and attention on one, single, healthy image? Will you focus your single-hearted devotion on God alone? You need to make the choice before it is made for you. For your choice will determine the direction, purpose, and outcome of your life.

CLEAR VISION

The writer of Hebrews makes the object of our focus crystal clear: Jesus. We are urged to run the race God has set before us. Then he adds, "Here's how you do it." There is a requirement. There is a precondition if, in fact, you are going to endure a difficult distance run.

That precondition is to possess a single focus. *"We do this by keeping our eyes on Jesus, the champion"* (Hebrews 12:2). The Son of God who came from heaven to run His race on earth for us. The Messiah. The King of the road. When your road is hard and the conditions weigh heavy upon you ... focus. The salient point is to fasten your eyes on Jesus so that your mind blocks out any distractions. And run! You'll recall how Robert Cheruiyot (Mwafrica) developed into a champion distance runner, despite numerous obstructions, disruptions, and hurdles in his life, because he centred his attention on a true champion, Paul Tergat. Similarly, if you want to run like a champion, keep your eyes fixed on Jesus, the true champion of your faith.

One day, three separate individuals approached Jesus and asked if they could follow Him. Their intentions were probably sincere, but after a brief discussion with Jesus, each one changed his mind. Why? Distractions. The priority of the comforts of a home. The duties and responsibilities of family. Family relationships. Jesus responded, *"Anyone who puts a hand to the plow and then looks back is not fit for the Kingdom of God"* (Luke 9:62). Now Jesus was not teaching that to follow Him, one must deny obligations and responsibilities and go live in a cardboard box on a street corner somewhere. He used a metaphor from the farm to emphasize the point that to follow Him meant single-focused devotion to Him.

During my years on the farm, I tried my hand at plowing. Now I would never win a plowing match, but I did learn to turn over a pretty straight furrow. I did it by keeping my eye fixed forward on one particular object, like a tree or a rock, at the far end of the field. I learned the hard way that if I looked back to admire my straight furrow (yes, plowing is an art), by the time I looked forward again, my focal point was gone and my straight furrow was no longer. I also discovered that if my focus was distracted and drifted off to some other point ahead, then my tractor also drifted in that direction. I shouldn't really blame the tractor. But we tend to drift where our focus fixates. This doesn't only apply to driving tractors, but also racing cars. Racing car drivers are taught not to look at the wall that borders the track. Why not? They will tend to move toward it and collide with it. It's the same with life. You gravitate toward what you focus on.

113

A New Paradigm

I have conducted many funerals. There is something I say at a funeral service without fail. I remind the mourners that, while they gather to remember and grieve the loss of a loved one, at such an occasion, they also come face to face with their own mortality. One looks at the casket and is cognizant that one day that will be *me*. We must all pass this way. There will be a memorial service conducted in your memory and friends and relatives will get up and read what is called a *eulogy*. They will say ... well, what? Usually, it's nice things whether true or not so true. Wouldn't you love to be a fly on the wall at your own funeral when people stand to give you honour and express feelings of love, gratitude, indebtedness, and appreciation? Unfortunately, most eulogies are comprised of sentiments that would have been extremely beneficial for the departed loved one to be told when he or she was alive. It would be a source of encouragement for the person if they knew the impact they had on the lives of others. The words, too often, are spoken to the wrong people.

But think about it. What would you like to hear expressed about you and your life? When all has been said and done, the last lap is finished and the race has been run, what do you want said? The end is a good place to begin. Because if you focus on where you want to end, that will impact exponentially how you run your race and live your life. Focusing on the finish is a shield against busily accomplishing goals, reaching success, and building recognition around things that in the end prove meaningless, leave you empty and barren, and rob you of achieving what really mattered most, but now is lost. Stephen Covey writes:

> How different our lives are when we really know what is deeply important to us, and, keeping that picture in mind, we manage ourselves each day to be and to do what really matters most. If the ladder is not leaning against the right wall, every step we take just gets us to the wrong place faster. We may be very busy, we may be very efficient, but we will also be truly effective only when we begin with the end in mind.[4]

Beginning at the end will possibly require a paradigm shift in your life. A paradigm is both the focus and source of your life. It defines who you are. It is the spring out of which flow your values, attitudes, thinking, and behaviour. It is the glasses you wear through which you view the world. If the lens is red, you will see a red world. If the lens is yellow, you will see the world as yellow. It governs your worldview. It puts everything in your life in perspective. It is the rock upon which the foundation of your life is built. The magnetic pole to which the compass needle of your life spins and points. The map for your life. Your focus.

There are many core paradigms around which people centre their lives. Spouse. Self. Money. Career. Friends. Church. Religion. Recreation. Family. Your core paradigm will impact everything. The Bible leaves no doubt about the one viable core paradigm for your life: Christ. As you run the race of life, fix your eyes on Jesus. Jesus told a story about a wise person and a foolish person. The wise person built a house upon the rock and the foolish person built a house upon the sand. When the rain came in torrents and the floodwaters rose and the winds beat against the houses, the house on the rock stood firm while the house on the sand collapsed. I think Jesus was comparing a person who constructed a house up on the rocky cliff to a person who conveniently erected a house down in the wadi. The wadi may be protected and dry today but is vulnerable to the floodwaters that tomorrow could come raging down through the gullies and gorges with uncontrolled fury. The contrast was between one person who listened to His teachings and followed them, with another person who ignored them. They both built the same kind of house. They experienced the same storm. The difference was upon what they centred their lives. Their core paradigms.

Let me give you an illustration of how one's core paradigm influences one's thinking. If my core paradigm is *family*, as a father I will concern myself with such reasonable questions as, "What career choices are my children making? What college should they attend?" Good questions. But if *Christ* is my centre, I will concern myself primarily with, "What is God's call on my child's life?" If *family* is my centre, I will ask, "Are my children growing and developing physically, emotionally, and socially?" If *Christ* is my centre, I will ask the same question, but begin by asking,

RUN! THE AMAZING RACE

"Are they growing and developing spiritually?" If *family* is my centre, I will ask, "Am I being the best dad I can be?" If *Christ* is my centre, I will concern myself with, "Am I a godly dad?" If *family* is my core paradigm, I will mull over the amount of inheritance I should leave to my children. On the other hand, if *Christ* is my core paradigm, I will be preoccupied with the spiritual legacy I leave. There's a difference.

THE STORY OF A PARADIGM SHIFT

There is an incredible story one would guess came right out of the plot in a Hollywood movie. The main character in the story had an exponential impact on this world. His name was Saul. Saul defined himself as a pure-blooded Hebrew, a believer in the one true God, faultless in his obedience to the Jewish law down to the minutest detail, respected and well-educated in the school of Gamaliel, the greatest teacher of the day. Saul was a card-carrying, no-nonsense, righteous-living Pharisee. He was so zealous about what he believed that he harshly persecuted the young growing movement of Christ-followers. Jesus of Nazareth had been crucified but then resurrected three days later, and witnessed alive by hundreds of people for 40 days after His resurrection. The evidence for His resurrection was overwhelming and thousands of Saul's fellow Jews believed Jesus to be the Messiah, the Christ. Saul saw this faith as a heresy within Judaism and something that needed to be purged. He was determined to eradicate the movement and began to wreak havoc in the Christian church everywhere he went.

Then something totally unexpected happened. Saul was on his way to Damascus to harass the Christians there, when a blinding light blocked the road before him. Saul's horse sprang up, sending Saul sprawling onto the ground. It was Jesus. The resurrected Christ whom he was persecuting. You can read the story from Saul's own account in Acts 26. This startling revelation shook Saul (later renamed Paul) to his core. Everything changed. The Christ-hater became a Christ-believer. The Christ-persecutor became a Christ-proclaimer. This one who had devoted himself to eradicating the new faith became its greatest defender. He was given a new identity.

116

A NEW IDENTITY

Paul described it himself in the book of Philippians. In Philippians 3:7–11, Paul mentioned the name of Christ nine times, in just five verses. That says something significant in itself. The paradigm for his life now centred on Christ. *"Everything else is worthless when compared with the infinite value of knowing Christ Jesus my Lord. For his sake I have discarded everything else, counting it all as garbage, so that I could gain Christ"* (Philippians 3:8). Everything his paradigm embraced before he met Jesus was disposed of. Everything he valued before was now considered meaningless. He had many accomplishments and good things in his life, but these things were no longer the ultimate end for him. When Christ becomes the paradigm for your life, you become a new person. You get your genes from your parents, but you get your identity from Christ. You know *who* you are. You are in Christ. You are a child of God. You are confident in His acceptance of you. You are not defined by your successes or your failures; you are defined by your relationship with Him. Your intrinsic worth is rooted in who Christ is within you and what He has done for you.

One of man's most basic human needs is security. A healthy identity is supported by a strong sense of security. The cup of security is filled by unconditional love. This cup is filled when you know you are in Christ and are unconditionally loved by Him. Paul reminded the Roman Christians that God had chosen and called them. He had given them right standing with Himself by not even sparing the life of His own Son, Jesus. Jesus died for you, was raised to life for you, and lives in heaven today for you. When Satan accuses you, Jesus pleads for you as your advocate. There is nothing more God can do to demonstrate His unconditional love for you (Romans 8:31–39). When you truly comprehend this reality, you will live with the knowledge that nothing can separate you from His love. Life's painful realities, personal failures, man's evil intentions, and the powerful unseen forces of evil combined are not enough to separate you from the love Christ has for you. That's security. Embrace it.

117

A NEW PURPOSE

Not only do you need to know *who* you are, but also *why* you are. Paul wrote, *"I trust that my life will bring honour to Christ, whether I live or die. For to me, living means living for Christ"* (Philippians 1:20–21). It couldn't be clearer. The purpose of his life was to live for Christ and to bring honour to Him. Paul added, *"I press on to possess the perfection for which Christ Jesus first possessed me"* (Philippians 3:12). What a fantastic purpose! To become everything Christ called you to be. To acquire and accomplish everything in your life that Christ possessed you for. The second basic need within the soul of every human being is to possess a strong sense of purpose. A question lingers within all of us. *Why am I?* We all need to know our purpose for being alive. Your ultimate significance is found in Christ.

A NEW DIRECTION

When Christ is the centre, you also have a strong sense of *where* you are going. *"I focus on this one thing: forgetting the past and looking forward to what lies ahead, I press on to reach the end of the race and receive the heavenly prize for which God, through Christ Jesus, is calling us"* (Philippians 3:13–14). We are pulled in many directions by many voices. However, the inner voice of God's Spirit calls us forward in the direction that leads us to Jesus, the end of this race down here and an eternity with Him. We can't imagine what that day will be like, except that the good we enjoy here is only a foretaste of the good we will enjoy there.

At the 1998 Winter Olympics in Nagano, Japan, Norwegian Bjorn Dahlie was the first of the 92-man field to cross the finish line in the 10,000-metre cross-country skiing event, winning his sixth lifetime gold medal. Rather than rushing away to celebrate his victory, he waited. Waited for Philip Boit of Kenya, lagging in last place. The Kenyans are renowned as distance runners, but this was a first for the African country. At last, Philip struggled into view. Only a few spectators remained to applaud his arrival. But Philip could see the great champion, Bjorn Dahlie, standing at the finish line cheering him in. As Philip crossed the finish line, Bjorn greeted him with a tight grip of respect and congratulations. He took him by the shoulders and communicated his admiration for one who was determined to finish.

Christ completed His course long ago. He was born, lived, died, rose from the dead and ascended to heaven. Today He stands at the finish line, eyes focused on you, intensely attentive to how you are running. Calling your name. Ready to welcome you in. He'll be there when you get there. So don't give up. Fade the distractions and focus on what lies ahead. Focus on Jesus cheering from the finish line. Keeping the end in sight will significantly impact how you run the race.

A NEW SOURCE OF STRENGTH

When Christ becomes the core paradigm for your life, you know where you are going, and also *how* you will get there. You draw from the source of deep, divine strength that fills the cup of your human frailty. It exceeds your weakness. It more than counterbalances your inability to run the distance. In Philippians 3:10–11, Paul stated that his earnest desire was to suffer with Christ, sharing in His death, so that he would experience the same power that raised Christ from the dead surging through him. Resurrection follows death. The struggles and severities of life are God's way of killing the self-life. Accept these trials, because when you die to yourself through the adversities of the run, you begin to experience the resurrection power of Christ empowering you to endure and go the distance. It's one of the great paradoxes in the spiritual life. The way up is down. Surrender is the prerequisite to victory. Life sprouts out of death. God's power works best in your weakness and inadequacy.

Paul wrote, *"I can do everything through Christ, who gives me strength"* (Philippians 4:13). Paul lived with strong confidence. But it wasn't self-confidence. It was Christ-confidence. Paul humbly understood and accepted his human limitations because Christ was his centre and the source of his strength. I emphasized this truth in a previous chapter, but I touch on it here again because it is relevant to the subject under discussion.

While it is critically important to rely on the power of Christ within, power is relative to focus. It is imperative to focus on the person of Christ, the source of your strength and inspiration. The writer of

119

Hebrews urged us to run with endurance by keeping our eyes on Jesus. He then added an interesting comment: *"Because of the joy awaiting him, he endured the cross."* Jesus ran with a focus. I think that the *joy that awaited Him* was the forgiveness of our sins. Our eternal salvation. He focused on an eternity with us awaiting Him at the finish line of His earthly mission. He endured by keeping His focus on us; we endure by keeping our focus on Him. We are why He persevered. He is why we persevere.

Then we read, *"Think of all the hostility he endured from sinful people"* (Hebrews 12:3). The word *think* means to "count up" all the ways Jesus endured the hostility of sinful people for your sake. Add it all up. Think about it. Ponder it. He didn't quit when He was criticized, misjudged, and ridiculed. He didn't quit when His friends bailed on Him. On the night when His path to the cross wound its way through Gethsemane, the knowledge of what was about to occur weighed heavily upon Him. He hit the wall. Would He run through the wall? Gethsemane was an olive grove and a location of the oil press. A large millstone crushed the olives, breaking the skins and releasing the finest oil. Then, in phase two of the process, the crushed olives were scooped up and dumped into burlap bags. The bags were placed under a heavy stone pillar called the olive press. The pillar pressed down upon the crushed olives, releasing more olive oil. The precious oil ran down channels and into containers to be sold and used for cooking, light, and medicinal purposes.

I can imagine Jesus reaching up and grasping the olive press. He was anguished and distressed. The sheer terror of what this night would bring was crushing. The torture of the cross that would mercilessly break His body and bleed it of its life's blood. The weight of every possible sin ever committed by man, the weight of the sin of the world. The fierceness of God's wrath poured out upon Him. The unfathomable dread of being abandoned by His Father because of the filth that He would carry in Himself. He cried, *"My soul is crushed with grief to the point of death"* (Matthew 26:38). Just as the olive press crushed the olives and pressed the valued oil from their flesh, so the weight of His grief would crush and press His life from Him. He prayed, *"My Father! If it is possible, let this cup of suffering be taken away from me. Yet I want your will to be done, not mine"* (Matthew 26:39). No! Not this cup! If it's possible, let this one pass! But it wasn't possible. This was why He had come. Jesus made a choice. And He ran through the wall.

He stayed the course when He was arrested, mocked, beaten, tortured, and crucified with five-inch spikes driven through His wrists and ankles. He didn't quit as the blood drained from His veins and dripped onto the ground. Where would we be if Jesus had quit before the end of the race? But He didn't. He powered His way through every obstacle, adversity, and sorrow. At the finish line, He cried out, *"It is finished!"* He accomplished everything His Father in heaven had sent Him to do. He lifted the cup of suffering, turned it upside down, and drank every drop. Every last drop. He emptied it. For you. *"He endured the cross, disregarding its shame. Now He is seated in the place of honor beside God's throne"* (Hebrews 12:2). He crossed the finish line for you and for me.

The reason for pondering all the hostility Jesus endured for you is to find your inspiration in Him. Inspiration means to have new strength and life breathed into you. You get your second wind. *"Then you won't become weary and give up"* (Hebrews 12:3). When you feel like giving up (and we've all been there), be inspired and strengthened by Him. Run for Jesus like He ran for you. He kept going for you; now you keep going for Him. *"After all, you have not yet given your lives in your struggle against sin"* (Hebrews 12:4). You have not yet given for Him as much as He gave for you. There's more that you can give. So, fix your eyes ahead, down the track. Do you see Him? He's there … at the finish line. Waiting for you. Stay the course. And one day, not far off, you will fall into the arms of the One who gave His all for you.

NINE

THE RACE OF FAITH

DEAN KARNAZES WAS APPROACHING THE 85-MILE MARK OF THE WESTERN
States 100-Mile Run. He had begun the race somewhere in the middle
of the pack of 379 runners. He was now running in 20th place. Darkness
had settled in, making the narrow trails much more difficult to maneuver.
The small flashlight strapped to his forehead beamed light several yards
beyond, making it almost impossible to distinguish the contour of the
terrain. Without warning, his small headlight dimmed. Dean stopped to
change the batteries. The new batteries, however, made little difference.

He continued to run, but his world was becoming strangely darker
and darker. Tree branches appeared out of nowhere, swatting him in the
face. Everything had gone black except for a peculiar green glow that
outlined the image of the foliage along the trail. The problem was not
the flashlight, but a condition called nyctalopia, or night blindness. It
is a temporary impairment and it threatened to bring Dean's dream to
an abrupt end with only 15 miles to go. He had overcome obstacle after
obstacle on this grueling, punishing run, and now he sat on the side
of the trail weighing his options. The options were two. Run blind, or
call it quits. But the same determination that had brought him this far
would not let him quit. He would keep going ... somehow.

Dean wasn't in denial. His plan was to sit and wait for the next
runner to come along and ask him or her to send back help from the
next aid station ahead. He soon nodded off. It was just a few minutes

but it was a deep doze, and when he came to, it was like climbing out of a black, bottomless cavern. His confusion was soon replaced by the splendor of a starlit sky. He suddenly realized he could see again. He began to run again. But the reprieve was short-lived. The eyesight began to dim again. He arrived at the next aid station where he was checked over. The volunteers encouraged him to rest until morning, at which time they would get him out on horseback. It seemed like a plan, except for one thing. Dean was determined to keep running. He had come this far. There had to be a way!

Someone brought Dean some brownies laced with espresso beans. He felt the rush. The caffeine and sugar surged through him, restoring his energy and vitality. What was even more amazing, his eyesight seemed to be recovering. Dean wondered what was really in those brownies. He was firing on all cylinders. He wolfed down another brownie and got up to continue the last fourteen miles. Someone called to him and asked skeptically if he really knew what he was doing. He didn't. Dean says, "I really had no idea what I was doing; this was entirely uncharted territory for me. At least I now had *hope,* which is more than what I'd had an hour ago."[1] And he headed off into the dark.

RUNNING IN THE DARK

Faith is only relevant when you are in the dark. If you could see, you wouldn't need faith. You'd run by sight. Faith is running in uncharted territory. You have no idea what lies around the next bend or what is waiting up ahead. *"Faith is the confidence that what we hope for will actually happen; it gives us assurance about things we cannot see"* (Hebrews 11:1). Faith is exercised in your blindness. It reaches beyond your limits. It stretches beyond your own control. There is something about man that he likes to hold control over everything happening in his life. We don't like to move outside the sphere of our control. Well, welcome to life! There are lots of things going on that affect you and that are outside of your control. You need to be willing to trust beyond your limits and confines. To trust beyond yourself. But let's be cautious here. Faith is not stupidity. Faith is not just a leap in the dark. It is not a dive into nothingness.

Authentic faith is embedded in the bedrock of truth. It is built on something substantial. After the writer of Hebrews tells us what faith is and that we cannot please God without it, he says that we *"must believe that God exists and that he rewards those who sincerely seek him"* (Hebrews 11:6). You must believe that God exists and that He makes the difference. The Bible teaches that He is self-existent. The Creator of everything. All-powerful. All-knowing. Sovereign. Providential. The Bible teaches that He loves you and has a purpose for your life. Ravi Zacharias writes, "God has made it imperative, in the design of life, to be willing to trust beyond yourself. Walking by faith means to follow Someone else who knows more than you do, Someone who is not only all-powerful but also good."[2] Trust Him.

Hebrews 11 is all about faith. People who believed God existed and that He made the difference. They trusted beyond themselves in Someone they believed knew more than they did. The proof of their faith was in their obedience to God. The book of James tells us that true faith is an action word. The faithful are action figures. God told Noah to build a huge boat on dry land with no water in sight. God gave him detailed instructions about how to build the boat. But, despite the detail, there was no directive about a rudder or a sail. These two items were omitted. The other thing missing was, of course … water. It made no human sense. But Noah did everything exactly as God directed him. Can you imagine paying your money to go for a voyage on a cruise ship the size of the Queen Mary, sitting on dry land, miles from any shore, with no way of budging, sailing, or steering her? But Noah obeyed. And God rewarded Noah. You know the rest of the story.

"It was by faith that Abraham obeyed when God called him to leave home and go to another land that God would give him as his inheritance. He went without knowing where he was going" (Hebrews 11:8). He had no map and no directions. Just a promise from God, who knew more than he did. So he packed up and moved.

When Abraham and Sarah finally arrived at God's destination for them, they lived there by faith. They put down no foundation for a permanent house surrounded by sturdy walls. They lived in tents, moving from place to place with their flocks and herds in a nomadic lifestyle. But Abraham had a promise and a faith that he was part of a much larger divine plan and purpose. And so the chapter continues with person after person who believed that God existed and knew more than they did. They trusted beyond themselves and acted on their faith. They ran in the blackness of the night. In their blindness they pressed on with confidence in the One who could see. They charted unfamiliar territory. And so can you.

With the example of those who have run the race of faith in times past, we are urged to run our race of faith with endurance. We are directed to keep our eyes fixed on Jesus, *"the champion who initiates and perfects our faith"* (Hebrews 12:2). Yes, faith is critical to the race. Not a kind of faith that leaps into the dark unknown, but a faith that centres completely on Jesus from beginning to end. A faith that rests on everything we know about God, through Christ, in the Bible and everything we have experienced about Him in life.

Jesus ran the course. He experienced all the struggles that you do along the route. The stress and fatigue of busyness. The desertion of friends. Misunderstanding. Ridicule. In fact, He had to get past the torture and shame of a Roman cross. And a cold, sealed tomb. Death itself. He ran the race and championed over everything. He understands your weaknesses, for He faced all the same tests and trials you do in your run; yet He never succumbed or sinned. And now He offers to you hope and help (Hebrews 4:14–16). You cannot see or know what lies ahead. Nyctalopia is part of the human condition. You may not understand why something is happening the way it is. But by faith you can have assurance about things you cannot see. You can keep your spiritual senses tuned to the One who knows the course. The terrain is uncharted from your perspective, but He has mapped out the way for you. Trust Him.

SKIING BLIND

It was the finish line of the grueling 50-K Nor-Am classic cross-country ski race during the Olympic trials at the Canmore Nordic Centre in Canmore, Alberta. A skier, in red and white gear, ski poles tucked under his arms, jaw set with the look of pain and determination, came into view and burned his way across the finish line in a time of

2:21:08—more than a minute ahead of his nearest competitor. What had just happened was amazing. You see, 30-year-old Brian McKeever was legally blind. With only 10 percent vision, he crossed a finish line he could not see.

From boyhood, McKeever dreamed of being an Olympian skier. By the time he was 18 years old, he was well on his way to seeing his dream realized. But then genetics kicked in. Brian's father had Stargardt's disease, a genetic condition that robs children of most of their sight. Brian had a 50-50 chance of inheriting the gene, but by 18 it seemed he had possibly beaten the odds. Then, over several years, his eyesight clouded over and gradually disappeared except for the little he could see on the periphery. "When he looks straight ahead, it's as if he's just had a flash bulb go off in his face, though in his case the flash never stops … much like seeing the corona of the sun when the moon eclipses it. Or, as McKeever puts it, in his all-Canadian fashion: 'I see the doughnut. I don't see the Timbit.'"[3]

Rather than allowing depression to take control of his life and dreams, however, as happens to so many, Brian determined to pursue his dreams. He asked his brother, Robin, to help him train. Brian and Robin had never been particularly close. Robin was six years older and busy with his own career travelling the world as an Olympian skier. Robin had beaten the genetic odds. But now Brian's blindness drew them together. Brian knew he needed Robin if he was to continue competing successfully. And something inside Robin told him that he would be there for his brother to help him keep his dream alive.

They made a great team. Robin would ski ahead of Brian, blazing a trail, as was allowed in the Paralympics. Brian would follow the blur of his brother's image and listen to his voice and the sound of his skis cutting the snow. With his brother as guide, he won four gold medals at the 2002 Paralympics in Salt Lake City and 2006 Paralympics in Turin, Italy. Paralympians train just as hard as able-bodied athletes, but Brian harboured the dream inside him of one day competing against the world's best able-bodied skiers. He knew that he could compete for Olympic gold. To many, Brian's dream was sheer fantasy; for Brian it was more than possibility.

The Nor-Am classic race in Canmore was critical to his quest. He was competing against able-bodied athletes with the same Olympic pursuit. Brother Robin led the pack on the first lap. Robin was skiing well, and when Robin was skiing well, Brian was skiing well. But then Robin began to lag. Another contender who had been challenging the brothers moved into the lead and Brian began to pursue the sound of his skis. Then, in the final stretch, Brian stepped out and took control. He melted the snow under his skis as he pushed for the finish line. He won. Winning the 50-K in Canmore brought him ever so close to his dream. Cross Country Canada chose him to compete in the 2010 Vancouver Winter Olympics for Team Canada. That made him the first disabled athlete to potentially compete in both a Winter Olympics and Paralympics. It wouldn't be easy. His brother, Robin, wouldn't be there to guide him. He would have to rely on the images of other skiers in front of him. And if he got out in front? Well … he would have only his memory of the course.

Disappointment is part of the journey. Two days before the prestigious Olympic 50-K race was slated to go, Canadian ski coaches decided not to start Brian. Under International Ski Federation rules, only four skiers are allowed to compete for each country. Four others from the team were chosen. Brian was extremely disappointed but remained positive. His very presence on the team was historic and he had drawn worldwide attention. In reality, it's when disappointment strikes or we square off with adversity that the real race is won or lost. The real race of life is not a 50-K classic that is won with strong legs, but a life-long endurance run that is won with strong character and tough faith. Adversity is a pathway. More often than not, adversity and disappointment are the fuel that helps us transcend our limitations.

BLIND SKIER'S EDGE

Watching a blind downhill skier following his guide in perfect sync, skis only two metres apart, carving arcing turns down the steep slopes of a mountain is an unforgettable sight. It is an amazing image of the race of faith. Actually, most blind skiers are guided from behind. The argument for this is safety. But it also limits the progress of the blind skier as he must keep craning his head back to hear the commands. It is difficult to accelerate forward when one is focused backward. It weakens confidence and certainly diminishes the enjoyment and thrill of the slopes.

New programs such as Blind Skier's Edge are educating blind skiers and guides in the keen advantage of focusing forward down the slope. Blind Skier's Edge was developed by blind adventurer Erik Weihenmayer and his ski guide, Jeff Ulrich. Weihenmayer is the only blind person to have climbed to the summit of Mt. Everest and the "Seven Summits." He is qualified to speak to the matter because he also skied blind from the summit of 18,000-ft. Mt. Elbrus, the tallest peak in Europe, skiing 10,000 feet from the summit to the base camp. He is a strong proponent of focusing forward. When the guide is in front, the blind skier is able to focus on *following* the voice commands and the sound of the guide's skis. This is proving to be a clear advantage. Eventually, the blind skier can learn to actually ski in the identical track of his guide. Remarkable!

Specific commands are given to signify humps and dips in the trail. Other commands indicate a steep downhill grade or a gentle grade. In an emergency, the guide commands, "Sit!" Most guides call turns in two syllables: "Turn left...turn right!" Erik Weihenmayer and Jeff Ulrich have discovered that three-syllable commands work best.

> When learning, blind and sighted skiers are taught about the three sequential parts of a turn: getting the skis up on edges to initiate the turn, facing down the fall line, and bringing the skis around for the finish. When guiding, each word in the three-syllable command should translate to a specific part of the turn. Jeff's command may sound like this: "Turn...a...left! Turn...a...right!" With each syllable, the blind skier knows precisely where to be in the position of the turn. Jeff will also elongate or shorten the call to indicate what size turn to make. For instance, a gradual turn, "Tuuuuuuuurn...aaaaaaaaa... leeeeeeeeeft." In addition, by drawing out different syllables, he can navigate the blind skier around obstacles.[4]

Watching two skiers, one blind, the other both eyes vigilant, moving fluidly together in total unison is a profound picture of faith. Jesus goes before. You follow. He sees ahead. You don't. He knows the way. You don't. But you know your Guide. You have a relationship with your Guide that runs so deep that you would trust Him with your life. And you listen intently to His voice, the voice of His Spirit. Jesus said of the Spirit, *"He will guide you into all truth"* (John 16:13). The apostle Paul wrote that the children of God follow the Spirit of God. We *"no longer follow our sinful nature but instead follow the Spirit. ... You are controlled by the Spirit if you have the Spirit of God living in you. ... All who are led by the Spirit of God are children of God"* (Romans 8:4, 9, 14). You listen forward to the movement and voice of the Spirit. He speaks through the Scriptures, other people, circumstances, prayer, and in numerous ways. He directs in and through the spiritual disciplines that we discussed in an earlier chapter. Sometimes the command is loud; most often it is a quiet voice you learn to distinguish from the many other voices around you.

We resemble the blind skier in so many ways. You may possess skill, energy, strength, and ambition, but you cannot see and do not know what lies ahead in your life. You have no idea what life will bring tomorrow or further down the course. But blindness is not a race-stopper. Like a blind skier, you move forward by voice commands and the sound of your Guide's presence in front of you. You know what it takes to confront any challenge the path of life presents, and to thrive. Because you trust beyond yourself. Your confidence is in your Guide. You know Him. You trust Him. This is the blind skier's edge.

FROM STRING TO CABLE FAITH

If you cannot please God without faith, then you know He will do everything it takes to develop it. Faith is like a muscle. Rest it for too long and it will deteriorate. Exercise it and it is invigorated and grows strong. All athletes are preoccupied with exercising the necessary muscles to compete on the field. All athletes running the race God has set for them are preoccupied with exercising and building the kind of faith that will give them endurance over the distance. Faith is meant to grow and develop.

When the first suspension bridge was erected across the turbulent Niagara River many years ago, it began with a kite. A kite was lifted and landed on the opposite bank. A thicker cord was attached to the thin kite string and drawn across the river. Then a rope. And then a small cable. The size and strength of the cables grew until an iron cable strong enough to support and suspend a bridge was stretched from shore to shore and fixed in place. Interestingly, the same procedure is put into practice today.

On Friday, June 15th, 2012, Nik Wallenda of the famed Wallenda family walked into history by crossing on a high wire over Niagara Falls. The crowds watched as the breathtaking feat was accomplished. Days before the walk, however, a heavy cable had to be stretched across the gorge. The cable was 550 metres long and weighed nearly seven tons. Too heavy for a helicopter to carry. The contractors hatched a plan. A chopper flew a lighter, high-tension Ultrex-rope from one side of the gorge to the other. Once strung across and secured, they attached the heavier cable to the end of the Ultrex-rope and pulled it across the expanse. It took 20 hours of preparation time to be ready to pull the seven-ton cable across, and 10 hours to execute the procedure. The rigging on each side was secured by huge anchors drilled deep into the bedrock. Without the light Ultrex-rope, there would have been no cable. And with no cable, there would have been no historic high-wire walk across the falls.

Similarly, faith builds upon faith. It begins small and grows. Growth is a process over time. The thin Ultrex-rope is like the saving faith that reaches from your heart into heaven and connects you to Jesus. It is the beginning of a life of faith. But it is only the beginning. Living faith is growing faith. True faith grows stronger over a lifetime and takes you on a journey with God. It leads you to becoming a conqueror over the difficulties of this life and takes you to the other side. James reminds us:

When troubles come your way, consider it an opportunity for great joy. For you know that when your faith is tested, your endurance has a chance to grow. So let it grow, for when your endurance is fully developed, you will be perfect and complete, needing nothing (James 1:2–4).

Do you see what James is saying? Trials are opportunities for growth. Adversity exercises faith. The strain and pain of adversity is needed to grow strong faith. Exercised faith reinforces your ability to endure. And as you endure through the trials, this grows strong, healthy character. You become whole and complete, like Jesus, ready for anything.

THE SCHOOL OF SPIRITUAL GROWTH

When Jesus called His disciples, He enrolled them in the school of spiritual growth. The classroom of faith. You will recall from a previous chapter that Jesus' disciples were *talmeid*. They were students who followed Him, learned from Him, studied Him, and became like Him. They grew in their understanding of what it meant to follow Jesus. They grew in their knowledge of who Jesus was and His mission. They grew in their faith. Jesus often turned everyday situations into a classroom experience to deepen spiritual understanding and grow faith.

The classroom was sometimes a field. A wedding dinner. A mountaintop. A boat. Three times Jesus used the fishing boat as a classroom. Each time, Jesus used the unique situation to stretch the disciples' faith a little further. As I discussed in a previous chapter, the introductory class in "Faith 101" occurred one day on the shore of the Sea of Galilee. It was a busy morning along the shoreline. Crowds pressed around Jesus trying to get close to Him. Children chased each other up and down the paths, stopping now and again to hurl a stone into the water. Fishermen were busily engaged washing and mending their nets. Normally, fishing was done at night, but Peter and his partners had had an unsuccessful night.

That particular morning, Jesus told Peter to push out where it was deeper and let down the nets to catch some fish. Peter protested a little but agreed since it was Jesus who was giving the directions. And Jesus had that look in His face like … just trust Me on this one. In a simple act of surrender and faith, Peter pushed out and let down the nets. Immediately, so many fish began to enter the nets that they began to tear. Peter called for help and a second boat was launched to the rescue. In the end, both boats were pulled to shore, sitting so low in the water that each was on the verge of sinking. Peter and his partners, James and

John, were stunned and humbled. Just a small act of obedience to what Jesus had said. But look at the outcome. What a faith lesson! But there would be more lessons. Harder lessons.

In lesson one, it was daylight. The sea was calm. Jesus was present and awake in the boat. In lesson two, it was also daylight and Jesus was present in the boat. But two features would change that would deepen the perplexity and increase the learning curve. The day began with the sun shining down on a peaceful, still lake. Jesus told His disciples to get into the boat and sail to the other side. It began well. But none of us know what any day will bring. Jesus was exhausted and settled down for a nap in the boat. Then it happened.

A fierce storm descended on the lake without warning. The sea swelled as the wind incited the waves into a rage. They lashed against the sides of the small craft and began to fill the vessel. Panic began to set in upon everyone as they realized the extreme danger. That is … everyone except Jesus. He was sound asleep, despite the water sloshing around Him. The fear intensified as the wind grew stronger and the waves rose higher, threatening to upset the boat. This time in the classroom, the sea was stormy and Jesus was asleep. Have you ever felt that way? The storm is blowing all around you. You reach points of deep discouragement, even despair. You feel a debilitating sense of hopelessness. You are paralyzed by fear. And Jesus? He seems asleep, unaware of the situation.

Someone shouted, "Wake Him … or we're all going down!" Another began shaking Jesus, waking Him from His sleep. As Jesus stirred, He lifted His head and saw the situation for what it was. He rose to his feet at the bow of the boat and commanded the wind and waves to stop. The storm immediately ceased and everything became calm. Jesus then turned to His talmeid and asked a question. "Where is your faith?" The men were both terrified and amazed. They recognized that here was Someone who could command wind and waves and they obeyed. Here was Someone inside their boat who was stronger than the storm assailing them. Here was Someone who was sovereign *over* the storm and *in* the storm. Who was He?

There was still one more faith lesson from the classroom of the boat. This one would pale the others. Would the students receive a passing grade, or a failure? *Faith 101* … the lake was calm and Jesus was present and awake in the boat. *Faith 201* … it was daylight, but the lake was stormy with the risk of the small fishing vessel capsizing. Jesus was in the boat but fast asleep. Now, settled into the classroom of *Faith 301*, Jesus, the Teacher, was about to stretch their faith to the breaking point. You can read the full story in Matthew 14:22–33.

Jesus sent His students out onto the lake in the boat without Him. Like before, unexpectedly, a strong wind began to sweep across the lake, whipping the waves into a fury. But this time, the blackness of night descended upon them. The situation was not good, even for those accustomed to the lake. A violent night storm. They rowed hard against the wind, all to no avail. The waves battered the sides of the boat blow by blow, each with increasing intensity. Both wind and wave swirled around them while the sea seemed intent on swallowing the little boat and its terrorized crew down into its dark watery stomach. It couldn't get worse. And Jesus was nowhere to be seen.

And then, about three o'clock in the morning, a figure was spotted walking on the water. One of the men shrieked, "A ghost!" After all, what would be your explanation? They had not experienced anything like this. There seemed no other possible rationalization. Things had just gotten a whole lot worse. It was like all your worst nightmares coupled together. But this was *Faith 301*. Don't expect it to be easy. As you will discover in any faith lesson, however, experiencing the worst can prove to be a window to the supernatural. Faith stretches you from the safety of your boat to the extraordinary. What looked like a ghost was really Jesus.

SITTING ON THE EDGE AND STEPPING OUT

Immediately, Peter stepped to the front of the class. Peter called to Jesus and said, *"Lord, if it's really you, tell me to come to you, walking on the water"* (Matthew 14:28). Jesus told Peter to step out of the boat and come. I can imagine Peter balancing himself on the side of the boat, white-knuckled, and gripping the edge. Should he? This would take a faith step. Jesus had never failed him before. Would He this time? There is a big difference between being in a storm while inside the refuge of the boat and being in a storm outside the shelter of the boat. Jesus was the difference-maker. Would it be the boat, or Jesus? Faith said, "Jesus." So Peter *"went over the side of the boat and walked on the water toward Jesus"* (Matthew 14:29). Peter had just passed the test with an A grade.

And what about the other 11 students still taking up space in the boat? Well, I'll let Jesus do the grading. But if you're not sitting on the edge, you're taking up too much space. Faith will take you to the edge. Faith will challenge your courage.

Returning to Hebrews 11, faith led Abraham to leave the familiar and to set out into the unknown. This faith step was the first of a number of graduated faith steps that God would lead Abraham through. That's why Abraham was called the father of faith. The final test of faith God introduced to him was a big one. *"Take your son, your only son—yes, Isaac, whom you love so much. ... Go and sacrifice him as a burnt offering on one of the mountains, which I will show you"* (Genesis 22:2). Human sacrifice was an accepted practice in Abraham's day. But God abhorred such rituals and had no intention that Isaac would be subjected to this pagan practice. This was a faith test. By this time in his life, Abraham had such a deep, profound faith in God that he was prepared to obey. Faith led Abraham to ascend the mount to sacrifice his only son, Isaac, believing that God was able to bring him back to life again (Hebrews 11:19). Faith led him to the edge of believing in something unprecedented to that point. Faith led him to the edge of raising the knife. And God called, "Halt!" God's response was like a graduation congratulations: *"Now I know that you truly fear God. You have not withheld from me even your son, your only son"* (Genesis 22:12).

Faith led Moses' parents to disobey the king's command and to hide their son, believing that God had given them this boy for a unique purpose. Faith led Moses to give up all the pleasures and privileges of Egypt and to head out into the unknown. Faith led the Israelites to the edge of the Red Sea to see a path open up for them to cross. Faith led Rahab to hide the Israelite spies at risk of her own life, to learn that God would save her life and to discover her greater purpose in God's larger design. Hebrews 11 is brimming with the stories of people who, by faith, sat on the edge and stepped out to encounter the unfamiliar, square off with the challenges, face the unknown, and accomplish the extraordinary for God. They are examples of how we are to run the race of faith.

Peter stepped off the edge of the boat to experience the extraordinary with Jesus. He launched off from the side of the boat to go on a *faith walk* with Christ. It wasn't all smooth walking; he even began to sink at one point. He got his eyes off of Jesus and onto the circumstances. The waves began to swallow him. But he quickly learned the critical importance of keeping his eyes focused on Jesus. A terrified Peter cried out, *"Save me, Lord!"* Jesus immediately reached out and grabbed him and asked another question: *"You have so little faith ... why did you doubt me?"* I don't denigrate Peter at this point. When Jesus reached out and took Peter's hand, I see a diploma of graduation in His hand. Peter wasn't perfect, but he was present, out there on the waves with Jesus. One graduate in a class of 12. Tough lesson. Tough test. Tough faith.

The waves of adversity are the circumstances in your life that threaten to drown you. But these same waves are the very stair-steps that can bring you closer to Jesus. The outcome is a matter of focus and faith. Christ uses every unique adversity to increase your faith step by step, grade by grade, degree by degree. A growing, enlarging faith will take you beyond your limits. It will enable you to trust beyond yourself. Faith will lead you from the safe to the supernatural. From the predictable and the secure to standing on the water where Jesus is. From white-knuckled survival in unfamiliar and uncomfortable circumstances to the peace and tranquility of knowing that God is present. He is your refuge and strength, always ready to help in times of trouble (Psalm 46:1, 10).

I recall one particular classroom of faith. It was a crib. I was a busy pastor running here and running there. Doing this and worrying about that. Evaluating yesterday and preparing and planning for tomorrow. It was Sunday night. Our beautiful daughter, Rebecca, was an infant. I was changing her diaper on the bathroom counter, when suddenly the pupils in her eyes rolled back and her body went limp. I panicked. I didn't know what to do. I grabbed her and tipped her upside down. I don't know if that was the right thing to do or not ... but it worked. She came to. She looked at me and smiled as though nothing had happened.

I gave a sigh of relief and called Diane to share what had just happened. Then, without warning, it happened again. Her eyes rolled back, her body went limp. I grabbed her and did the same thing as before. And, sure enough, she revived a second time. Well, as you can imagine, we wrapped her up quickly and rushed her to the hospital. She was under close monitoring in intensive care for a week.

When we finally were allowed to take her home, we were told by the doctor to watch her closely. To tell parents to *closely watch* their infant daughter is like prescribing no sleep for the indefinite future. We placed her in a crib right beside our bed. And listened. I lay with one ear on the pillow and one ear aimed at her crib like a satellite dish to receive any microwaves being transmitted from that direction. If there was a small noise, I jumped up. If there was no noise, I jumped up. We went sleepless for a week until we realized that this could not go on. I remember the night we placed her in her own room and gave her to God. When we placed her in her own crib, we placed her in His love and care. We told God we loved her and wanted her with us, but that she belonged to Him. We would trust beyond ourselves. And we went to sleep with the peace and tranquility of knowing that God was present. It never happened again. But it was one more step in my faith journey. One more faith lesson in the school of spiritual growth. Learning to hold on to what is precious with an open hand and trusting that everything is in His hands. Trusting when I can't see. Trusting beyond myself. Enjoying what is in my arms right now. Embracing the blessings in my hand. Without fear of loss.

In Psalm 46, the Psalmist reminds us that when faith rests in God who is our refuge and strength, this faith eliminates fear. *"We will not fear when earthquakes come and the mountains crumble into the sea"* (verse 2). Life can threaten with some pretty fearful circumstances. But when you exercise a quiet confidence in God, fear begins to erode and give way to joy. *"A river brings joy to the city of our God"* (verse 4). Many ancient cities had a river flowing through them. The river sustained life. But not so with the city of Jerusalem. No river. There was something better: God. When God is present and flowing in your life by faith, He is all you need.

TEN

RUNNING BEYOND THE LIMITS

THE DESERT IS A BEAUTIFUL PLACE, BUT IT IS ALSO A DANGEROUS PLACE. Many have been lured into its deadly, deceptive trap, like an insect crawling over the tiny hairs on the inner surface of an attractive pink and yellow Venus Flytrap. The leaf closes, trapping and digesting the unsuspecting creature. The magnificence of the wilderness gives a false sense of security. And yet the course God has called us to run winds its way through the desert. The desert is not a place of weakness or defeat; it is a place of strength and conquest. In the words of Shakespeare regarding the ambition of Julius Caesar to accomplish great things, even impossible things: "Bid me run, and I will strive with things impossible."[1] Running in the desert of life is where you strive with things impossible.

BADWATER

In the opening chapter, I told the story of Scott Jurek, winner of the Badwater Ultramarathon in 2005. There was another leading runner in that race. Ferg Hawke, a 48-year-old Canadian from New Westminster, British Columbia. His age dictated against a successful finish, but he was determined to turn the odds on their head. Ferg began running after a doctor's visit in which he was told that he was overweight, consuming too much beer and wings after slow-pitch, and needing medication for high blood pressure. So he started running. I have spoken with Ferg, and one quickly perceives in his voice and mannerisms a strong determination

RUN! THE AMAZING RACE

that is obviously transferred to the way he runs and to his approach to life. Kenyan running sensation Paul Tergat speaks of the three Ds of running. Dedication. Discipline. Determination. Ferg Hawke embraces all three.

Death Valley, California, is a desert of salt ringed by mountains that bottle up the summertime heat to temperatures exceeding 130 degrees Fahrenheit (the brain boils at 110 degrees F). The desert floor burns under the relentless sun to a temperature of 200 degrees, enough to melt the rubber on your running shoes in less than an hour. The feet blister as they pound the black pavement. The dry air sucks the sweat from your body so quickly that you can become dangerously dehydrated before your throat even feels thirsty. Every July, 90 runners push their bodies beyond the limits, following route 190. The highway of asphalt runs like a scorching black ribbon along the desert floor for 135 miles. They run along the white line that edges the roadside so as to prevent the soles of their shoes from burning down. The race leads the runners from Badwater Basin, 282 feet below sea level, the lowest point in North America, up 13,300 feet on Mount Whitney. The distance must be completed within the official cutoff time of 60 hours. Before the end of the race, each runner's foot strikes the pavement 300,000 times, subjecting the body to an overall impact of four million pounds. It is called the world's toughest footrace. The ultimate test of endurance.

Ferg ran in third position for the first seventeen miles. Mike Sweeney ran in first, like a rocket. Scott Jurek was running second. During the second leg of the race, at mile 42, fellow Canadian runner Ray Zahab made a pit stop and urinated what looked like coffee. He was experiencing severe pain in his muscles and kidneys and was forced to stop. It was the lowest point in his running career to that point. Jurek was also labouring, and fell into an ice chest to cool off. Ferg passed him into second place. In Leg 3 of the race, Jurek continued to flag, falling into an ice chest for the fourth time. Ferg continued running a strong second, following lead runner Mike Sweeney.

As darkness descended and temperatures cooled, Scott Jurek began to revive. At the 72-mile mark, Jurek passed Ferg into second place. Ferg kept pace with Jurek two minutes behind him. Then Ferg moved back into second position, vomiting as he passed the younger runner. Both runners made headway on Sweeney who was beginning to wane. Soon all three front-runners were minutes apart. Ferg passed Sweeney into the lead.

Leg 4 of the race is all uphill. It is during this leg that lots can go wrong. The normal systems that transmit critical data to the brain begin to malfunction. The body and brain become disconnected. One needs to drink lots of water to prevent dehydration. But there is a difficult balance to maintain. If you drink too much water and not enough sodium (salt), or vice versa, you can throw off your balance of electrolytes. Up to 25 percent of the runners suffer from hyponatremia. This is a condition where the water intake dilutes the sodium in the body fluids, causing confusion and sometimes hallucinations. Hypoxia is another threat. The blood is depleted of oxygen, causing shortness of breath. When these conditions impact the brain, as they are prone to do, they can cause confusion, seizures, even death.

Sweeney became a victim of Leg 4 and his doctors advised him to stop. He stepped out. At the completion of Leg 4 and the 90-mile mark, Ferg was running in first place with Jurek following close behind. Ferg was suffering badly, however, from severe blisters on his toes, soles, and heels. The blisters had to be lanced with a small sterile scalpel, which can make you wince with pain, and then the skin was stuck together and taped to prevent further deterioration. One method used to seal the skin was to insert the tip of a tube of Krazy Glue into the broken blister, glue it shut and then tape it. Duct tape will work. The throbbing pain was extreme. His face grimaced with every limping step. Scott Jurek, 31 years old, was running strong. Ferg was not running with any misconception. He knew that the young competitor just behind him was the best long-distance runner in the world. Ferg told himself that, while he was not Scott Jurek, maybe he could "out suffer" him. Whether he hobbled, shuffled, staggered, or crawled on his hands and knees across the finish line, he would endure. The battle of endurance is won or lost depending on what you do when the pain sets in.

It was a long night, but by morning light both runners were still going. Scott Jurek had taken the lead and was on a record pace. Dusty

Olson, Jurek's pacer, had been flown in to pace for him and encourage him. Ferg's son, Carter, ran at his side, pacing and encouraging his dad. Five miles separated the two runners as they moved closer to Mt. Whitney. Again, the course ran all uphill. Ferg wouldn't quit. This was not about winning; it was about enduring. Sheer fortitude. Finishing. Ferg says that you run the first half of the race with your legs and the last half with your heart. The odds were stacking up against him. Festering blisters. Missing toenails. Aching muscles. The body was breaking down, but the spirit grew stronger. Long after the body cried, "Stop," the spirit cried "Go!" Despite the odds against him, his spirit clutched the smallest bit of lingering hope.

Scott Jurek crossed the finish line, setting a new course record for Badwater of 24 hours, 36 minutes, 8 seconds. Ferg learned of Scott's achievement. He kept moving forward. His face showed the strain as he struggled with each step. But his eyes showed his true spirit of resolve to push his body beyond the limits of physical endurance. That look of determination that refused to surrender and quit. His pacer sprayed his head with water. As he got closer to the finish line, his daughter, Connie, ran out to meet her dad. Before long, his wife and children were running alongside him. What an inspiration! Ferg ran with renewed vigour. A huge smile filled his face. What an inspiration to all that day who watched Ferg and his family, in one long line, holding hands as they crossed the finish line together.

RUNNING THROUGH THE DESERT

Some things can only be learned in the desert experiences of your life. When God led His people out of Egypt and through the Red Sea, the path led right into the desert. And it wasn't the shortcut through. It was the long way. The reason? While He had gotten His people out of Egypt, He needed to get Egypt out of them. They needed to get the Egyptian gods out of their heads and hearts. They needed to learn to trust God against the odds stacked against them. They needed some character-building. God needed to change them from a group of slaves into the army of the living God. They needed to learn to obey Him so they could become a nation that showed Him to the world. They needed to understand that they had a divine purpose in the world. They needed to feel His deep love and care for them and learn to respond to His love like a bride to her husband. They needed to fall so passionately in love with Him that they were singly devoted to Him above everything else. God needed their course to follow through the desert for all these reasons. It wasn't just about the destination; it was about the journey.

Remember how the Lord your God led you through the wilderness for these forty years, humbling you and testing you to prove your character, and to find out whether or not you would obey his commands. Yes, he humbled you by letting you go hungry and then feeding you with manna, a food previously unknown to you and your ancestors. He did it to teach you that people do not live by bread alone; rather, we live by every word that comes from the mouth of the Lord (Deuteronomy 8:2–3).

Note that it says, "God *led* them through the wilderness." When the path you follow runs through the wilderness, you may think you have lost your way. Somewhere along the path, God went right and you went left. And now you are wandering in a wasteland. Your life is going nowhere. But you are not lost. God is leading you. Your path runs through the desert for a purpose. It's not just about the destination; it's about the journey.

Yes, the desert is a wasteland. But what that means to your life depends on how you look at it. The most valuable things in life are often hidden and uncovered in the most obscure, barren places. The desert represents the struggles, the pain, the dryness, and the perils in your life. The course of your race runs through these places. You realize in these places just how fragile and vulnerable you really are. But the desert is the place where you find a source of life greater than yourself. The place where it is necessary to trust beyond yourself. The place where bread falls out of the sky and water flows out of the rock. It is the place where you learn to run beyond the limits of human endurance. It is a place like none other where you discover God's power, provision, faithfulness, care, and presence. You thought you were alone? You have never once been on your own. Never do you feel the presence of the Shepherd more keenly than when you walk through the deep, dried-up wadi of the shadow of death. You become increasingly cognizant that every step you take is by His grace and strength.

In the desert you learn that without God you are finished, but with Him you can finish. So you cling to what little hope there is. You determine that, whether you hobble, shuffle, stagger, or crawl on your hands and knees, you will endure. The battle of endurance is won or lost when the pain sets in. You feel the pain. You choose to keep going. It is a defining moment.

THE PROOF IS IN THE PERSEVERING

There is an old proverb that says, "The proof is in the pudding," which, in the way it reads, is meaningless. The full proverb makes more sense. "The proof of the pudding is in the eating." The evidence of the true value or quality of something is demonstrated when you experience it. The proof of the quality of a pudding is revealed when you eat it. The proof of the quality of a vehicle is revealed when you take it for a test drive. Similarly, the proof of a genuine runner is demonstrated in the persevering. A true runner perseveres despite the conflicting odds.

This is not to say a runner cannot be injured and fall to the side of the path. Many runners become exhausted. Discouraged. Wounded. Some are judged or misjudged for their failure. But in the race of faith, the genuine runner will get up and get going again at some point. We are to endure like Jesus endured (Hebrews 12:1–2). *"God blesses those who patiently endure testing and temptation. Afterward they will receive the crown of life"* (James 1:12). We are encouraged to *"follow the example of those who are going to inherit God's promises because of their faith and endurance"* (Hebrews 6:12). These faithful and enduring runners are the ones whose names and stories are recorded in Hebrews 11. The writer of Hebrews introduced these faithful runners, whom we are to follow, with these words: *"We are not like those who turn away from God to their own destruction. We are the faithful ones, whose souls will be saved"* (Hebrews 10:39). True faith is an enduring faith.

Dietrich Bonhoeffer was one of the few church leaders who stood up against the evils of the Nazis in Germany during the 30s and 40s.

He endured imprisonment and severe interrogation, but throughout bitter persecution, maintained a noble disposition, a hopeful spirit and enduring faith. He often repeated to his fellow prisoners that "the only fight which is lost is that which we give up."[2]

It is noteworthy that, when Jesus addressed the seven churches in Revelation who were enduring great persecution, He made the same promise to all seven. He promised eternal life to those who overcame to the end. One could argue that the saved ones are the ones who endure. This does not mean it is up to you to endure in order to be saved. That would be works and not grace. But it means that if you truly belong to Christ, then the presence and power of the Holy Spirit within you strengthens, inspires, energizes, and guarantees that you will endure until the end. Romans chapters 6, 7 and 8 are worth reading to understand the power and impact of the Holy Spirit within you.

Ferg Hawke endured Badwater to the end. He is a true runner. The proof is in the persevering. And there were others who endured against great odds. Jeffrey Hilton Barber was the first blind man to complete Badwater. He is a true runner. Dan Jensen, a Vietnam vet, was the first athlete to cross the finish line wearing a prosthetic leg. He finished the distance in 55:44. He returned five years later at the age of 60 and finished Badwater in 36 hours. He is a true runner. Jack Dennis became the first 70-year-old to complete the race. He ran the distance in 57:52. Amazingly, he returned five years later and completed the same race in 59 hours, one hour before the cutoff time. He is a proven true runner. The proof is in the persevering. And the Scriptures declare the same to be true for authentic runners in the race of faith.

LIVING EXTRAVAGANTLY

I have noted something else in my interaction and communication with truly great distance runners. *The proof is in the pushing.* They push themselves beyond the limits of human endurance. Beyond what seems the limit of human possibility. Beyond the norm. It is not a self-inflicted demand. It is who they are. It is their passion. And running in the desert best brings this evidence to light, verifying one to be the *real deal.*

So it is in running the race of faith. The genuine runner embraces the challenge of *pushing beyond the limits*. It is not merely a self-inflicted demand or expectation. It is who we are. It is our passion. It is *living* beyond the limits. One could call it extravagant living. The word *extravagant* is derived from the Latin and means *to wander outside*. Extravagant living means to live outside the lines. Living beyond the normal. One is not satisfied with just surviving, but thriving. Stretching beyond the bare minimum of what is expected or acceptable to what we could call maximum living.

Caleb was one of the 12 spies that returned from scouting out the land of Canaan for Moses and the Israelites. Ten of the spies returned with an unfavourable, faithless report. They said, *"We are like grasshoppers in their sight."* But Caleb, along with Joshua, refused to adopt the *grasshopper complex*. Forty-five years later, after Israel had conquered the land, Caleb, who was now 85 years old, asked for the opportunity to attack and defeat the inhabitants of the hill country (Joshua 14). The inhabitants of the hill country lived in great, walled towns. The sons of Anak, a family of giants, lived in these walled towns. Yet 85-year-young Caleb had such faith in God that he wanted the challenge of leading the charge against this region. And he pulled it off! He lived beyond the limits. He lived extravagantly.

EXTRAVAGANT GIVING

In 1 Kings 17, Elijah the prophet, along with the whole nation of Israel, was in the midst of a devastating famine. Elijah saw a widow at the edge of a village and asked her for some bread. She replied that there was no bread in her humble home. In fact, she was about to use up the last handful of flour in the flour jar and the little cooking oil remaining in the bottom of the jug to cook the last meal for her son and herself. Then they would die. This was desert living. God told Elijah what to say to her. So Elijah presented her with a challenge. Bake him some bread first, and then use whatever was left to prepare a meal for her and her son. God promised her that He would provide just enough flour and olive oil in their respective containers until the famine was over. She took a faith step and obeyed. After that, until the end of the famine, every time she went to the flour jar, there was always a little more lying at the bottom. And there was always just enough oil for the next meal. That's maximum living. Even when you have little of this world's resources, you can live extravagantly. When you give by faith beyond the limits, you live by faith beyond the limits.

Another widow, in the New Testament, lived beyond the limits. Jesus was sitting near a collection box in the Temple one day, watching people drop their money into it. The boxes were trumpet-shaped receptacles that looked like inverted megaphones. There were 13 of them situated around the perimeter of the Temple. Many rich people were dropping in large amounts. You could hear the money tumbling down into the catch basin below. But it didn't impress Jesus. Then a poor widow quietly dropped in two small lepta. Lepta were the smallest and least of all the coins. Something like a penny. Her gift drew an immediate response from Jesus. *"This poor widow has given more than all the others"* (Mark 12:43). How could that be? How could two pennies be more than bags of money the rich were giving? Jesus gave the reason for His evaluation. *"For they gave a tiny part of their surplus, but she, poor as she is, has given everything she had to live on"* (Mark 12:44).

While they gave more quantity, they gave only a tiny portion of their surplus. There was a lot left over at home. On the other hand, the poor widow gave everything she had. God looks not at what you give to Him; He looks at what you have left over for yourself. He looks not at what you put in the collection box for God, but at what you put in the bank account for yourself. He measures not the amount of the gift, but the sacrifice of the giver. One is minimum giving; the other is maximum giving.

When the apostle Paul travelled through the first-century Roman world on his third journey, he had a clear purpose in mind. He was collecting a monetary offering from the Gentile churches to give to the impoverished Christians back in Jerusalem. The Macedonian believers were not wealthy folk, but their financial state was not reflected in the way they gave. Paul commended the Macedonian churches for their exceptional liberality. He said that though they were very poor, they excelled in rich generosity. *"They gave not only what they could afford, but far more"* (2 Corinthians 8:3). They were examples of maximum giving. It is noteworthy, however, that Paul writes, *"their first action was to give themselves to the Lord"* (8:5). They had first discovered the joy of maximum living. Generosity flows out of maximum living.

Extravagant giving has nothing to do with one's monetary wealth. The poor can give out of their poverty. The wealthy can give out of their riches. One day, a very wealthy woman named Mary walked up to Jesus and broke a 12-ounce jar of very expensive perfume over Jesus' head and feet. The house was filled with the fragrance. The perfume was valued at a year's wages. Yes, one year's wages. So extravagant was this act of devotion that it resulted in immediate criticism. But she did this in anticipation of Jesus' burial and to publicly declare her faith in Him as the Messiah, the King. The fragrance of such costly perfume would have lingered not only in the house, but into the garden of Gethsemane where Jesus was arrested, into Caiaphas' chambers where Jesus was illegally tried, into Pilate's judgment hall, along the narrow streets as Jesus carried His cross, in the nostrils of the soldiers as they bent over Him to nail His hands to the cross and into the tomb. The aroma of the King.

Extravagance is a response to the great gift of Jesus on the cross. Extravagant giving was God sending His Son from the riches of heaven to the poverty of this world, so that we could inherit the riches of heaven one day. It was stepping down from the throne of heaven and up to the cross of Calvary so that we could obtain eternal life. Jesus took our sin so we could have His life. *"Though he was rich, yet for your sakes he became poor, so that by his poverty he could make you rich"* (2 Corinthians 8:9). This is the story of grace, and grace exceeds all limits. Where sin abounded, grace super abounded. Maximum giving is rooted in the greatest super abounding gift of all time. Jesus.

MAXIMUM RECEIVING

Initially, one might deduce that giving creates a deficit. You give, you lose. But the Bible teaches quite the contrary. Paul continued to instruct the Gentile believers that maximum giving reaps a generous crop. In other words, God responds to generosity with generosity. *"A farmer who plants only a few seeds will get a small crop. But the one who plants generously will get a generous crop"* (2 Corinthians 9:6). The Bible pictures the giving of one's resources not as withdrawing from a bank account, but like a farmer planting seed. The more seed you spread around, the greater harvest you reap. *"And God will generously provide all you need. Then you will always have everything you need and plenty left over to share with others. … He will provide and increase your resources and then produce a great harvest of generosity in you"* (2 Corinthians 9:8, 10).

God takes note of giving beyond the limits. You will always have enough for yourself and to share with others. Generosity begets generosity. I think of the widow who provided for Elijah. She always had just enough for herself and her son … and enough left over to share with Elijah. Generosity is not a recipe for getting rich. There are much greater riches than money. But you will always have enough of whatever resources you need. And enough is plenty.

THE CHALLENGE TO GO BEYOND THE LIMITS

Let us not lose sight of the ultramarathoner running through the desert. Straining with every step. But in a peculiar way, every painful stride brings with it a sense of inspiration and exhilaration. Why? Because one is crossing beyond the normal. This is about more than persevering. This is about experiencing the atypical. Like an early explorer discovering new land on the horizon through his telescope. Like a mountain climber getting closer to the summit of Mt. Everest. Like an astronaut rocketing into space. Like a scientist on the verge of discovering a remedy for a debilitating disease. It's about going beyond the limits. And that's how Jesus taught that we should live. The lives of Jesus' followers should exceed the limits of what the world expects or considers good enough. We should be pushing beyond the limits of minimal acceptability or tolerability.

In what has become known as the Sermon on the Mount, Jesus taught principles for living as citizens in His Kingdom. Throughout the sermon, He drew the comparison between minimum and maximum living. *"You have heard … but I say."* They had heard that one should not murder. But He went beyond the act of murder to thoughts of anger. They understood that they should not commit adultery. But He went

147

beyond the act of adultery to thoughts of lust. He pushed beyond the visible deed to the invisible thought. *"Anyone who even looks at a woman with lust has already committed adultery with her in his heart"* (Matthew 5:28). You can't help the first look unless you're blind. But be careful with the second look. That's when the seed of lust germinates. You can't help a bird flying over your head, but you can prevent it from building a nest in your hair. So go beyond the deed to your thought life. Jesus taught us to move beyond guarding our actions to guarding our hearts.

Minimum living asks how little you can do to meet man's approval. Maximum living asks how much can you do to meet God's approval. Minimum living directs its attention to the outward requirement. Maximum living directs its attention to the inner condition of the heart knowing that true righteousness and virtue spring from the heart. Minimum living pays attention to the hundreds of rules calculated to keep you out of trouble. Maximum living is motivated by love. Christ's indescribable love for you and your passionate love for Him. Love grips your heart and drives your words and actions from the inside out. The heart is surrendered in love to God, and as a result, the attitudes and actions directed toward our fellow man exceed the limits of what is expected.

As I mentioned, running in the desert is the proof of a true distance runner because this is where the ultramarathoner pushes oneself beyond the limits. One runs outside the lines. One strains beyond the normal. Similarly, loving your enemies pushes you outside the lines. Beyond the limits. Enemies are people who have hurt or opposed you in some way. These are the ones who are not easy to love, which is an understatement. In fact, they are downright easy to hate. Jesus knew that. And so He used it in His sermon on the mountain as an illustration of going beyond the limits.

"You have heard the law that says, 'Love your neighbor' and hate your enemy. But I say, love your enemies" (Matthew 5:43–44). It was acceptable and reasonable to love your neighbour. But to love your enemy was an unreasonable stretch. It even qualified to be posted on the *RidicuList*. But Jesus always pushed His followers beyond the limits. We would agree that it is right and reasonable to cut your grass so as to keep the

weeds down. But Jesus would add that you should cut your neighbour's grass also, so as to keep his weeds down. If your sister asks to borrow a particular piece of clothing from you, it is reasonable and kind to lend the article of clothing to her. But Jesus would add that you should open your wardrobe to her and ask if there is anything else she would like to wear.

The law demanded that when someone harmed you, the punishment should equal the crime. An eye for an eye and a tooth for a tooth. But Jesus added that you should *"not resist an evil person"* (Matthew 5:39). Jesus was not speaking about the issue of self-defense or the application of justice. That would be taking His words out of context. He was speaking about personal retaliation. He was teaching about returning good for evil. That's what God does. To return evil for good is devilish. To return good for good is human. But to return good for evil is godly. That's extravagant living. Living outside the lines.

Jesus continued, *"If someone slaps you on the right cheek, offer the other cheek also"* (Matthew 5:39). Jesus exemplified this in His own life at His trial. *"If you are sued in court and your shirt is taken from you, give your coat, too"* (Matthew 5:40). The shirt was an undergarment. The coat was an outer garment and needed for warmth. One could take your shirt but was forbidden to take your coat. But Jesus added that if you lose your shirt to an enemy, offer to give them your coat as well. Excessive? Yes, but Christ-like.

"If a soldier demands that you carry his gear for a mile, carry it two miles" (Matthew 5:41). If a Roman soldier demanded that you carry his gear for him, by law you must carry it for one mile. Your legal requirement went no further. But Jesus added that one should offer to carry his gear for an extra mile. Can you imagine turning to the soldier at the one-mile mark and asking if you could go another mile for him? That's where your testimony begins. The first mile is obligatory. The second mile is grace. And grace lives outside the lines. During the second mile, the soldier is wondering, what makes you tick? Why are you different? During the second mile, you can share about the difference Jesus makes in one's life. That's when you can share about God's love for everyone. The principle of the second mile can be applied to so many areas of your life.

"Give to those who ask, and don't turn away from those who want to borrow" (Matthew 5:42). The context is still about how to treat one whom you consider an enemy. Someone has treated you unfairly, even maliciously. And now, they have a need and they are on your doorstep asking for help. What should you do? Jesus taught that all of your possessions, your house, money, vehicle, clothes, food, and everything you own are resources for generosity. If you have the resources to bless an adversary, do it. If you have an opportunity to show compassion, show it. Rather than retaliate, bless. But you may ask, isn't there a risk? Aren't I vulnerable to being taken advantage of? The answer, of course, is yes. But let me come back to that in a moment.

We noted earlier in the chapter that generosity begets generosity. That is a biblical principle. Jesus said that God responds proportionately to the degree of your giving. Giving is not a recipe for disaster; it is a path to blessing. A key to maximum living. *"Give and you will receive. Your gift will return to you in full—pressed down, shaken together to make room for more, running over, and poured into your lap. The amount you give will determine the amount you get back"* (Luke 6:38). The picture is that of a marketplace. A homemaker goes down to the souk to buy some flour for bread making. The merchant presses the flour into a measuring bin. He then shakes it down so that there is room for more and fills the container until it is spilling over with flour. When the container can hold no more, the customer pulls her outer garment up to act as a basket and the merchant pours the flour into the buyer's "lap." The lesson? You cannot out-give God.

Jesus reduced the whole law to one thing. Love. Love God. And love your neighbour as yourself. Someone asked, "And who is my neighbour?" Jesus answered with a story. A Jewish man was walking along the road from Jerusalem down to Jericho. Somewhere along the way, he was attacked by robbers and badly beaten. Two Jewish brothers, religious men, saw him lying by the side of the road and passed by on the other side. Then along came a Samaritan man. Why would Jesus use a Samaritan in the story? Well, that was the point of His story. Jews and Samaritans were enemies. Despite the disregard, even animosity, the Jewish victim would have shown to the Samaritan, if the situation had been reversed, the Samaritan crossed the road, bent down, and cared for the injured man. He bandaged the man, lifted him up onto his donkey and transported him to an inn where he provided money for his care until he had recovered. So, who is my neighbour? Your neighbour is anyone, even an enemy … especially an enemy … whom God brings across your path who needs your help and compassion. You can read the whole story in Luke 10.

"In that way, you will be acting as true children of your Father in heaven" (Matthew 5:45). *"If you are kind only to your friends, how are you different than anyone else? Even pagans do that. But you are to be perfect, even as your Father in heaven is perfect"* (Matthew 5:47–48). Meaning, at no point are you more like your Father in heaven than when you love an enemy … especially an enemy. That is exactly how He loves us. God's love goes beyond the limits. And when you love like He loves, you are living outside the lines. Extravagantly.

I like the way Paul teaches the same truth:

Never pay back evil with more evil … never take revenge. Leave that to the righteous anger of God. … Instead, "If your enemies are hungry, feed them. If they are thirsty, give them something to drink. In doing this, you will heap burning coals of shame on their heads." Don't let evil conquer you, but conquer evil by doing good (Romans 12:17–21).

The words, "of shame," are not in the original Greek. And I think the addition of these words by the translators throws off the intended meaning of the passage. We do not overcome evil with shame, but by doing good. In Paul's day, warmth was provided and bread was baked in an oven that held burning coals in its belly. One morning, your neighbour wakes to discover that his coals have died out during the night. What is he going to do? As neighbours, things have been less than amicable. In fact, your neighbour is listed on your inventory of enemies. You want him to get what's coming to him. You would secretly celebrate his calamity. And now your neighbour needs your help to get his fire going again. He sheepishly knocks on your door and asks for assistance. You know that if the shoe were on the other foot, he would slam the door in your face.

151

You have three choices. You can slam the door on him. Or, you can give him a coal ... one lone coal ... and watch him spend the rest of the day trying to ignite his dead coals with the one live coal that you grudgingly gave him. Or ... you can give him as many live coals as he needs and more. People carried buckets on their heads. Heap burning coals into his bucket so that when he returns with his bucket on his head he has more than he needs to get his fire going. Let love and generosity take you outside the lines. Live beyond the limits. That is how to overcome evil. That is godliness.

EXTRAVAGANT FORGIVING

One day, Peter asked Jesus how many times he should forgive someone who had offended or injured him? Seven times? Why did Peter throw out the number *seven*? Maybe because it is the number that represents completeness. Whatever the reason, Peter considered it a good number. Certainly a safe number. I'm sure that in Peter's mind, he was being generous. But Jesus used the question as an opportunity to stretch Peter from minimum to maximum thinking. Jesus replied, *"Not seven times ... but seventy times seven"* (Matthew 18:22). Jesus was alluding to something mentioned only one other place in scripture.

In Genesis 4, a braggart named Lamech was boasting to his wives about how he had defended himself against a younger man and killed him. *"If someone who kills Cain is punished seven times, then the one who kills me will be punished seventy-seven times!"* (Genesis 4:24). The number can also read *seventy times seven*. It was a boast of excessive revenge upon anyone who tried to harm him. Jesus picked up on this story and drew a sharp contrast.

> His followers should be as eager to forgive as Lamech was to take vengeance. Just as Lamech was vowing a punishment that far exceeded the crime, we should let our forgiveness far exceed the wrong done to us. We should be Lamech's polar opposite.[3]

And Jesus' exact likeness. We are to give and to forgive beyond the limits. We are to live outside the lines. Extravagantly.

RUNNING THE RISK

There is always risk when you go beyond the limits. Any runner who sets off across Death Valley, running Badwater, knows the reality of running the risk. The risk of injury. Wrecked knees. Pulled hamstrings. Acute tendonitis. The unpredictability of a hostile environment. A relentless sun beating down upon the head with temperatures excessive enough to cook your brains. Dehydration. Hyponatremia. Hypoxia. Confusion. Growing despair. Sleep deprivation. Seizures. And even death. But if one does not assess the risks, prepare to meet them and set out to confront whatever the journey brings, one will never know what depth of courage and strength lies within the human spirit. One will never experience the thrill of the run or the elation of triumph.

Life is full of risks. Many people fear risk. In fact, some are paralyzed by the fear of risk. And they will never reach their full potential if they do not step outside the wall of security, or should I say wall of insecurity, that fear has built around them. If you were to ask an unborn child if he or she wanted to leave the warmth and security of the mother's womb, they would probably say, no thanks. Outside the womb you run the risk of new challenges, uncertainties, failures, trials, sorrows, life. But, on the other hand, inside the womb you would never live life to its full as God intended. You would never thrive at your full potential.

I have had couples say to me that they do not want to beget children because of the kind of world they would be bringing their children into. There is the risk of subjecting a child to evil, moral decadence, harm, and suffering. There is the risk of losing a child to disease. The risk of personal pain. Yes, there are risks. But if one does not run the risks, then who will carry the truth and witness of Christ to the next generation? Who will be the world-changers of tomorrow? Who will be the light of Christ in a dark world? The potential for good and for God far outweighs the risks.

Marriage is a risk. You bring together two worlds, two cultures, two personalities, two histories, two family backgrounds, two genealogies, two viewpoints, two brains, two genders, and two of almost everything into one inseparable relationship. You make a commitment to one person for the rest of your life with very little idea of what you are doing and no idea of what lies ahead in life. You don't know what lies around even the next bend in the journey. But the joy and fulfillment of marriage far overshadow the risks. The synergy of two exceeds the risk. *"Two people are better off than one, for they can help each other succeed. … A person standing alone can be attacked and defeated, but two can stand back-to-back and conquer"* (Ecclesiastes 4:9–12).

I see a strong parallel between life and the spirit of the early frontier people and pioneers who moved west to open up new lands for settlement. While I abhor the greed of the white man and am repulsed by the political treachery that accompanied westward expansion, I appreciate the spirit of taking the risk and pushing beyond the limits, expanding the margins of one's life. In life you don't know exactly what is going to happen or where it will lead you. There are numerous dangers, tests, trials, and demands along the way. Stephen Covey writes:

> It takes an enormous amount of internal security to begin with the spirit of adventure, the spirit of discovery, the spirit of creativity. Without doubt, you have to leave the comfort zone of base camp and confront an entirely new and unknown wilderness. You become a trailblazer, a pathfinder. You open new possibilities, new territories, new continents, so that others can follow.[4]

Accepting and responding to new possibilities and challenges, along with the risks that accompany them, is critical to thriving in life.

When I speak of risk, I am not referring to foolish risk-takers who will bet the whole farm. I am not talking about a "jumping off the cliff" nor a "sleeping on the white line in the middle of the road" kind of risk. But neither should we be risk-averse. We should be prepared to calculate the risk. It is this kind of risk calculation that keeps you on the edge of the boat considering something like going beyond the limits and walking on water to Jesus in obedience to His call. It keeps you on the edge of growth. It is the means of enlarging your self-imposed boundaries to the threshold of where God calls you. It multiplies the blessing. It increases your faith and expands your productivity.

Almost all the stories in the Bible are stories of risk and faith. Check out the Hall of Faith in Hebrews 11. And there are many others. There was a young Moabite woman who fell in love with and married the son of a wealthy Israelite rancher. The Israelite rancher had immigrated to Moab with his wife and two sons and settled there quite comfortably. Then the unexpected happened. The father suddenly died. The burden of the business fell upon the two sons, who managed it for about 10 years. Then, one heartbreaking day, tragedy struck the family again. The young woman's husband and his brother died without warning. Maybe they were killed in an accident out in the field. We're not told. But needless to say, the woman and her mother-in-law lost the family business. To make matters worse, neither woman had any means of support. No social programs. No life insurance. Whatever could go wrong had gone wrong, and it couldn't get worse. That was when her mother-in-law decided to move back to her homeland in Israel, and the young woman was faced with a huge dilemma. Should she go with her mother-in-law? Or stay back?

Everything she was familiar with was in Moab. Family. Friends. Cuisine. Culture. She had never travelled more than 20 miles from her hometown. To add to the problem, she had no particular skills to mention with which to pick up a job in a new country. In fact, in a male-dominated society, she was the wrong gender to step out too far into the unfamiliar. And, of no minor significance, Moabites were despised by Israelites. But she had become very attached to her mother-in-law. In fact, her mother-in-law had led her to become a believer in the God of Israel. And she had a persistent feeling inside that God had something special in mind for her life. So she made the decision. She would take the risk. She would act in faith upon what she believed God was saying to her. She would leave her familiar surroundings and go.

The woman's name was Ruth. There is a book in the Bible named after her. It never entered her wildest imagination what God had in mind. On her part, a willingness to take a calculated risk, to pull up stakes and move with her grieving mother-in-law to a foreign country. A readiness to take a faith step. A choice to surrender her future to the living God. On God's part, Ruth would meet and marry Bethlehem's

155

RUN! THE AMAZING RACE

most eligible bachelor, Boaz. She would become the great-grandmother of Israel's greatest ruler, King David. One millennium later, the long-awaited Messiah would trace His earthly lineage back through her. When you understand Ruth's story and the stories of so many others, you begin to understand that thriving spiritually embraces putting faith into action and taking the risks, allowing God to prove Himself faithful.

Jesus' body was hanging lifeless on the cross. The practice was to take the bodies of crucified victims down from each cross, throw them into the back of a wagon, and dump them in a waste disposal site just outside the city walls. A man named Joseph intervened and requested permission from Pilate to retrieve Jesus' body and bury it in his own personal tomb. It is significant to note who Joseph was. He was a member of the Sanhedrin. The Sanhedrin was like the Jewish Supreme Court. Seventy elder statesmen who were extremely powerful and influential. The Gospel of Mark records, *"Joseph of Arimathea took a risk and went to Pilate and asked for Jesus' body"* (Mark 15:43). He stepped out of the shadows and made a public demonstration of his faith and loyalty. The Sanhedrin was responsible for condemning Jesus to death. And now one of their own members (actually two members, as Nicodemus also came forward) broke rank with the prestigious rulers and joined the small band of persecuted Christ-followers. They removed Jesus' body from the cross, and, according to Jewish burial custom, wrapped the body with about 75 pounds of perfumed ointment and spices in long layers of linen cloth. They laid His body in the tomb and sealed it, rolling a large stone across its mouth. Both men stepped forward and stood out from the rest. Both men risked their reputations. They risked ostracism, even reprisal from the Sanhedrin. They risked their safety and wellbeing. They may have risked financial ruin. But that day at Golgotha, Joseph and Nicodemus put faith into action despite the risk. And their actions supplied strong evidence for Jesus' resurrection three days later.

Jesus said that, to follow Him, you may risk the loss of everything. Possible rejection from friends. Potential ostracism from your family. It may cost you your inheritance. You may even risk your life. He advised you to calculate the cost (Luke 14:25–33).

Going beyond the limits accepts risk. Loving your enemy embraces risk. When the Good Samaritan crossed the road to help out the wounded Jew, there was the risk of being assaulted, beaten and robbed himself. And, for who? Someone who probably wouldn't have done the same for him. Is there the risk of being taken advantage of when you give to a needy person? Isn't there even a greater risk giving to the needs of someone who has treated you maliciously? Certainly. Is there risk in going the extra mile? Is there risk in turning the other cheek? Is there risk in forgiving? Is there risk in showering compassion on the ungrateful? Certainly.

Risk jumps into the front seat of the moving van when you move from one part of the country to another. It sits in your backpack when you enter high school or march off to college. It settles in your mind when you accept a new job. Risk may mean giving up your second car to a single mom who needs a vehicle to keep her job. Opening your home to a family that needs a temporary shelter. Risk may mean being treated like a narrow-minded bigot because you speak up against pornography or abortion. Alienation because you share your faith at work. There is risk in moving to the inner city to provide a Christian presence there. Giving your blessing to your teenager to follow God's call to serve Him in a country known for terrorism or disease. Giving up your well-paying job to cross the threshold through another door that God has opened and called you to enter.

Running the risk always holds the chance of failure. Running the risk always holds the possibility of adversity. But when you fail, you won't fail alone. When you endure adversity, you won't endure it alone. He is with you. It's the godly, Christ-like way to live. Without risk, you won't budge from where you are. Life will become stale. Unproductive. You will pass up the chance to run beyond the limits.

ELEVEN

ONE STEP AT A TIME

THE MESSAGE OF THE BOOK OF HEBREWS IS ABOUT FIXING YOUR FOCUS on Jesus and patiently enduring. *"Let us run with endurance"* (Hebrews 12:1). This is not passive, patient endurance; it is active. William Barkley writes that this kind of endurance is not:

> [that which] sits down and accepts things but the patience which masters them. It is not some romantic thing which lends us wings to fly over the difficulties and the hard places. It is a determination, unhurrying and yet undelaying, which goes steadily on and refuses to be deflected. Obstacles do not daunt it and discouragements do not take its hope away. It is the steadfast endurance which carries on until in the end it gets there.[1]

Sometimes the struggle of the race gets down to just putting one foot in front of the other.

Gordy Ainsleigh was the pioneer of the 100-mile (160 km) trail ultramarathon. The Western States 100-Mile Endurance Run in California is a form of extreme long-distance trail running, but began originally as a horse race called the Western States Trail Ride. Competitors raced on horseback through the mountains, attempting to complete the 100-mile distance within 24 hours. But that all changed on August 3rd, 1974. Gordy Ainsleigh, a chiropractor, had trained hard with his horse all year in preparation for the 100-mile challenge. Just prior to the race, however, his horse went lame.

Gordy was crushed but not undaunted. He wrote:

> There are defining moments in every person's life when he or she must decide either to be sensible and do the reasonable thing or to embark on a perilous journey through a fog of uncertainties and attractive unknowns that cannot possibly be estimated for their risk potential. Faced with such a choice, we make our best guess and then either turn back or press forward.[2]

He made his choice. He announced that he would compete in the race without his horse. The decision certainly raised eyebrows. Was this courage or lunacy? On the morning of the race, bare-chested Gordy stood at the starting line with dozens of horses. Amused bystanders made comments like whether he was suicidal or just "horsin' around." One friend jokingly asked whether he wanted a ham sandwich or a feedbag. Another onlooker contested Gordy's qualifications for running. He questioned an official as to whether or not this particular race was reserved exclusively for animals. The official replied, "Yes, exclusively for animals … so Gordy qualifies!" No one seriously thought he would go very far. When the starting gun fired, off he ran on two legs amidst the dust and dirt shooting up from the hoofs of his four-legged fellow contestants.

He began running with vigour. Through the canyons, across ridges, over rivers, jumping ditches and dodging rocks. It felt good to be running, and especially energizing to be running as the *underdog*, or whatever you would call him in such a race as this one. Underhorse? But soon the intense heat began to exact its toll. He became tired and dehydrated. As he ran through the trailside town of Cool, the temperature hit 108 degrees Fahrenheit. It felt like his body was baking and his brains were boiling. His eyes couldn't focus. Every step seemed like it would be his last. As he neared the 43-mile point of Last Chance, he questioned whether, at his rate of deterioration, he could realistically make it to the finish before the 24 hours elapsed. The answer appeared obvious. No! Never! Could he make it to Michigan Bluff at the 55-mile point? No!

So then, could he make it to Devil's Thumb at mile 48? Even though Devil's Thumb was only several miles ahead, it was perched high on a ridge between two canyons. The answer was painfully apparent. No! Not possible! He seemed done. So, should he quit? His mind screamed, "No!" Then what should he do? He couldn't go on and he couldn't quit. That was when he heard a little voice of desperation deep inside his soul. Could he still put one foot in front of the other? For once the answer returned … "Yes!"

Gordy wrote:

> This was the defining moment, with everything that had gone before building toward it, and everything afterward forever changed by it. And, as such things so often are, it was so simple. The decision formed in my mind, and I made a commitment to it: I would keep putting one foot in front of the other until I could no longer put one foot in front of the other. It didn't take a genius. All it took was complete and total commitment.[3]

And that's how he ran the last 58 miles … one step at a time. At 23 hours, 42 minutes—eighteen minutes before the clock ticked down, Gordy's head popped over the hill. He was somewhat incoherent and barely shuffling, but he was on both legs. He even beat some of the horses.

Sometimes the path is an endless winding trail of corners and hills. At other times, the road seems to stretch out into eternity as straight as an arrow. Sometimes you have to run through hell to reach heaven. Difficulties and distance, however, do not crush a true runner; they make them. It is overwhelming sometimes to think about how far you have to go. The road to recovery can be a long one. The goal can seem a long way off. The difficulties fall like a torrential downpour. There seems no end to the demands. You can't plan every step. But you can take the next step. And then the next. Persevere one step at a time and you'll go the distance.

Baby steps. Set your goal as that next bush. Or, the log lying across the trail 10 metres ahead, not the rest station 10 kilometres in the distance. That street sign 50 feet ahead, not the finish line 50 miles away.

Just get to the street sign. Just do the next thing on the list. Take on that one next challenge. Deal with the struggle in front of you today. Centre your attention on the distance you need to go in the next hour, not the distance you need to run over the next week or month. Break things down into smaller units and pace yourself to that point. You will learn that the next step is not a race-stopper. Take baby steps and focus on closer, attainable goals. Your pace will begin to quicken. You'll feel the endorphins kicking in. Baby steps.

Nudder Hill

History is filled with stories and evidence that supports the "one step at a time" principle. The greatest achievements have been accomplished one failure and one breakthrough at a time. Wars have been won one battle at a time. New lands were discovered one voyage at a time. Archaeologists unearth entire ancient cities one spade of dirt at a time. The longest, most difficult marches were completed one step at a time.

Canadian history is overflowing with amazing stories that grew out of the incredible challenges of a young nation pushing westward against every possible obstacle. Geographical barriers. Physical and topographical barriers. Climatic barriers. Social, racial, political, and cultural barriers. And the sheer expanse of the country. French, English, Métis, and Native Peoples caught in a tangled web of self-interest, deceit, hostility, survival, and conflicting visions, while endeavouring to carve out a nation that would accommodate everyone in as peaceable a way as possible while satisfying no one.

By the late 19th century, the inhumane and sometimes brutal treatment of western native people by white traders was a problem getting the attention of the politicians back in the east. The end of the American Civil War had unleashed huge numbers of adventurers, whiskey-trading scoundrels, fur traders, murderers, wolfers, gold-diggers, and unprincipled, unscrupulous characters onto the western plains. Drunkenness, debauchery, and violence were on the rise. The newly formed Canadian government feared growing lawlessness, inevitable atrocities, and an all-out Indian war, so it decided to send a police force to maintain British law. To *maintien le droit*.

Young men from all over southern Ontario applied to go west for the adventure and intrigue. Soon a ragtag group of 250 to 300 ill-trained, poorly-equipped men was assembled and dispatched to Fort Dufferin in Manitoba. The new force was named the North-West Mounted Police. This period of history brought names like James Macleod, James Walsh, Sam Steele, Jerry Potts, Louis Riel, Gabriel Dumont, Crowfoot, Sitting Bull, Big Bear and many other significant players to the same table.

The Great March West began from Fort Dufferin, Manitoba, on July 8, 1874. There were 395 constables, officers, and scouts. Each policeman wore a scarlet tunic, grey riding britches, shiny black boots, white buckskin gloves, and a white cork helmet. The whole troop was divided into six divisions, each division riding horses the same colour, distinct from the other five. Following the six divisions came a long string of ox carts, cattle, agricultural equipment, wagons, field guns, and mortar cannons that stretched out for a distance of eight miles. It was called an "astonishing" scene. But it would all go downhill from here.

Not too far out onto the plains, the miseries mounted to what could be called extraordinary. Heat stroke. Dust inhalation. Blisters. Lice. Cold rain and wind that chilled the men to the bone. Water holes were scarce or dried up. Many water sources were despoiled by buffalo feces and urine and the water was putrid. The men were so thirsty, however, that they boiled the awful-smelling water and made tea to drink. They often regurgitated it as quickly as they swallowed it. Dr. RB Nevitt wrote in a letter:

> I have been examining the water that we were forced to drink—with a microscope & there are animals in it that look like large fleas—nice it is not—Some of them are not animal culae, but are visible individually to the naked eye. However when boiled and tea made with them you can't distinguish the animals from tea leaves so it don't matter.[4]

The result was typhoid and dysentery. And long line ups at the medical tent.

Storms created mud so deep that the wagons sank to their axles. Grasshoppers were so thick at times that they blotted out the sun. Prairie fires had depleted the plains of forage for the cattle and horses. Horses were dying every day. Supply wagons fell so far behind at the rear of the train that the men had nothing to eat at supper time. Constable James Finlayson wrote in his diary: "Camped on the open plain near a swamp. No water, no wood, no supper. The supply wagons did not get in till after midnight, therefore no provisions."[5]

But they did it! The treacherous, epic journey westward took them 1,300 kilometres across prairie grass, flatland, wooded coulees, and rolling hills. Without the help of bridges, roads, or supply stations. They did it. Mile after mile. Coulee after coulee. Hill after hill. Step by step.

They hired the help of guide Jerry Potts, a bow-legged, hard-drinking son of a Scottish clerk and a woman of the Peigan tribe. Potts spoke French, Cree, Sioux, Blackfoot, and very little English. He never spoke in a full sentence, but his scouting skills and knowledge of the territory were unrivalled by anyone. He was indispensable to the Mounted Police. When he was on the hunt for someone and had their scent in his nostrils, he kept his nose to the trail and kept moving, undaunted, step by step by step until he had hunted his prey down. One day, an officer rode up to Potts on the trail and asked impatiently what he thought they'd find over the next hill. Potts answered, "Nudder hill." He taught them to just focus on the hill in front of them. And then the next hill after that.

Whether it is the Great March West or the amazing race of life, the extraordinary begins with a step. One step at a time. One obstacle at a time. One challenge at a time. One hill at a time.

ONE RAIL AT A TIME

Another fascinating story from Canadian history is the construction of the transcontinental railway. It began from both ends of the country. About 22,000 men, many of them brought from China, began from the west coast, dynamiting their way east through the mountains. They constructed 600 bridges and trestles over rivers and gorges. They dynamited 27 tunnels through the rock. They endured snowstorms, avalanches, raging rivers, and dynamite blasts. Some days, they progressed only six feet. On average, two lives were lost for every mile gained. But

163

they advanced bridge by bridge, tunnel by tunnel, mile by mile, foot by foot, step by step and rail by rail.

In the east, more than 7,000 workers laid the track westward from Lake Superior. They blasted their way through the swamps and muskeg of northwest Ontario out on to the plains. To prevent the railway from being buried in the winter snowdrifts, the tracks were laid on embankments four feet high and edged on either side by ditches twenty feet deep. The work of laying the tracks pushed the men seven days a week, often leaving them restless, agitated, and exhausted. The dangers were many and the benefits few. Food was rotten, meat was rancid, blizzards were harsh, clothing was insufficient, and pay was irregular. Alcohol was the easy escape, and drunkenness often led to brawling, violence, and debauchery in the camps and shantytowns.

In March 1885, the unrest escalated and unpaid workers threatened a mass strike. A mob gathered as troublemakers incited strikers to violence. Inspector Sam Steele of the NWMP was in bed sick with a fever and barely able to lift his head. But when the report came to him about what was transpiring, he dragged himself out of bed and hurried with several other officers to a bridge where the mob was heading. Steele and his men stood on the bridge and, with rifles raised, read out the *Riot Act.* Steele wrote in his journal, "Seizing the Winchester rifle from the constable on guard at the gaol [jail], I ran to the bridge, and as the crowd was on the point of making a rush onto it, I covered them with the rifle and called upon them to halt or I would fire."[6] There was something in his weakened voice that communicated his intent and determination to back up his words with action if they did not concede. The mob backed away. Steele wrote, "By the next day, the area was as quiet as a country village on a Sunday morning at dawn."[7]

The challenges were staggering. But the immense project pressed forward mile after mile until both sides came together high in the mountains of British Columbia on November 7, 1885. East and west met and a nation was symbolically brought together by a string of steel. A small group stood by when the final spike was driven into the last of a million ties laid across an expansive country. An eerie silence fell upon the onlookers when the sound of the sledgehammer stopped. Once again, history had given evidence that monumental feats begin with a single step. And then another. Endurance is a choice, a complete and total commitment to put one foot in front of the other, to lay one rail after another… until you arrive. A profound life lesson.

GRACE FOR THE NEXT STEP

Paul wrote, *"I run with purpose in every step"* (1 Corinthians 9:26). He recognized that the race is run and won one step at a time. The distance is covered step by step. God gives the grace to sustain you through the next step. The next step may be laughter after the loss. Favour after the failure. Peace after the pain. Joy after the injury. Or another unwelcomed struggle and the strength to endure it. I love the encouragement Paul gives out of his own experience of weakness. God reminded him, *"My grace is all you need. My power works best in weakness"* (2 Corinthians 12:9). When Paul considered the power and grace of God working in and through his own personal weakness and inadequacy, he rejoiced, because *"when I am weak, then I am strong"* (2 Corinthians 12:10). I believe God provides His sustaining grace for the next step, not the whole race. He meets you at the point of your weakness and takes you to the next step.

One of my favourite songs is *Never Once* by Matt Redman. In that song, Redman reflects upon his life from a mountaintop. He speaks for all of us who walk with Jesus. He gazes back at how far we have come through the adversities and challenges of life. Without doubt, it hasn't been easy. But there is a reality that has proven true, that for every step we took, Christ was there with us. We have never once walked alone. Not once. Even when life was a battleground and we struggled with things that wounded, hurt, disappointed, and defeated us, we were ultimately victorious, not because of our strength, but because of His power in us. When we were weak, He was strong. The angel of the Lord fought alongside us. The line that catches my attention is, "Step by step we are breathing in His grace."[8] Every step you take, though exhausted, and gasping more than breathing, the air you breathe in is *His* grace. A grace that empowers and sustains you for the next step.

Jesus taught us to pray, *"Give us today the food we need"* (Matthew 6:11). Many first-century labourers lived a precarious day-to-day existence. They depended on their wages at the end of each day's work so that they could go and purchase the bread and food needed to provide for the family. It's not difficult to imagine what that would mean for a family if the "breadwinner" became sick for several days or weeks. The family would not eat. People lived one day at a time. The prayer, *"Give us today the food we need,"* is a recognition that we rely on God's grace and provision for this day. This hour. This minute. This step.

God taught this lesson to the Israelites in an awesome way. As they travelled through the barren desert, He miraculously provided the daily bread they needed. Every morning, a white flaky substance like frost blanketed the ground. They named it *manna*. The people went out and gathered as much manna as they needed for that specific day. God had instructed that they gather just enough for one day. It became the staple ingredient in their diet. They took it home and used it in every meal. They soon had more manna recipes than we have pasta dishes. The honey-tasting pancakes were particularly delicious. Some Israelites gathered huge quantities of manna to supply for the needs of a large family while others gathered just a little in their baskets. Everyone collected up just enough. *"Those who gathered a lot had nothing left over, and those who gathered only a little had enough. Each family had just what it needed"* (Exodus 16:18).

God was teaching His people that while they trekked through the wilderness He would provide for them. Morning by morning. Day by day. Those who took more than what they needed for one day woke up the next morning to find the manna crawling with maggots and a terrible odour wafting through the tent. That's like grace. There's enough for your needs today, not for tomorrow. There's enough for the next step, not for the entire race. His grace is sufficient for one step at a time. And when His grace is all that you've got, it is enough. It's all you need.

THE STEP-BY-STEP REMEDY TO WORRY

Worry is looking at tomorrow's problems with today's grace. Jesus said, *"So don't worry about tomorrow, for tomorrow will bring its own worries. Today's trouble is enough for today"* (Matthew 6:34). Jesus isn't saying we shouldn't plan for tomorrow, or prepare schedules or set goals for tomorrow. It is healthy to have a plan of action. But worry immobilizes. There is no action. Only a lot of thinking, imagining, and allowing fear to drive one's thoughts in any conceivable direction. There's little you can do about tomorrow's problems. But just think about all the emotional energy that is sapped just thinking about them. Worry is looking too far down the path. It is thinking about the hill you have to climb before you have arrived there. Worry is wondering what is over the next hill or around the next bend. Jesus said to just take the next step. Today's trouble is enough for today. And God's grace and provision is enough for whatever you encounter today. Tomorrow will bring tomorrow's problems. And you will discover, as you did today, that tomorrow's divine grace and provision will be enough for tomorrow's problems. It will be all you need.

Perhaps you have heard about the clock that had an emotional breakdown. At first everything was going great. It was keeping good time and all its little wheels were turning as they should. But then the clock began to think about the number of ticks that it had to tick before it ticked away with old age. Two ticks a second would add up to 120 ticks per minute. That would add up to 7,200 ticks per hour, 172,800 per day, 1,209,600 per week, and 62,899,200 ticks for the whole year. And this would be for how many years? Just thinking about it brought the clock to the point of emotional exhaustion, and one day it simply stopped working. The clock was rushed to the clock doctor who opened it up. There was nothing wrong with the mechanism, so the doctor asked the clock what was ticking. The clock told him about the stress it was carrying just thinking about all the ticks it had to tick in a year, let alone a lifetime. The doctor asked, "How many ticks do you have to complete at a time?" "Just one," the clock replied.

An imaginary story? Yes, but not as imaginary as one would like to think. Many of us are right there. We borrow trouble from tomorrow. We think over and over again about the seemingly insurmountable barriers ahead, only to discover when we get there that God has taken them away. We worry about *what if*, but when we get to that point, we find that God's grace is more than sufficient. Read Matthew 6:25–34 where Jesus teaches that worry is needless, senseless, useless, pointless, faithless, and godless. Your heavenly Father will provide for your needs and emergencies today. If He does not meet the material and physical need, He will give you the grace and strength to accept and endure the situation. He cares for you one day at a time.

There are two days in every week about which we should not worry. The one is *yesterday,* with its failures, blunders, aches, and pains. Yesterday has passed forever beyond your control. We cannot change it. Nothing can bring it back. It has forever gone. The other day is *tomorrow,* with its adversities, challenges, and uncertainties, some or all of which may never happen. A person with cancer is often asked, "How do you live with the uncertainty?" But the reality is that we all live with uncertainty. The only difference is that some people's uncertainty has a name. Cancer. Joblessness. Tomorrow's sun will rise. The sun may be shining or be hidden behind rainclouds—but it will rise. Until it does, you have no stake in it. This leaves only one day—*today.* Anyone can handle *today.* God's grace is available for you today. It's when you and I add the burdens of those two seemingly dreadful eternities, *yesterday* and *tomorrow,* that we break down. You can't live your life thinking about the "what-ifs," or you will disregard the "what is." So learn to trust your Father in heaven for today—the step you are taking right now.

There is a wonderful promise given to us in Scripture: *"God is faithful. He will not allow the temptation to be more than you can stand"* (1 Corinthians 10:13). The word *temptation* includes enticements, troubles, challenges, and burdens. And the promise is that God will not allow today's troubles to be more than you can carry. The old British cargo ships had a line painted all around the hull. It was called the load line. As the ship was loaded, the ship would sink further and further down into the water. But when it reached its load line, it was considered full and nothing else could be loaded on. The captain commanded a halt to the loading operations. And God knows your load line. He will not allow you to be burdened beyond it. God's grace carries you, covers you, sustains you, and keeps you from sinking below the water level. So run with today's grace. Don't borrow from yesterday or tomorrow. Don't add the burdens of either to your load limit for today.

GREEN MEADOWS

As emphasized before, the desert or wilderness teaches us much about going forward one step at a time. One of the most well-known passages in Scripture is Psalm 23. You have read the line about the shepherd leading the sheep into green meadows. The prophet, Ezekiel, also writes that the Lord is a Shepherd who will give His sheep good pastureland and feed them *"in the lush pastures of the hills"* (Ezekiel 34:14). Of course, this is speaking about God's provision. I have travelled amongst the hills spoken about here, however, and I have found very few rich green meadows. Certainly none knee-deep in alfalfa. In fact, as you watch a flock of sheep grazing up the side of a hill, you can't help but wonder what they are eating. Do these sheep eat rocks?

When you take a closer look, however, something becomes noticeable. Tiny clumps of grass concealed amongst the rocks. Tufts of green peeking up through the stony landscape. Growing without apparent nutrition or moisture. But the table has been specially prepared. The early morning humidity condenses along the edges of the rocks, and that is where the grass takes root. The tiny shoots drink in the moisture and establish morsels of green. The good shepherd finds a pasture where the sheep can feed on these blades of grass. The sheep nibble a mouthful here and a mouthful there as they make their way along the hillside. The psalmist writes that the Shepherd's goodness and unfailing love pursues me *"all the days of my life"* (verse 6). Your Shepherd provides for you one day at a time. Every day. One hillside at a time. One tuft at a time. You don't need to worry about tomorrow's green meadow while you nibble on today's green hillside. Tomorrow there will be the provision of another green pasture. Over the next hill somewhere. Your Shepherd knows where. Trust Him. There will be enough for your daily needs.

RUNNING ON EMPTY

Marshall Ulrich has been described as the ultimate extreme athlete. In 2008, Ulrich completed a transcontinental run from San Francisco to New York City. He ran a distance of 4,929 kilometres (3,063 miles), averaging 96 kilometres (60 miles) a day for 52 days straight. More than two marathons every day for nearly two months. He had previously climbed Mt. Everest, but said that an average day running across the continent was as difficult as his toughest, most challenging day on Everest. He was 57 years old.

Ulrich wrote the story of his amazing run in a book entitled *Running on Empty*. A most appropriate title, because for many of those miles he seemed to be running on an empty tank. Emptied of physical stamina, reason, purpose, emotional reserve, passion. He recalls, "Nearly every muscle in my body rebelling against the daily grind of my current reality, I desperately craved relief. *I just need to hang in there for a few more days,* I'd tell myself. *Soon this will be over.*"[9] No doubt you have been in that spot and told yourself the same thing. Ulrich recalled some tough Russian mountaineers who once told him that there was to be no complaining or else you were finished! One needed to disregard the negative whispers and say only what you meant. For instance, don't say that you want to stop unless that is what you *intend* to do with the very next step. Don't say you are "done" unless you are going to pack it in … *now!*

Whether it is running across America or running the race of life, it takes resolve to keep going one step at a time, come what may. Ulrich writes, "Face forward and take the next step. Don't flinch when the road gets rough, you fall down, you miss a turn, or the bridge you planned to cross has collapsed. Do what you say you'll do and don't let anything or anyone stop you. Deal with the obstacles as they come. Move on. *Keep going, no matter what, one foot in front of the other, millions of times.*"[10]

DISTANCE OF TRUTH

In the last chapter, I detailed the amazing race that Ferg Hawke ran in the 2005 Badwater Ultramarathon. The run was captured on camera for a documentary called *The Distance of Truth*. The title caught my attention. What did it mean? At the end of the movie, filmmaker Rob Letson wrote some thought-provoking words that must be pondered over and over in order to grasp the meaning and interpretation for one's own life.

"The distance of truth speaks for itself without words … where we strip away the layers and remove all that is meaningless.

Where our status is no longer symbolized by our material accomplishments but measured by the strength of our character. Where the trivial things we stress and strain over begin to disappear and we get to our roots—the place—where after all the questions are answered—we discover—it was never really a question—at all."[11]

I asked Rob Letson for the meaning of the passage. He responded that the meaning is open to personal interpretation. Something like a piece of contemporary abstract art. The confluence of shapes and colours differ in meaning according to the experience and interpretation of the individual observing the canvas. Similarly, this passage will have different meanings for different individuals.

So, what does it mean to me? I believe it has something to do with coming face to face with yourself. It stirs you to answer some fundamental questions about yourself. Who are you? Why are you? How do you define yourself? Many people define themselves by their material and physical accomplishments and successes. Who are you? I am a successful businessperson. I am a powerful and prominent person. I am an influential person. Who are you? I am a rich person. I am a famous person. I am a hard worker. I am a good student. But if these things were taken from you, who would you be? Receiving a significant promotion is not who you are. The first time your personal wealth reached one million dollars did not define who you are. "Closing that lucrative deal" is not who you are. All of these things are influential incidents and events in your life, but they do not define who you are.

Then there are those people who define themselves by their pain, disappointments, adversities, and losses. They define themselves as a failure. The betrayed. A victim. The black sheep in the family. A bereaved parent. A cancer patient. Divorced. A couple who *couldn't* have children. Admittedly, you may have experienced a painful and demanding moment in your life. You may have experienced an incident that you grieve, regret, or for which you feel shame. But, while that incident may have had a huge impact on your life, it is not your *life*. That episode in your life may *refine* you but it does not *define* you.

Everyone's path inevitably winds down through the desert. I am not thinking here of the desert as a place you experience but a point you reach in your life. The point in your life where you come face to face with the frailty of your human existence. The layers are stripped away. Your material accomplishments. Your successes and even your failures. Everything is stripped away. Everything. You are unmasked. You stand naked, alone, vulnerable, face to face with yourself in the mirror. It's just you … and God. Who do you see? This is the defining moment in your life. Running the distance through the desert gets you to the root of who you are. It is the process God uses to lead you to your true measure as a man or woman.

God wants to unravel the uniqueness, richness, potential, and beauty that lie within each of us. We are His creation, made in His image. But these things will not be unravelled until we understand our absolute need of Him and discover His all-sufficiency in our lives. We are meant to live, not just exist. And living is inseparably linked to the life of Christ in us. The apostle Paul wrote, *"Everything else is worthless when compared with the infinite value of knowing Christ Jesus my Lord"* (Philippians 3:8). There's no way around it. When you are running on empty, you need His filling and His power surging through you. Running the distance through the desert brings you to the point of absolute reliance upon Christ Jesus and unconditional surrender to Him. *"Christ lives in me,"* and *"living means living for Christ"* (Galatians 2:20; Philippians 1:21). This is the distance of truth.

The lens of the camera captures the magnificence and beauty of an ultradistance runner running against the backdrop of a large red sun disappearing behind a barren ridge and casting long eerie shadows across the path. The silhouette of a human being heading into the night. Following a path that is tough, demanding, and risky. But not deterred. Conscious that he or she runs not in one's own strength, but in the power of the Spirit of God. Ever so mindful that one does not run alone, for the Lord is close beside you. This is the distance of truth. It is your story. You are the runner, and the distance of truth speaks for itself, in your life, without words.

TWELVE

RUNNING WITH THE HEAD

RAY ZAHAB IS ONE OF CANADA'S BEST. A LONG-DISTANCE ADVENTURE runner who boasts a list of achievements as long as his arm, Ray exudes an extremely high level of energy, and his days and weeks quickly fill as a husband and father, trainer and serious runner. He organizes expeditions to some of the world's most inhospitable terrains, takes on endless speaking engagements, and talks with people like me who call him up on the phone. Recently, Ray was highlighted in the documentary series *Finding Sarah,* where he trained and accompanied the Duchess of York, Sarah Ferguson, on a flesh-numbing –50-degree Celsius expedition to Yellowknife in Canada's Arctic. Ray lives in the Gatineau Hills in Quebec and runs endless kilometres through some of the most picturesque countryside in Canada. As I mentioned in an earlier chapter, Ray can often be seen on a winding road threading his way through the hills, pulling a tire behind him. One of his primary passions and life goals is to channel his energy into making a difference in people's lives. He founded *Impossible2Possible,* an organization that aims to inspire and educate youth through adventure learning. The organization is designed to help youth learn how to move beyond their perceived limits and succeed in life.

I spoke with Ray just after he had completed the Atacama Extreme Expedition in February 2011. He began near the Peruvian border and ended in Copiapo, Northern Chile, 20 days and approximately

1,200 kilometres later. He ran through the "rainless" Atacama Desert, one of the driest landscapes on the planet, following the trails of the ultrarunning messengers of the ancient Incas. Ray told me that this had been his greatest challenge to date. The topography and geography. The heat rising to 50 degrees Celsius. And the aloneness. He ran alone and at times the loneliness was overpowering.

90% MENTAL AND 10% IN THE HEAD

If you check out Ray's website, a statement jumps out at you. *"The Challenge is believing that overcoming obstacles is 90% mental and the other 10% is all in our heads."* [1] There is certainly a physical component to running. You need to train and be in shape physically. But Ray focuses on the mental component. That you push yourself beyond your perceived limits by *willing* yourself beyond these points. It is critically important to set your *mind* to the extraordinary. Every ultrarunner comes to the point where one thinks he or she is done. At that pivotal point, however, you are probably only 40 percent into what your body is capable of doing. It is the mind that breaks through those self-imposed limits and pushes you past the threshold.

Ray Zahab was a 37-year-old, self-described "pack-a-day smoker and couch potato," who came to his senses and admitted that he needed to change his life. He made up his mind that he would train hard to become the kind of runner who could reach his limits and then go beyond them. He was soon running two marathons a day.

Ray had been running for only two-and-a-half years when he envisioned something that would test the limits … an epic run across Africa's Sahara Desert. The proposal was to run two marathons a day for 80 days … without a day off. The course would run from the Atlantic to the Red Sea through six countries: Senegal, Mauritania, Mali, Niger, Libya, and Egypt. Ray invited two other experienced runners to accompany him: Kevin Lin from Taiwan and Charlie Engle from the United States. The run was captured on a documentary film, *Running the Sahara*, produced and narrated by Academy Award winner Matt Damon, and directed by another Academy Award winner, James Moll. The purpose of the journey and film was to draw awareness to the drinking-water crisis in Africa and the clean-water initiatives directed at trying to remedy the crisis. The decision to execute this ambitious plan was not made lightly. The journey was fraught with risks. The question that kept running through Ray's mind was whether or not it could really be done. Who would watch a movie about running *part* of the Sahara? Who would be interested in a movie entitled *A Failed Attempt to Run the Sahara*? No one. This needed to succeed.

The three runners began their ambitious quest with their feet in the Atlantic Ocean, in St. Louis, Senegal. Ahead of them waited 7,500 kilometres of some of the driest, hottest, most inhospitable, hostile real estate on earth. They began running at 5am every morning and ran until noon. They would take a siesta for three to four hours during the hottest time of the day. Then, at 5pm, they would run again for four more hours. At day's end they would fall exhausted into their sleeping bags and sleep until 5am, when they would get up and do the same thing all over again. The filming crew were like flies on the wall. From a logistical point of view, it was amazing what the film crew accomplished. They had to keep up with the runners, moving all the camera equipment along, setting up, taking down, and running ahead. At times they were hopelessly stuck in the sand up to the axles of the trucks. But through everything, they captured the agony and exhilaration of the run, the beauty of the desert and the people living there.

By Day 6, they had completed 219 kilometres. They were enduring dehydration, blisters, 140-degree temperatures, stress fractures, shin splints, cramps, diarrhea, and kidney failure. At times, they lay prostrate on their backs thinking they were going to die. A doctor was always at hand to give medical attention. When the body cried "stop," Ray would remind his companions that overcoming obstacles was 90% mental and 10% in your head. They had come into this knowing there would be a lot of suffering. They should not dwell on the negative, but think about getting the job done. One cannot do everything, so ask yourself: *What is important to me? Why am I here?* They were here to complete running the Sahara. He encouraged them to think one challenge at a time, one step at a time, one day at a time. Set your mind to keep going.

On Day 39, they reached the 2,579-kilometre mark. They spotted a seven-year-old boy sitting alone up on a sandy ridge. He had been sitting in that spot for two days while his parents were gone to find water. He had never seen a white person before and was afraid as he witnessed these strange figures run in and out of his life. The runners gave him food and water.

Day 44, they reached the Mali-Niger border. This was the most unforgiving part of the Sahara. The region was ravaged by drought. The people were nomadic tent-dwellers, believing that houses are the graves of the living. The runners stopped to assist some desert nomads who were digging a well. The divergence was rewarding. Their efforts helped to deliver clean water to about 1,000 people; water that would change their lives forever. Divergence is healthy for the mind. Similarly, the mind is revitalized by fun and relaxation. Christmas Day arrived and the men opened a box with an unexpected surprise inside. Snow. One of the wives had packed snow as a gift. The three amigos showered themselves with the white stuff, creating their own blizzard, laughing and carrying on like young boys. For the rest of the day, they ran inspired by the music of Elvis Presley, *Walking in the Winter Wonderland*. In the middle of the Sahara Desert.

KEEP YOUR HEAD IN IT

The lightness of the moment was short-lived. As they approached Libya, everything became unpredictable. A sense of uncertainly expended their energy. The Niger-Libya border was officially closed. There was the risk of treading upon land mines or encountering insurgent forces. And then there was the unremitting, suffocating assault of wind and sand blasting their faces like tiny needles. They wrapped themselves from head to foot and peered out through their goggles, looking like aliens running along the surface of some far-off planet. Sand filled the air like a heavy mist, giving a sense of isolation from one another. The support vehicle kept about three to four kilometres ahead of the team. The idea was to follow the tire tracks. But they had not accounted for the blowing sand covering the tracks, making it ever so easy to lose their way. A GPS was needed to keep them moving in the right direction in this sea of nothingness. Their bodies were weakened by sickness and their minds tormented by a growing sense of hopelessness. Charlie had lost 40 pounds, Ray 30 pounds and Kevin 25. No one had any fat reserves left. It was paramount that each man eat and drink as many calories as possible. They ate mammoth dinners and loads of candies, energy bars, peanut butter, and cookies. Actually, $700 worth of cookies.

On Day 59, the Tenere Desert in Niger stretched out before them. Miles and miles of arid, empty space, and yet some of the most beautiful landscape they had ever seen. An expansive ocean of red sand. They had run 3,500 kilometres, a total of 84 marathons. That night, sitting in the tent, tension filled the air. At least it wasn't sand. But it was something more incapacitating: fear and discouragement. Kevin was within a hair of quitting. He said he would be withdrawing from the run in the morning.

Ray tried to encourage him. "You've fought back from painful knees and sickness. You've got to fight whatever this is."

Charlie Engle, who was fighting his own battle with a blister on his foot the size of a baseball, admitted, "All I want to do is get to the finish line, and all I can think about is stopping." He then looked Kevin in the eye and said, "But we aren't going to stop. We are going to finish. And we want you with us. We're a team. You don't want to quit. And you *can* do this." Kevin looked down, biting on his finger. Charlie got up and put his arm around Kevin. "Don't quit!"

His words remind me of the encouragement the writer of Hebrews gave to the Hebrew Christians who were enduring a very difficult faith journey. Many were within a hair of giving up. He used the promises and truth of Scripture to inspire them with courage and set their minds to keep going. *"Patient endurance is what you need now, so that you will continue to do God's will. ... We are not like those who turn away from God"* (Hebrews 10:36–39). Don't quit!

"Just run as far as Libya, 10 more days," urged Charlie. Kevin wiped tears from under his dark glasses. There was silence. Both Charlie and Ray fixed their eyes on Kevin. Kevin continued staring down at the ground. "Then, if you want to quit ... you can quit."

Kevin sat motionless, speechless. He straightened his shoulders a little. Then agreed with a nod. Charlie pulled him in and held him tight. "Thank you," he said, "thank you."

On Day 74, with 108 full marathons and 4,500 kilometres behind them, they reached the Libyan border. Kevin made the commitment to keep running with the team. Every day was an act of desperation. On Day 93, they ran 80 kilometres but only moved forward 26 kilometres toward their destination. They encouraged one another and their own spirits with five words: *Keep your head in it.* They washed their minds of any negative toxic thoughts with these words, over and over and over again. *Keep your head in it. Keep your head in it.*

Day 110. They crossed the Egyptian border at the 7,275 kilometre mark. Exhilaration pumped in their chests as they saw the pyramids of Giza loom up in front of them. Their course wound its way between the giant triangular tombs and the three broke their pace to embrace. But they were not finished yet. They decided to run the final 160 kilometres to the Red Sea non-stop regardless of the pain. Charlie was still nursing a blister that had become abscessed. They shifted into autopilot and focused on running one step at a time. They were soon running through the streets of Cairo. The busy streets streaming with traffic and thronging with people made them feel less safe than in the desert.

As is so often the case when completing the final miles, the challenge is to overcome the barrier of the brain. To the last onerous stride, they needed to intentionally keep their heads in the run. They needed the head to command the legs to take the next step. To accept the pain and mentally "gut it out." In the end, the entire journey was the triumph of mind and will over body. The mind succeeded in overcoming the obstacles and breaking through the self-imposed limits. They did it. On Day 111, their feet touched the warm waters of the Red Sea. They had run a total of 7,500 kilometres. That was the same as running across Canada from St. John's, Newfoundland to Vancouver, British Columbia. More than 170 marathons without a day off.

Ray Zahab told me that not too long ago he was just a regular dude who decided to start running. If he were betting, he would have bet against himself ever being able to accomplish such a challenge. But standing knee deep in the waters of the Red Sea, he declared, "I was able to finish. I was able to convince myself to finish. And that's a fact. I ran the miles. I did it!" He affirmed what he believed, that most limitations we have are ones we set upon ourselves. If you *think* you can run only five or 10 kilometres, you'll probably run only five or 10 kilometres. Too often we set the boundaries in a safe, non-threatening place, usually far too low and way too short. Our goals are feeble and our growth is stunted. The target can be set further out. The bar can be positioned higher. Your dreams can be supersized. Your mind is a command centre for blasting beyond your perceived limits.

A MENTAL BLUEPRINT

In Jeff Galloway's book, *Marathon: You Can Do It*, he talks about rehearsing the marathon in your mind so that you can immerse yourself mentally in the experience. Draw upon past experience to construct your mental marathon so that you will be mentally conditioned for anything you encounter in the marathon itself.[2] Play it out first in your mind. Instead of just waiting for things to happen, be mentally prepared for unexpected encounters. Be mentally prepared for what could go wrong. Be mentally prepared for how you will respond to challenges and adversities. Plan mental solutions for every conceivable problem. And do the mental rehearsal regularly. When you do this, you are wisely setting up a mental blueprint for running the marathon.

There is a profound parallel here for running the race of faith. When God called the second generation of Israelites to enter and conquer the land of Canaan under Joshua, He gave them a mental blueprint. The Book of Deuteronomy means *the second law*. This was a second chance. A new opportunity. A new generation. A new leader. The book of Deuteronomy was a review of what God had done for the first generation and of what He had commanded. It was a story of God's provision and protection for Israel and of Israel's lack of faith and regard for God. An unbelief that prevented them from experiencing the joy of conquering the land and consigned them to merely existing in a hostile world until they had died off.

The review of the failed past was intended by God to be a rehearsal for what God expected as they encountered the challenges ahead. The new generation was to review its paltry beginnings as wandering nomads. It was to rehearse the nation's dire situation of slavery in Egypt and how God had heard their cries and seen their hardship, toil, and oppression. They were to remember how God had delivered them from Egypt with a strong hand and powerful arm with miraculous signs and wonders. They were to recall how God had led them to their new land of abundance. They were to rehearse what God expected of them as they moved in to conquer and settle the Promised Land. Wholehearted obedience. If they obeyed, they would be His special treasure, blessed, renowned, and high above all the other nations (Deuteronomy 26:5–19; 30:11–20).

There were failures that should not be repeated. There was need of a fresh commitment to trust, love, and obey God. There were promises to hold on to. Blessings to embrace. Courageous choices to be made. There was faith to act upon. Moses was rehearsing the imminent marathon through the land of Canaan, mentally preparing the people for the challenges, dangers, tests, and temptations ahead. Deuteronomy was a mental blueprint for conquering the land.

The blueprint was to be rehearsed regularly. Moses wrote everything in a Book of Instruction. The book was to be read to everyone, including the children, every seven years. In those days, there were no books, Bibles or newspapers for people to read, so they relied on word of mouth to communicate the Word of God to them. They also relied on memorization (Deuteronomy 31:10–13). What a reminder for us. The entire Bible is God's blueprint for our lives to understand and follow if we are going to run the race God has set for us. But we need to rehearse its content and substance over and over again in our minds and hearts.

Immediately after Moses died, God spoke these words to the new leader, Joshua. "Study this Book of Instruction *continually*. Meditate on it *day and night* so you will be sure to obey everything written in it. *Only then will you prosper and succeed in all you do*" (Joshua 1:8, italics added). The message? God has given the blueprint for living. Continual rehearsal of the blueprint will give you success in the race you are running for God. Keep your head in the Book and God will keep your legs in the race.

STAYING ON THE RIGHT SIDE OF YOUR BRAIN

The left hemisphere of your brain is the centre of logic. It solves problems, organizes, and structures things into compartments. It does not like to deviate too far from the beaten track. It values reason, consistency, security, order, predictability, and comfort. It steers you away from stress with subtle warnings and negative messages. "Slow down." "Don't push yourself." "Look after yourself." "You'll never get through this." "What have you gotten yourself into?" It nags you to stay within your limits. It is usually a voice of negativity and doubt. It reminds you that you are halfway between here and there. Congratulations! You have arrived nowhere, and probably don't have the reserves to make it somewhere. Maybe it's time to stop. It's not very adventurous or daring, and is certainly not a risk-taker. Now take care not to ignore the voice of the left brain. It is a reliable compass. It is your danger alert system. It is the voice of reason. It is the source of rationale and order in your life. It will help you solve a math problem or organize a filing system. It's just that when it comes to running, you need to tap into the right-brain track.

The right hemisphere of your brain is very different from the left. It sits under the same skull but gets you out of the box. The right side is the spring of creativity. Whatever barrier or challenge you face, the right side can come up with a creative solution to solve it. It says, "Try this." "It would be fun to try that." "Let's test something novel." "You can do it." It is a risk-taker. It balances the rigidity of the left brain with trying something original or going on an adventure. It is able to adjust to the situation and adapt to the challenge that suddenly confronts it. It encourages you to push through the obstacle, to keep going and *gut it out*. It says, "You may be outnumbered, but you have the mental resources and ability to get it done."

In the early periods of the French and Indian War in 1755, it was a battle between left and right-brain thinking. The British military strategy was European in nature, meaning an entire army of Redcoats lined up in a straight column and fired volley after volley of musket balls directly ahead. Now that may have been successful on a *field* of battle. But in a wilderness forest, it was totally ineffective. Musket balls ricocheted off trees, crashing through limbs and splintering bark in every direction They fractured rocks and spat clumps of dirt into the air. Everything that had breath took cover, from man to the smallest fur-bearing or feathered forest creature. But there was little loss of life. The clouds of gunpowder smoke from the muskets grew so dense that no one could see his hand in front of his face let alone what he was shooting at. But still, the British kept firing volley after volley. Why? This was the system. This was how a battle was fought. This was the way it had always been done. This was what was learned in military school. Stick with the plan. That's left-brain thinking.

On the other hand, the French and Indians darted, lunged, crawled, materialized unexpectedly and disappeared just as suddenly and illusively as phantoms, completely camouflaged among the trees. They moved from tree to tree, taking cover when necessary, and firing at the red-coated targets standing before them in plain view from behind the protective shield of those same trees. They adapted to their environment and used it to their advantage. They defeated armies five times their size. That's right-brain thinking.

And when it comes to running and living the race God has given you, you need to stay on the right side of your brain. Whereas the left side of the brain finds running hard work, the right side of the brain finds it inspiring, exhilarating, and fun. The left side is the brakes; the right side is overdrive. The left side sees the run as a stressful experience; the right side as a challenging journey. The left side counsels you to stick with the routine; the right side counsels you to adjust to the situation. The left side warns you to stay within your capabilities (and this should not be ignored); the right side stirs you to stretch beyond your perceived limits. Jeff Galloway, an Olympic athlete and running teacher, writes, "The left side of your brain has a million logical reasons for why you can't do something. The right side won't try to argue; it will just try to get the job done using its unlimited supply of creative, spontaneous, and imaginative ways of steering you in the direction of your abilities."[3]

The apostle Paul attempted to motivate Timothy to tap into the right side of his brain when he wrote to his younger disciple. Paul was nearing the end of his life and wanted to encourage Timothy to persevere running his race. Paul wrote two letters to him. Timothy seemed to be committed to running a good race, but struggling with a timid and reticent nature. He allowed others to look down on his youthfulness and this had a way of reducing his effectiveness for God. He was available to God but felt inadequate. Paul encouraged him to faithfully teach the truth about the living God. Then he added, *"Don't let anyone think less of you because you are young. Be an example to all the believers in what you say, in the way you live, in your love, your faith, and your purity. ... Throw yourself into your tasks so that everyone will see your progress"* (1 Timothy 4:12, 15). *"Endure suffering along with me, as a good soldier of Christ Jesus"* (2 Timothy 2:3). In other words, Timothy, ward off the negative messages you are listening to and get on to the right track.

DON'T RING THE BELL

In his book, *Running on Empty,* Marshall Ulrich describes the infamous training camp for all potential Navy SEAL recruits. It is appropriately called Hell Week, and is designed to demonstrate that the human body can endure more than the mind normally believes it can. This survival week is intended to challenge the mind to rise above normality and push the body beyond its perceived limits. Trainees are exposed to cold, heat, rain, mud, wind, and sand as they undergo a series of unforgiving tests calculated to break their spirits or build their endurance. They suffer 132 hours of exhausting physical labour, and are only allowed a weekly total of about four hours sleep. As they endure each grueling test and punishing hour, the instructor's voice is continually echoing in their ears, reminding them they can drop out at any moment. It resonates with their inner voice pleading with them to stop. No one *has* to put up with this. All any recruit has to do is ring a shiny brass bell that hangs in a prominent spot, visible for all to see, luring any weakened soul to bring an end to its torment. Ring the bell? You declare that you're done. Finished. For good.[4]

The battlefield is the *mind.* The enemy is *the voice.* The voice that urges you to quit. *I can't do this. I don't have to put up with this. Ring the bell! Find something easier, lighter, more comfortable, more reasonable. I'm done!* One silences the voice in one of two ways. You either ring the bell, or you mentally shut the voice down. You mentally block the negative messages. Marshall Ulrich was asked to counsel potential Navy SEAL recruits regarding how to win the battle of the mind and overpower the voice. So he formulated a battle strategy. A series of commands that some called *Marshall Law.*[5] Some of these laws hold a clear resemblance to the instructions Paul gave to Timothy in the last known letter that he wrote. They are most helpful to anyone running the race of faith. They are principles that steer you to the right side of the brain and ward off negative messages that threaten to rob you of your God-given potential and prevent you from possessing everything Christ possessed you for. Principles that will keep you from *ringing the bell.*

MARSHALL LAW

1. *Expect a journey and a battle.* The fact is that life is hard. It is filled with challenges, trials, and disappointments. But the critically important first step is to accept this reality. When you don't, your mind easily withdraws to the reservoir of negative messages, such as how much your body is hurting, how slowly the time passes and how far you still need to go. The mind tends to accentuate the negative and ignore the positive. When you accept your reality, however, you own responsibility and that both increases your pain threshold and empowers you to endure more suffering.

Suffering is okay. And it is inevitable. Paul reminded Timothy, *"Everyone who wants to live a godly life in Christ Jesus will suffer persecution"* (2 Timothy 3:12). That's the reality. If you live for Christ, it will not be easy. It will be a battle. It will be a journey of failures, defeats, victories, blessing, and growth.

2. *Don't dwell on the negative.* The mind runs to the negative like water runs to the lowest point. So, when the mind runs there, don't dwell there. Set your mental hooks into the positive. Paul gave Timothy the positive reminder of his own personal example. *"But you, Timothy, certainly know what I teach, and how I live, and what my purpose in life is. You know my faith, my patience, my love, and my endurance. You know how much persecution and suffering I have endured ... but the Lord rescued me from all of it"* (2 Timothy 3:10–11). Paul reminded Timothy of the

faith of his mother and grandmother. Then he challenged Timothy with these words: *"And I know the same faith continues strong in you. This is why I remind you to fan into flames the spiritual gift God gave you. … For God has not given us a spirit of fear and timidity, but of power, love, and self-discipline"* (2 Timothy 1:5–7). The writer of Hebrews did the same thing. He set before us the examples and stories of men and women who encountered many trials and challenges and yet endured by faith. They give a positive example of how to run the race. We draw from the legacy of their faith and strength.

There are other ways to dwell on the positive and tap into the right side of the brain. Good, wholesome, inspiring music. Music is something God has given to reach down and touch the deepest parts of the heart. When you feel the negative messages surfacing, turn on the music, put on the headphones, fall into the rhythm, and let the words and melody flow healing, hope, and encouragement into your mind and heart. If one song speaks particularly into your life, play the same song over and over again. The continual rehearsal will refresh and restore God's mental blueprint for pushing your race forward.

You can tap into your right brain by rehearsing success stories. Your own personal stories. Not just the big ones, but the little successes along the way. But also draw from the success stories of other runners. I have always found it extremely inspiring to pick up a good biographical book. As I read, I live the life of another person. I feel their pain and loss. I drown in their failures. I confront their challenges with them. I celebrate their successes. Biographies give hope and set you back on the right track. They are food for the right brain.

And don't underestimate the power of a good laugh. Someone has said that humour greases the wheels of learning. It is equally true that humour greases the right brain. Connect with people who make you laugh. Tell a good joke. Learn to laugh at yourself. Laughing uses far fewer facial muscles than frowning. It has a way of relaxing the whole body. I had an uncle who had a laugh so contagious it made everyone around him break into fits of laughter. He would hold his belly and go into convulsions until the tears flowed down his cheeks. His laugh was like the roar of a large wave breaking against the rocks, followed by the sound of air being sucked like a rip-current back into his lungs, creating a vacuum that would explode again with a gut-wrenching howl. Everyone around him laughed so hard it hurt. But it was a good hurt. When it was all over, the body felt completely relaxed. Solomon wrote, *"A cheerful heart is good medicine"* (Proverbs 17:22). Laughter is medicine that relieves stress. It increases pain tolerance. It boosts enthusiasm for life, lightens the load, and generates a positive outlook. And it is fun, free, and easy to use. Try it.

3. *Have confidence that you will succeed.* Paul wrote to Timothy because he was confident that Timothy was the real deal. Paul wanted timid and fearful Timothy to feel the same confidence for himself that he would succeed in what God had called him to do. So Paul penned these confidence-building instructions: *"Preach the word of God. Be prepared, whether the time is favorable or not. Patiently correct, rebuke, and encourage your people with good teaching. … Don't be afraid of suffering for the Lord. Work at telling others the Good News, and fully carry out the ministry God has given you"* (2 Timothy 4:2, 5). What God calls you to do, He will empower you to do.

4. *Know that there will be an end.* Create a mental picture of yourself crossing the finish line. You are standing on the podium and your face is reflecting the glow of a shiny gold medal hanging around your neck. The aches have given way to achievement. The struggles have given way to satisfaction. Such mental images put you on the right side of the brain. Immediately after Paul urged Timothy to not shrink away from suffering, but to fully carry out his God-given ministry, he said, *"I have fought a good fight, I have finished the race, and I have remained faithful. And now the prize awaits me"* (2 Timothy 4:7–8). This mental image was as much for Timothy as it was for Paul. He was reminding Timothy that there would be an end.

5. *Quitting is not an option.* No, it's not. So shut the voice down.

The Power of a Renewed Mind

I am not speaking about the power of positive thinking, but about something much more powerful. The power of God-focused thinking. A mind oriented to biblical truth. Psalm 1 is the introductory psalm to the whole Book of Psalms. It lays the foundation for the rest of the book. It lays out life's two roads. The path of the godly and the path of the ungodly. The path that is run by those who believe and follow God, and the path run by those who don't. As you run the race, you are following one of these two paths.

The godly *"delight in the law of the Lord, meditating on it day and night"* (Psalm 1:2). To *delight* in the Scriptures is like a starving person devouring a delicious meal. To *meditate* on it is to focus or concentrate on it. Don't let the idea of meditating conjure up ideas of your mind floating like a cube of ice on a sea of nothingness, drifting who knows where. Rather, it is the discipline of focusing on a particular thought, word, passage, or principle over and over again so that its truth is planted firmly on the mind and begins to grow into godly living. Rick Warren calls it "focused thinking."[6] He compares it to the exercise of worry, an exercise that comes so naturally that none of us need to practice doing it. "If you know how to worry, you already know how to meditate. Worry is focused thinking on something negative. Meditation is doing the same thing, only focusing on God's Word instead of your problem."[7]

Those who run on this path *"are like trees planted along the riverbank, bearing fruit each season. Their leaves never wither, and they prosper in all they do"* (Psalm 1:3). Even in the hot, arid, inhospitable desert of their lives, their roots go deep into the underground living waters of truth. Therefore, they grow fruit in times of abundance and times of drought. Their leaves never wither. The truth of Scripture refreshes their spirits. When they feel themselves fading due to the difficulty of the path, they go deep and don't wither and collapse. They prosper. They keep going. They don't merely survive; they thrive.

Paul implored followers of Christ: *"Don't copy the behavior and customs of this world, but let God transform you into a new person by changing the way you* think" (Romans 12:2, emphasis mine). The voices call out, "Join in!" "Everybody's doing it." "It's not hurting anyone." "It makes sense." "It feels good." "It feels right." All of these statements are flawed by sin. Rather, let God transform you into a new person by changing the way you *think.* You are what you *think.* So fill your mind with God's Word. God's thoughts. God's truth. And that will govern your will. Paul continued, *"Then you will learn to know God's will for you"* (Romans 12:2).

THE POWER OF AN EXERCISED WILL

God made every person a living soul. The soul is comprised of three essential elements … mind, will, and emotion. We know and believe with the mind. We act with the will. And we feel with the emotions. The will acts on the basis of what the mind tells it. The mind says, "I believe such and such." The will responds: "Then this is what I choose or will to do."

There are two types of people. Firstly, there are *reactive* people. These people blame the circumstances, the past, other people, and hurts. The primary influence in their lives is what has happened to them. They live out the script handed to them. They find it difficult to take responsibility and make choices that will create change and move them forward. They just react to what comes their way.

Then there are *proactive* people. Such people refuse to be controlled. They choose to take control. My running friend, Jim Willett, who was undergoing chemotherapy for his cancer at the time, said to me: "It's not what happens to us, but what we *make happen*." The will of a proactive individual refuses to be acted upon, but to act upon. It chooses to make something happen. "I will exceed the limits." "I will outdistance the voices of discouragement and negativity." "I refuse to accept this situation any longer, but choose to rise above the circumstances." "I choose to move forward." "I choose to forgive." Or, as the apostle Paul said, *"I press on to reach the end of the race"* (Philippians 3:14). *"I can do everything through Christ, who gives me strength"* (Philippians 4:13). Therefore, set your mind to the extraordinary and exercise your will to go there.

The good news is you are not alone in exercising your will. The power of God is in you, giving you the willpower to make choices that are right and good for you and pleasing to Him. *"For God is working in you, giving you the desire and the power to do what pleases Him"* (Philippians 2:13).

In Romans 6, the mind and the will are seen working in unison to break the power of sin in your life. Paul addressed first the power of a renewed mind. *"We* know *that our old sinful selves were crucified with Christ so that sin might lose its power in our lives. … And since we died with Christ, we* know *we will also live with him. … So you also should* consider *yourselves to be dead to the power of sin and alive to God through Christ Jesus"* (Romans 6:6, 8, 11, emphasis mine). The emphasis is on the *knowing.* The mind. If you are a believer in Christ, you have died with Christ by faith, meaning you have died to the power of sin over you. And you have been raised with Him, meaning you live a new life. This is your spiritual position in Christ. Understand this. Know it. Believe it. This is the truth. And the truth sets you free.

When your mind knows the truth, then the will is freed to act accordingly. To exercise its power to make right choices. Note what Paul writes next: *"Do not* let *sin control the way you live; do not* give in *to sinful desires. Do not* let *any part of your body become an instrument of evil to serve sin. Instead,* give *yourselves completely to God, for you were dead, but now you have new life"* (Romans 6:12–13, emphasis mine). The renewed mind and will operate inseparably and fluidly as a powerful mental and spiritual force to guard you against ringing the bell. The head pushes you beyond your perceived limits. And you run, and run, and run.

THIRTEEN

RUNNING WITH THE HEART

THE SOUL IS BROKEN DOWN INTO THREE COMPONENTS ... MIND, WILL, and emotion. You don't *have* a soul. You *are* a soul. Your true self is mind, will, and emotion. Of the three, emotion is probably the least accentuated. Emotions are considered unreliable or untrustworthy. They are considered a sign of weakness. People confess, "Oh, I don't want to get all emotional." We disparage people from making an emotional response. It is regarded as shallow and lacking in commitment. We value logic and a strong will, but emotion is the weak link. Or is it? Maybe emotion is simply not understood or recognized for the dynamic power it possesses. Emotion is related to passion. And passion is powerful and influential.

Passion is certainly recognized when it comes to sports. Winning teams are not only skilled and persistent. Winning teams are passionate. No team will go very far with only talent. But add a good dose of passion, and watch out! It's interesting how sports generate passion both on and off the field or the ice. How many so-called "unemotional" guys go silly with euphoria and excitement when it comes to the Super Bowl? Or the NHL playoffs? Emotion reigns. Passion explodes. They high-five and thump each other's chests. They scream and yell themselves hoarse with unintelligible sounds. When a goal is scored, they leap out of their chairs, jump into the air, speak in ecstatic languages, and cry like babies. Then when it's all over, they walk back into life saying, "Now don't get all emotional on me."

When I was a teenager living in Northern Ontario, the long winter meant hockey. And more hockey. And then more hockey. We had short days and long hours to fill. I lived in a small village with an outdoor rink. We would pull together as many guys as possible in the evenings and go the rink. There was a shed with a woodstove roaring hot and we would sit on the rough benches enjoying its heat as we joked, exchanged insults, and changed into our skates and whatever gear we had. Skates and a hockey stick were the necessities. Then out into the cold night air we would go. And did we ever *go*. There were few rules and no whistles. We just skated. And skated. And skated. The idea was to get that little black puck into the other team's net any way you could. The only time there was a break in the game was when too many of us were bending over with sticks resting on our knees, completely winded, chests wheezing and panting uncontrollably in and out, while steam exhaled from our nostrils like smoke from the shed's chimney. Until someone would throw the puck in the direction of one of the nets, and we all came to life and were at it again.

Skates and sticks were not the only necessity. Passion was essential. I can remember playing hockey in sub-zero Fahrenheit temperatures, and playing so hard I would peel my sweater off my back and play with nothing on above the belt. And the steam still rose from my back and shoulders. Yes, we played with passion. Hockey is about more than getting a little black puck into a net. It was about the love of playing the game. Hockey without passion is meaningless. And similarly, life without passion is meaningless. Life is more than reason, logic, choices, activity, performance, getting from point birth to point death, winning or surviving. It is about thriving. Loving life. It is feeling strongly about what you believe. Living and loving are meant to be wed together. Passion cares intensely. Passion carries a strong commitment. Passion runs deep.

Plants have life but no feelings. We are not plants. We have feelings. Feelings motivate you toward purpose. Passion motivates you to do what you were created to do. You feel more alive when you do what you are passionate about than what you are good at. It's a bonus if both are the same. Passion ignites dreams. Passion stimulates you to do things you

RUN! THE AMAZING RACE

have never done before. It was passion for Jesus that inspired Peter to get out of the boat and walk over the waves toward Him. Passion gives you the power to overcome the obstacles and pain in your life.

I once heard TD Jakes compare passion to the action of a bow and arrow. An archer positions the arrow into the string and, while holding the bow with one arm, pulls back hard on the string with the other. He then releases the string and the arrow is thrust and propelled forward. The pain and problems in life are the pull back. But rather than thinking of these *negative* events in your life as damaging or unconstructive, think of them as the digression of the arrow that leads to progression. The greater the digression, the greater the progression. These *negative* episodes influence the thrust and direction for your life. Your incarceration can help you discover who you are and help you find your way. Your illness can give you a genuine passion for others who suffer and lead you to the reason why you were put here. Life's setbacks can give your life purpose, something to live for. You are the arrow. Digression shoots you forward to hit the mark for why you were created. What seems to be against you is actually working for you. Digression produces thrust. Thrust propels forward thinking. And forward thinking creates passion.

THE RUNNING PEOPLE

Running has been critical to man's survival from prehistoric days. We ran to eat. We ran to avoid being eaten. We ran to communicate between communities. We ran to meet deadlines. We still speak in terms of "running here," "running there," "running away," "running off" and "running wild."

Deep in the Copper Canyon of Mexico, an extension of the Grand Canyon, live a peaceful, fun-loving people called the *Tarahumara*. Their real name is *Raramuri*, or *Running People*. They were called Tarahumara by the Spanish conquistadors who mispronounced their name. They survived the Spanish invaders merely because they could outrun them. They are great runners. Possibly the greatest runners in the world today.

The Tarahumara run for a living. They do not know on any given day what challenges or dangers they will encounter. They need to be prepared to run fast and far to catch dinner. They need to be prepared to climb steep canyon trails or to outrun a swelling flood after a torrential downpour. They sometimes even need to be ready to outdistance an enemy. Lifestyle makes the Tarahumara great athletes, and therefore great runners.

But despite the fact that they are the greatest runners in the world, you have never seen them run in any world competitions. They do not run on paved roads, but on canyon trails, terrain congested with sharp rocks and poisonous snakes. They don't consume sports drinks or protein bars; they live on a simple diet, primarily ground corn and barbequed mice. Yummy! There's no tapering, stretching, or warming up before the race, and no prize money at the end. They just show up laughing and joking, and then begin to run for as long and far as they want. It's as though running to death makes them feel more alive. They wear no Nike running shoes, no support or comfort, just leather soles strapped to their feet. They will often kick a wooden ball the size of a grapefruit as they run along, just for fun.

So, why are these tribal people with no training gymnasiums, fitness diets, sports technology, running shoes, or the latest in running gear the best runners in the world? The answer seems to lie in the fact that they run for the sheer joy of it. The passion. The heart. They enjoy the view as they run. They enjoy watching the sunrise over the canyon walls, the colours of the flowers and the feel of the breeze. Most of all, they enjoy each other. They take pleasure in running with their companions. They are intrinsically motivated.

In the west, sport is about receiving medals, trophies, and Nike deals. It's about becoming faster, fitter, and richer. In the west it's about winning; for the Tarahumara it's about running. In the west it's about competition; for the Tarahumara it's about community. In the west it's about running against; for the Tarahumara it's about running with. In the west it's about being the best; for the Tarahumara it's about being together. In the west it's about fame; for the Tarahumara it's about fun. In the west it's about the prize; for the Tarahumara it's about passion.

At the root of their passion for running is the sense of community. They run together to unite and strengthen the bonds of friendship. It's more like a family playing road hockey together on Christmas Day just before a sumptuous turkey dinner. Yes, it's competitive, but mostly, it's fun. Or playing hockey at the village rink on a cold winter night. The passion and the joy of it is being together. For the Tarahumara, the greatest joy is running with the pack and adding one's power and enthusiasm to the pack. That's why you'll never see a Tarahumara running in the Olympics or in a western competition. It's not about winning; it's about community and running for the sheer joy of running. And they don't need to leave the canyons to do that.

In his book, *Born to Run*, Christopher McDougall made this insightful comment about the Tarahumara:

> This was the real secret of the Tarahumara: they'd never forgotten what it felt like to love running. They remembered that running was mankind's first fine art, our original act of inspired creation. Way before we were scratching pictures on caves or beating rhythms on hollow trees, we were perfecting the art of combining our breath and mind and muscles into fluid self-propulsion over wild terrain. And when our ancestors finally did make their first cave paintings, what were the first designs? A downward slash, lightning bolts through the bottom and middle—behold, the Running Man.[1]

I love the truth that God has called us to be *Running People*. We were born to run. It's about more than running; it's about living. We were born to live. It's who we are … living beings. And God wants us to run the journey of life in the same way that the Tarahumara run the canyon trails. With passion, heart, and for the sheer love of it.

FOR THE LOVE OF IT

Life is a wonderful gift from God. Genesis 1:27 reads, *"God created human beings in his own image."* We are the pinnacle of God's creation, unique from every other form of life. We reflect His character. We can relate to God and commune with Him like no other created being. We can know God personally. We can love Him deeply. We can obey Him completely. Interestingly, it says in Genesis 2:7 that we were made from the *"dust of the ground."* There is nothing special about the chemical elements that make up one's body. There was nothing special about any human being until God breathed *"the breath of life"* into our nostrils and man became *"a living person."* This is who we are. Our worth is rooted in the fact that we are made in God's image and that God gave us the breath of life … the gift of His life. This is an incredible gift and one that should be celebrated by living life to the full.

Christopher McDougall tells the inspiring story of one of the world's most colourful runners, Emil Zatopek.[2] Zatopek was a Czech soldier. He ran with the style of a gorilla trying to climb up a descending escalator. But he loved to run. He loved running so much that when he was in army boot camp, he would grab a flashlight and run 20 miles through the woods at night. In his combat boots. In the winter. After a full day of infantry drills. Soon he was running 33 miles at full speed with 200-metre rest periods interspersed. His favourite workout was to jog through the woods in his combat boots with his wife riding on his back. When Emil ran his first marathon, no one told him that the way to complete a marathon was to run slow and steady. So he ran it in 100-yard dashes. The spectacle of his atrocious style became the joke of journalists. But Emil just laughed it off. Fortunately, he wasn't figure skating. He wasn't looking for points for style … just speed.

When Emil ran, he laughed and chatted continuously, sometimes causing other runners to complain about his incessant talking. But that was Emil Zatopek. He seemed to do everything wrong, except winning. And that he did, time after time, enjoying every minute of it. In the late '40s, he won every race he entered over a three-year period, going 69–0.

When he arrived at the 1952 Olympics in Helsinki, the Czech team was so thin that Zatopek was given the choice of what distance events to enter. So he entered them all. He ran the 5,000-metre and won gold, setting a new Olympic record. Then he did the same thing for the 10,000-metre. He had never competed in an Olympic marathon before, but why not go for it. It was a hot day, and Zatopek was up against England's Jim Peters, then the world-record holder. At the 10-mile mark, Peters was leading the field and using the high temperatures to make the other runners suffer. Zatopek pulled up beside him and asked rather innocently, "Excuse me, this is my first marathon. Are we going too fast?"

"No," replied Peters. "Too slow." Dumb question ... dumb answer. "Are you sure?" asked Zatopek. Then, to Peters' amazement, Zatopek took off, sprinting past him, and ran to his third Olympic gold. When he burst into the arena, the whole stadium stood and cheered him in like he was their own. He was the people's runner. Before his own teammates could get to him, the Jamaican sprinters had already hoisted him onto their shoulders and were parading him around the track. "'Let us live so that when we come to die, even the undertaker will be sorry,' Mark Twain used to say. Zatopek found a way to run so that when he won, even other teams were delighted."[3]

Infectious joy. Infectious love. Infectious passion. You can't compel, intimidate, command, or pay someone to possess that. When the Red Army marched into Prague in 1968, Zatopek was given the choice of becoming a sports ambassador for the Soviets, or cleaning toilets in a uranium mine for the rest of his life. Emil chose the toilets. The athlete vanished. But the enthusiasm persisted. It's like the faithful in Hebrews 11:35–38 who were tortured, beaten, chained, imprisoned, stoned, and inflicted with unspeakable atrocities for their faith. They were persecuted into oblivion, but their faith was infectious. They possessed a fervor and passion that could not be obliterated, that lived on past them and exists today. It was Tertullian, one of the great early apologists of the faith, who wrote: "The blood of the martyrs is the seed of the church." The more they persecute the faithful, the more their seed flourishes. How true. You can't kill genuine passion. When someone runs with the heart, you can cut him or her off at the knees, but the passion of the heart lives on.

Coincidentally, at the same time as Zatopek was disappearing from the running scene in 1968, his chief rival for the title of world's greatest distance runner, Australian Ron Clark, was experiencing problems of his own. His success was disintegrating and he finally choked when he failed to win the favoured 10,000-metre final at the '68 Mexico City Games. He was returning to Australia to face the disappointment and disgrace of his nation and decided to take a detour into Prague to visit his old friend and rival who had never lost a race. Emil, though enduring his own disparaging personal trials, endeavoured to encourage his friend and give him reason to hope. When Clark said goodbye, Emil slipped something into his suitcase, gave him a hearty embrace and said farewell with these parting words: "Because you deserve it." Clark thought Zatopek was referring to the embrace. But later, when he opened his luggage, he discovered Zatopek's '52 Olympic 10,000-metre gold medal. Clark extolled Zatopek, "His enthusiasm, his friendliness, his love of life, shone through every movement."[4] That's how you and I are to run. That's how we are to live. Through all the highs and lows, our enthusiasm, our friendliness, our love of life, should shine through every movement. That's running and living with the heart.

It is said of Jesus that He endured the severe agony and torture of the cross and disregarded its shame *"because of the* joy *awaiting him"* (Hebrews 12:2, emphasis added). His passion was to return to heaven having completed the work His Father had given Him to do. His passion was to open the way for us to be forgiven of our sins and to be one in relationship with Him in this life and the next. His passion for living and dying was us. Our passion for life and death should be Him.

THE SIXTH DEADLY SIN

There may be worse sins, but few that are more tragic than apathy. Not caring anymore. To get to the point in your life where you want to stay alive only because there is nothing to die for. A desert monk by the name of John Cassion (360–435 AD) codified the "deadly sins" and listed this one as the sixth deadly sin. He called it *acedia.* We could call it a sluggish heart. Inertia. Indifference. Apathy. Apathy simply means to have no passion. You lose your enthusiasm for life. You become demoralized. When this condition sets into the heart, the life drains away. You find yourself simply going through the motions and giving no more than ceremonial attention to God or how He wants you to live. The runner's legs become heavy. The arms drop. Failure is imminent. It is just a matter of time before you collapse and fall, a victim to the sixth deadly sin.

You become the polar opposite of the Tarahumara. The polar opposite of Emil Zatopek. Worse still, you begin living contrary to the way Jesus lived for you and the way He wants you to live for Him.

197

RUNNING TO WIN

Passion is critically important for the runner. That's why the apostle Paul exhorted the Corinthian Christians, *"Don't you know that in a race everyone runs, but only one person gets the prize? So run to win!"* (1 Corinthians 9:24). What did Paul mean? We are all in a race. But in a race only one runner gets the gold medal. Now, Paul knows that in the race of faith, all who run will receive a medal. So he isn't saying only one will win a medal. He is speaking about running with passion. Run *as though* only one runner can win. Run *in such a way* that if there is to be only one winner, it will be me! The exhortation goes out to all of us participating in the race. Christ wants all of us to run with passion. With heart. Like it really matters how I run the race. This is what I was born to do.

The city of Corinth was situated on a three-and-a-half-mile isthmus of land between the Aegean and Adriatic Seas. Every two years, the city played host to the Isthmian Games. These games were played in honour of the god Poseidon, or Neptune, chief god of Corinth. Poseidon was the god of sea and earthquakes. For a city whose welfare depended on commercial shipping and trade, it was very important to keep Poseidon happy. The Games were one way to stay on his good side. Runners ran to honour Poseidon. They ran to declare Poseidon as God. The Games were far more than a sports event. They were a religious extravaganza.

It was a similar event in Caesarea, the Roman capital on the eastern Mediterranean seacoast. One can stand in the ruins of Caesarea's ancient hippodrome today, and with just a little imagination, hear the cheering and roar of the spectators. The hippodrome was situated in the middle of town next to the amphitheatre and King Herod's impressive palace overlooking the Sea. The purpose of sport was to declare the gods as supreme and worthy of our worship and surrendered lives. In the days when the Caesars would demand acknowledgement and obeisance as Lord, runners ran to declare that Caesar was Lord and God.

The Games followed a prescribed program of events. First, the emperor would enter the stadium with his entourage surrounding him, dressed in a flowing robe with a sash across his chest. The crowds stood and cheered as he settled himself in the royal box. The emperor would wave to his worshippers and sit down. The Games were ready to begin. The first and most exciting events to open the games were the horse and chariot races. The hippodrome in Caesarea was 250 metres long and 50 metres wide with a long narrow spina running laterally through the centre. The spina was decorated with ornate columns and statues. The best place to sit was at the far end of the spina. If there were crashes, rollovers, spilt blood, or sprawling bodies, this was where they would occur. Next, the athletes paraded in, waving palm branches while the people cheered, "Caesar is Lord! Caesar is Lord!" Then the main events, the foot races, began. The runners ran to declare that Caesar was Lord. The way they competed honoured or dishonoured Caesar. So every runner would run with passion.

When Paul wrote, *"Run to win,"* he was drawing from this familiar scene. The runner is a Christian. The point of the race is to declare that Jesus is Lord. How dare we treat the race of faith as though it was a jog in the park. A mid-afternoon yawn. How dare we give up and quit. Paul wrote, *"I trust that my life will bring honor to Christ, whether I live or die. For to me, living means living for Christ"* (Philippians 1:20–21). Jesus *"is seated in the place of honor beside God's throne"* (Hebrews 12:2). He is seated in the royal box and watches you run your race. So run! Run, like Jesus is King! Run! Run! Run, until you have nothing left!

I love a particular story tucked away in the Old Testament in 1 Chronicles 11. It's a story of devotion and bravery driven by passion. David was hiding in the wilderness from the relentless pursuit of King Saul, while at the same time, avoiding hostile Philistine warriors. During this period, the Philistines occupied David's hometown of Bethlehem. Many outcasts and misfits had drifted into the hills and rallied around David. These men were completely loyal to David and became a powerful guerilla militia. One day, David was thinking out loud. He remarked longingly, *"Oh, how I would love some of that good water from the well by the gate in Bethlehem"* (1 Chronicles 11:17). It was a nostalgic wish. But some of his loyal followers decided to act on it.

Three unnamed men risked their lives, slipped through the Philistine lines, drew some of the favoured water from Bethlehem's well, and returned it to David. It was a perilous act of intense devotion. It was driven by passion for their beloved leader. David quickly recognized the risk for what it was. Instead of drinking the water, he poured it out as an offering to the Lord. He said, *"This water is as precious as the blood of these men who risked their lives to bring it to me"* (1 Chronicles 11:19). He recognized his unworthiness of their passionate devotion and re-designated the gift as an act of passionate devotion to his God. This is how passionate people think and act.

Living with Heart

Dean Karnazes was raising awareness for organ donation when he ran *The Relay*. *The Relay* is a 199-mile footrace that begins in Calistoga, CA, crosses the Golden Gate Bridge and ends in Santa Cruz. As the name suggests, it is run by relay teams of 12 runners each. Dean decided to tackle the entire 199 miles by himself. A one-man team. Team Dean. The most difficult leg of the race was the last four to seven miles. His legs were swollen and heavy. Every step got harder. Yet he completed the last mile of the race in less than six minutes. What kept him going? Dean tells us. "Immerse yourself in something deeply and with heartfelt intensity."[5] "The human body has limitations; the human spirit is boundless. I didn't need a wristwatch to set the pace; I needed to run with my heart."[6] Passionate, heartfelt intensity kept him going. There are times when you can no longer run with the legs; so you must run with the heart.

It's the same heartfelt intensity that drives a true artist to paint pictures. The motive is not to sell pictures. The motive is to create a picture that captures the beauty and inspiration of a mountain or a lake. A true musician plays an instrument or sings a song, not just to perform, but because he or she is inspired by the music and wants to inspire others. That is where the fulfillment lies. It's skill *and passion* that make great painters, musicians, runners, and people.

Few people were ever more passionate than the apostle Paul. *"My life is worth nothing to me unless I use it for finishing the work assigned to me by the Lord Jesus—the work of telling others the Good News about the wonderful grace of God"* (Acts 20:24). *"I focus on this one thing ... looking forward to what lies ahead, I press on to reach the end of the race"*

(Philippians 3:13–14). He wrote to the church in Corinth, "*I will gladly spend myself and all I have for you*" (2 Corinthians 12:15). On the last of his three missionary journeys, Paul stated his eagerness to go to Spain to take the Good News to the people there. Twice he wrote to the Romans that he planned to visit them on his way to Spain. In Paul's day, Spain was off the map. Even in his later years, his dreams took him off the map. That's passion.

"*I work and struggle so hard, depending on Christ's mighty power that works within me*" (Colossians 1:29). The word *struggle* is the word *agonizomai*. You can immediately recognize the word *agony*, the same word Paul used for *race*. The words *race* and *struggle* stem from the same root and refer to a long, hard distance run with all of its exertion against obstacles and pain. Paul's struggle is supported by two strong arms. One is the arm of Christ undergirding him and strengthening him from within. When the mighty power and passion of God gets inside you, anything is possible. The other arm is the pursuit of a passion. A passion for making Christ known to everyone and bringing them into a wonderful, mature relationship with Christ (Colossians 1:28).

Passion and purpose are inseparable. Passion drives purpose, and purpose fans passion. The pursuit of passion embraces the pursuit of an overriding purpose that surpasses every setback and obstacle in your life and gives you a reason, not only to keep going, but also to excel. It gives you a reason to live and a reason to die. You feel so strongly about it that it is the driving force for your life. For the apostle Paul, this supreme passion and purpose was summed up in Christ and making Christ known. This should be the overriding passion and purpose for every Christian. Once your overriding purpose and passion is settled, that passion will filter into every crevice of your life. It will influence how you view life and impact how you live life.

While an overriding passion and purpose for your life is extremely significant, God created you a living soul, meaning that passion is part of who you are. There are things that grow out of your passionate being. Things that bring sparkle to your eyes. When it comes to your life's career or work, you will find much greater fulfillment choosing what you are passionate about over what you are good at. If proficiency and passion are the same thing, that is a bonus. For many people, however, circumstances do not afford them to make that choice. You may be filling your days working at a job that is neither your passion nor your skill level. In fact, it is mundane, difficult, and maybe even oppressive. How can you experience any kind of passion in these circumstances? The Bible has an answer for that.

The apostle Paul addressed slaves who had become believers in Christ and were part of the church at Colosse. Now, no one would enjoy being a slave. No one says when I grow up, I want to be a slave. That's hard, thankless, demanding work. So Paul gave them a reason to feel passionate about the worst job in the world. *"Work willingly at whatever you do, as though you were working for the Lord rather than for people. Remember that the Lord will give you an inheritance as your reward, and that the Master you are serving is Christ"* (Colossians 3:23–24, emphasis added). He takes them back to their overriding purpose for life. Christ and making Christ known. Remember that whatever you do, you are really working for Christ in this life. He is taking note of your faithfulness and He will pay you good wages one day. Centre your heart on Him. Make Him known to others, right where you are, by the way you work and live. Be a bright light in a depressing place. When Christ is your focus, He will make you passionate about even the worst job in the world.

Many things in my life fan the flames of passion. Things that light up my life. Family. Friends. I am passionate about helping people with daily deeds of kindness. Every week, I look for small ways to bless others. Several weeks ago, I saw a couple trying to get a new mattress into their van. The woman was struggling on her end and the mattress dropped. I pulled my vehicle over and asked if I could help. They were amazed that someone would stop, and I was blessed. Soon after, I saw a small piece of paper blow out of a woman's fingers. She tried to retrieve it but the wind took it up over a hill and away. She looked distraught. I ran over and asked her if she needed the paper. "Yes," she cried, "it had an important email address on it!" I told her I would try to recover it. I knew it was a long shot. But off I drove. I drove through the expansive parking lot of the mall and across a road. I had never before stopped to actually take note of the myriad number of small pieces of paper blowing in the wind across a mall parking lot at any given moment. Which one should I chase? I saw one particular yellow fragment of paper blowing up a hill and thought, "Could it be?" Hardly. I chased it and would you believe it … a scrap of lined paper with an email address scribbled on it. The woman was overwhelmed and I was blessed. Those kinds of small things fill my passion tank.

Something else that fans the flames of passion in my life is to feel that God has used me to speak into the life of another human being. Whether it is preaching and teaching God's Word, leading a couples' retreat or sitting down face to face with an individual, it stirs my passion for life. While I sit with my computer on my lap writing this chapter, I am seven floors up, looking out over the ocean and breathing in the salt air. Just below me is a small park. On one particular bench sleeps a homeless man. He has been there much of the week. He is very thin, unkempt, and scruffy. He has worn the same old plaid jacket and brown pants for the last five days. He removes his boots to sleep and his feet are kept warm by a pair of grey wool socks. On his head is a ball cap over which he pulls an old knit hat for warmth. Every morning he positions the cap on his head in a very precise and intentional manner. Everything he owns is inside two plastic bags into which he reaches and pulls out a banana or apple he found discarded at the back of a grocery store. People walk past him all day, staring at the undesirable neighbour. Just another mysterious, unwanted, inauspicious figure to ignore and steer clear of.

This kind of person provokes something inside of me. Just yesterday, I decided to speak to him. As I approached him, I could sense numerous eyes watching me from the balconies above. But I kept going. His head was bent downward. I didn't want to startle him. I shuffled my feet a little to warn him of my intrusion into his space, and introduced myself.

"Hello," I said. "My name is David. What's your name?" I stuck out my hand toward him to shake hands.

He looked at me apprehensively, and then shook my hand. "My name is John," he responded.

I told him that I had walked past him many times, and felt guilty that I had not come over to him to say hello. After a few moments of preamble as we got more comfortable with each other, I asked him if he had ever had dreams as a young man. I saw a slight sparkle in his eyes as he replied, "Oh, yes." He went on to tell me how he had attended a Lutheran University and had a degree in philosophy and history. He had dreamed of becoming a teacher.

"So what happened?" I asked.

"What happened was the Vietnam War," he responded. "I was drafted into the army but could not fathom myself going thousands of miles away to shoot somebody that I had never met." He continued to tell a story of how he was imprisoned for his refusal to go. The tears began to stream down his cheeks. It was easy to tell that some very deep emotions lay buried inside. He made it clear that he didn't want to talk about it.

I moved closer cautiously. "Were you treated badly in prison?" I asked. He nodded. "Were you treated *very* badly in prison?" I continued.

He nodded again. The tears continued to well up in his eyes. "I would rather not talk about it," he repeated.

Whatever had happened to him inside the walls of the prison had so messed with his mind that when he was released, he never recovered. He retreated from life and lived on the streets for the next 45 years.

There was an awkward silence as I searched for something to say. It was then that God gave me the words: "John, you and Jesus have something in common."

That got his attention. He looked up and responded, "I've never heard anything like that. How's that?"

I answered, "Jesus was also homeless. He said that the foxes had dens and the birds had nests, but that He had no place to rest His head. He lived on the streets and in the fields. And do you know why, John?"

He didn't speak, but his eyes sought an answer. "Jesus gave up heaven where He had everything … to walk the roads of this earth with nothing … so that you, with nothing … could have everything in heaven with Him one day. He even gave up His life for you and me. That's how much He loved you, John. You are loved beyond what you could ever fathom."

There was a long period of quiet. Finally, John broke the silence. It took him a long time to say it, but he spoke with deep gratitude and introspection. "Thank you, David … I needed to hear that … I needed to hear that … thanks for taking the time with me … to speak to me … thank you."

We parted ways. He laced up his boots, shook my hand and strolled off with his two plastic bags. I don't know where he went. But I know that when I returned to my computer, I was pumped. Few things will better infuse you with passion than pouring friendship and love into someone's life. You sense that God led you to speak into someone's heart … someone who needed to hear from Him, and you were the one He used. You find yourself running with a full heart.

I fan the flames of passion in many ways. Reading. Writing. Studying biblical archaeology and history. Travelling in the lands of the Bible. Reading the stories of people and places in North American history between the period of 1754 and 1885. Setting out across a field or winding down a back road to discover and explore the sites that I read about. These are things that may do nothing for you. But that's okay. They do something for me. There are things that will work for you. Things that bring colour and fervour to your life. Begin by listing your interests in life. Cultivate these interests. You may discover that they fan the flames of passion. It might be music. Painting. Bird watching. Hiking. Fishing. Crafts. Cabinet-making. Building an ancestry tree. Or, of course, running. You name it. What works for you? Do it.

WHEN GOD GETS INTO YOU

There is an old Puritan prayer: "Lord, keep us from trafficking in unfelt truth." God didn't just save the world; He so *loved* the world that He gave His Son. Truth is accompanied by the deepest of emotion. Paul wrote, *"speak the truth in love"* (Ephesians 4:15). You can destroy someone with the truth. That is unfelt truth. Speak it, live it, and manifest it in a loving, compassionate way.

Lord, keep us from trafficking in unfelt *anything*. Compassion means to be filled with passion. When Jesus saw the crowds of people wandering about like sheep without a shepherd, we read that He was filled with *compassion*. Are we? When you give, don't give reluctantly or in response to pressure. *"For God loves a person who gives cheerfully"*

(2 Corinthians 9:7, emphasis added). The word *cheerfully* is the word *hilarion* in the Greek, from which comes our word *hilarious*. So we could call this hilarious giving. It is the kind of giving that is not motivated by pressure, but by excitement and passion. Paul exhorted God-focused, passionate living when he wrote, *"Always be full of joy in the Lord. I say it again—rejoice!"* (Philippians 4:4). *"Work hard and serve the Lord enthusiastically"* (Romans 12:11, emphasis added). That could also read, *let the Spirit excite you*. Enthusiasm means to *be filled with God*. God gets into you. And when God gets into you, life takes on a whole new meaning.

We must be careful to distinguish a passionate person from a person who is merely high-energy or overly busy. Or from someone who is optimistic, upbeat, or happy, happy, happy all the time. Neither is passion a denial or minimizing of reality in favour of a flight into fantasy. Passion is something God's Spirit plants within you. It is His life flowing in you. Jesus said that if anyone comes to Him, *"rivers of living water will flow from his heart"* (John 7:38). He was speaking of the abundant, bubbling, satisfying life of the Holy Spirit within you. I see passion here. Passion pours out of a sense of eternal purpose and a faith that distinguishes the bigger picture from the smaller, immediate one. It focuses on a God who is in control of the whole picture. This passion drives you to endure any circumstance with hope and joy because you know your life is in His hands.

I believe this is key to understanding the phenomena of why so many Christians over the centuries were able to accept and endure incredible suffering for their faith with such peace and even enthusiasm. The writer of Hebrews said that many were jeered at, whipped mercilessly, chained in prisons, stoned, cut in half with saws, and tortured in revolting ways. They endured such tortures, *"refusing to turn from God in order to be set free. They placed their hope in a better life after the resurrection"* (Hebrews 11:35–37).

Eusebius of Caesarea (c. AD 260–339) was a witness to the severe persecutions under the Emperor Diocletian and documented many of the deaths of martyrs in his *Church History*. Many recanted their confession of Christ to save their lives. I understand that. What I less comprehend is how many others not only stepped up to the plate, or should I say the torture rack, but did so with eagerness. He tells of an imperial servant named Peter, who refused to sacrifice a pinch of incense to the image of Caesar. "He was hoisted up naked and lashed with whips until he should give in. Since even this failed to bend him, they mixed salt with vinegar and poured it over the lacerations of his body where the bones were already protruding. When he scorned these agonies too, a lit brazier was applied, and the rest of his body was roasted by the fire ... little by little. Still he clung immovably to his purpose and expired *triumphantly* in the middle of his tortures" (emphasis added).[7] He writes about men and women being threatened with being roasted in the fires, "leaping on the pyre with *divine enthusiasm*" (emphasis added).[8]

Eusebius writes about how men, women, and small children were scraped to death with pottery shards, racked, ruthlessly whipped, dragged through the streets with ropes and metal hooks, given to the flames, roasted on hot gridirons or the iron chair, torn apart by wild bears, panthers, boars and lions, drowned, beheaded, crucified, even crucified head downward and kept alive until they died of hunger on the cross. Martyr's legs were fastened to the strong branches of separate trees that were bent down and released to tear the victim apart by the limbs. Amazingly, Eusebius gives an eyewitness account that he "observed a marvelous *eagerness* and a divine power and *enthusiasm* in those who placed their faith in Christ: as soon as the first was sentenced, others would jump up on the tribunal in front of the judge and confess themselves Christians ... they received their final sentence of death with *joy, laughter, and gladness, singing hymns of thanksgiving to God* until their last breath" (emphasis added).[9] True God-inspired passion enthuses people with courage and perseverance. It will support you through the worst times in your life. It gives you something to live for and to die for.

Historically, enthusiasm has been viewed as suspect by traditionalism, formalism, and controlled religion. The Anabaptists of the 16th century were a counter-cultural movement and were persecuted by the established church, both Catholic and Protestant. One of the primary reasons was their enthusiasm for their faith. They believed that if you were truly a believer in Christ, it should impact the way you lived your life. Faith changed culture, altered long-held practices, and transformed lives. Their passion for Christ caused them to live out their faith in public and made them willing to lay down their lives by the thousands. Between the years 1525 and 1535, more than 50,000 laid down their lives for their faith. Women were drowned and men were burned at the stake.

In the 1700s, the preaching of John Wesley brought revitalization to a faith that had grown stale and cold. An infectious enthusiasm ignited in people's hearts as *The Great Awakening* spread like fire across Britain and the British North American colonies. John Wesley grew up in a staunchly religious home, the son of a high-church parish priest. When John and his brother, Charles, attended Oxford University, they became devoted followers of Jesus Christ. Their intense devotion attracted other students such as George Whitefield, who would become the great preacher and revivalist in the Americas. A group soon gathered regularly to study the Scriptures, pray, and hold each other accountable for living holy lives. They were derisively labeled "the holy club," "the Bible moths" and "the Methodists."

The Church of England was suspicious of such radical and passionate faith. Parish pulpits were closed to John Wesley. So he began to preach in the out-of-doors. Masses of Britain's dispossessed … coal miners, maids, farmers, factory workers, sailors, and fishermen … gathered outside the towns and villages to listen to the novel preacher deliver heart-stirring messages. Without the assistance of a loudspeaker system, Wesley preached to crowds of up to 20,000 people. When criticized for preaching in other men's parishes, he responded that he looked upon the whole world as his parish. He described himself as someone who was set on fire and that people came to watch him burn. Wesley's enthusiasm was ignited by the love of God. He was overwhelmed by the love God had shown in sending His Son, Jesus, to this earth for him. He was in love with God. And if you've ever been truly in love with someone, you don't need to be told what passion is. Wesley's passion defined the faith of the people called Methodists. Passion distinguished their preaching and their singing. John's younger brother, Charles, was a prolific songwriter and published the words for more than 6,000 songs, setting the lyrics to popular tunes. The followers of Wesley were organized into local groups or classes, each with a leader. They met weekly to encourage one another and advance spiritual growth and holy living. The Church of England looked upon these new *Methodists* with distain as dangerous "enthusiasts." Such enthusiasm was discouraged. Written on one vicar's tombstone in England is the eulogy: "He faithfully performed his task *without* enthusiasm." These words were meant to convey a positive commentary on the way the vicar carried out God's work. But how can that be? How can one serve the living God without enthusiasm? How can one love God without enthusiasm? As I said, enthusiasm means to be filled with God. An enthusiastic person is somebody God gets into. And when God gets into you, you can never be the same again. You will run your race for Christ *with* enthusiasm.

Joe Louis, the famous boxer, is attributed with saying, "You only live once, but if you work it right, once is enough."[10] Live like once is enough. Run with the heart.

FOURTEEN

RUNNING ON EMPTY

I GOT THE TITLE FOR THIS CHAPTER FROM A BOOK BY THE SAME TITLE written by Marshall Ulrich, whom I have already introduced. Ulrich ran across America at the age of 57 and by doing so sealed his distinction as one of America's greatest distance runners. But he has much more on his record of achievements. He has run the infamous Badwater Ultramarathon multiple times. He celebrated his 50th birthday in 2001 by running across Death Valley four times in succession for a total of nearly 600 miles. That was followed in his 50s by climbing the world's Seven Summits, including Mount Everest. He climbed all of them successfully on the first attempt. He celebrated his 60th birthday by running Badwater again and then headed to the Alps where he scaled five peaks over 4,000 metres (13,000 feet). There is no doubt that Ulrich has experience with running on empty while finding a way to rejuvenate and go beyond the limits.

Even as you read the chapter title, you probably said to yourself, "That's me ... I've been there." In fact, all too often we seem to be running on empty. Physically. Emotionally. Spiritually. You can't run on empty for too long if you don't find a way to refuel. It's no different from your car. People are forced to stop because they become exhausted due to running too hard, too long and too far without sufficient fuel. They live so hard that they burn out and have to quit. Distance runners sometimes battle the problem of hallucinations. They begin jumping over boxes of chocolates (actually, rocks). Trees and shrubs appear to them as animals lurking on the sides of the trail. It's time to stop!

Earlier, I told the story of Ferg Hawke's run at Badwater. Running 217 kilometres (135 miles) in brain-boiling temperatures of up to 54 degrees Celsius (130 degrees Fahrenheit) where you can collapse onto the pavement and lie there unable to get up. You are cooked. Entirely spent. Comatose. Finishing the race is a distant, despairingly forlorn hope. And then there is the problem of injury. In that same race, Ray Zahab was forced to drop out when he experienced severe pain in his muscles and kidneys and he was peeing what looked like coffee.

The above reasons for stopping are reactive. But there are proactive reasons for stopping. We all need to stop from time to time to restore ourselves, or to prevent ourselves from burning out or suffering injury. Running across Badwater in temperatures severe enough to bake your brain, it may become necessary to stop and fall into a giant ice-filled cooler for a few minutes to bring your body temperature down. There are times to stop and take a breather. To stop and rest. To stop and eat. To stop going so that you can keep going. That's what I want to focus on in this chapter.

The race of life has its own set of challenges that can reduce one's tank to empty. Physical setbacks. Financial difficulties. Relational issues. Busyness without intention. Addiction to a task list. Hard work and commitment that seem to yield little fruit. We feel like we are trying to pull a wagon with square wheels, full of stuff, uphill. We cry, "What's the use?" We experience failures that expose our pride, self-centredness, self-interest, and utter inability to run the race in our own strength. Spiritual dryness. A sense of weakening aloneness. Unanswered prayer. Purpose without passion. Passion without purpose. We lose sight of our priorities.

As a pastor, I am amazed at the number of people to whom I give pastoral counsel who suffer from debilitating work-related stress. They are running on empty due to work overload, time pressures, role ambiguity, lack of job security, impeded ambition, conflict with the boss or co-workers. They receive little approval. They feel powerless and unfulfilled at work. Burnout is rampant. Growing numbers of good people are feeling physical and emotional exhaustion because they have low job satisfaction.

Many people in the helping professions, including many of my own pastoral colleagues, suffer from a condition that has been labeled as *compassion fatigue*. "Compassion fatigue refers to the profound emotional and physical erosion that takes place when helpers are unable to refuel and regenerate."[1] This occurs when you care for others without caring for yourself. You become preoccupied with filling the emotional tanks of others and fail to fill your own emotional tank. Soon, you find yourself laid aside in life's infirmary with such symptoms as anger, depression, apathy, isolation, moral failure, or substance abuse.

This kind of erosion and trauma can begin to define who you are if you don't find a way to move on. You need to find an oasis in the desert. A water source and some shade.

An Oasis

You'll remember the previous story of Ray Zahab's run across the Sahara Desert. It was Day 63, with 3,761 kilometres behind them. Ray was feeling weak and doubting himself. He was sore, exhausted, and the left side of his brain was shouting, "Stop!" But he kept going, running one step at a time. Just one step at a time.

Then they arrived at a little town called Fachi in Niger. Fachi was an oasis. Palm trees. Shade. Water. Mud huts. A community of welcoming desert-dwellers. The villagers ran out to greet them in their brightly-coloured clothing. Scores of children came streaming out of their mud huts and began to run alongside. Ray felt like the Pied Piper. The further he ran, the more children he collected. They seemed to be coming out of nowhere and everywhere. They grabbed hold of his hands and soon he was running along with strings of children cheering and singing. He entered Fachi tired, worn out, and empty. For just a few minutes. But what a difference a few minutes can make in the right place and space. A community came together. Refreshing water from the well and cooling shade from the palms. The exhilarating cheers and songs of children. People who had so little, but had given so much. He left Fachi feeling healed, energized, and refueled.

Matt Damon, the narrator and executive producer of the film, *Running the Sahara,* was quoted regarding this experience at Fachi: "When all hope seems to evaporate in the desert sun, there is the renewal of the spirit, the oasis, like a stepping-stone across the desert, drawing people for miles and for days, to its life-giving water."[2] When you are in a race, you don't live at the oasis. You run in the desert. The oasis is, as Damon describes, like a stepping-stone that your foot rests upon for a few minutes in time and space. And then you are on to the next stepping-stone. You receive what it gives. Renewal. Refreshment. Restoration. And then on and out into the desert again.

One day, Jesus took three of His disciples, Peter, James, and John up onto a high mountain. As they climbed, suddenly His appearance was transformed. His face and clothing began to shine as bright as the sun. And then two men, Moses and Elijah, long dead, appeared and began conversing with Jesus. The disciples were stunned. It was like the curtain that separated heaven from earth had been rolled up. This was a spiritually rejuvenating, refocusing, refreshing, renewing time for both Jesus and His disciples. The kind of place and space that you would like to linger in. But that was not to be. At least, not yet. There was still earth to walk. A cross to carry. The experience was like a spiritual oasis in the desert. Before long, it was over and Jesus and His three friends were on their way back down the mountain to confront the realities of life.

SHADE

The Wadi Rum is a deceptively beautiful desert in southern Jordan. Its moonlike landscape and high rolling hills of sand can easily lure the unsuspecting hiker into its lethal snare. Its overwhelming splendour is soon eclipsed by its suffocating heat as the sun rises over the mountain peaks and stares down upon you. Four of us were hiking in the early morning. We were doing some exploring and looking for a Bedouin camp where a young shepherdess, whom we had met the evening before, had led her flock of sheep and goats. We were making our way up the steep slope of a high sand dune. The heat intensified as we climbed higher. My wife, Diane, began to feel weak and shivery, and her breathing was becoming noticeably more rapid. We feared sunstroke and needed

213

to find shade as quickly as possible. There was a small broom tree close by, so we made our way over to it and crouched down under the shelter of its branches, and drank some cool water. A refreshing refuge in a sea of heat.

It reminded me of the story in the Bible when Hagar wandered with her son aimlessly in the wilderness of Beersheba. One does not wander long without water. And soon her water was gone. The relentless sun, debilitating heat and lack of water spelled certain death for both of them. She knew her son was dying and didn't want to watch him die. So she put him in the shade of a bush, walked a short distance away and burst into tears. God heard her cry and opened her eyes to a well full of water. What God led her to was probably an oasis. An oasis was a place where she could find water and shade for her and her son. And it meant the difference between life and death. *"She quickly filled her water container and gave the boy a drink"* (Genesis 21:19).

The Bible portrays God as our oasis. Our source of shade and water. When the relentless trials beat down upon you, the debilitating heat of life's adversity saps your emotional strength, and the lack of relief threatens to drain you of hope, these words hold true: *"The Lord himself watches over you! The Lord stands beside you as your protective shade"* (Psalm 121:5). The psalmist cried out to God, *"My soul thirsts for you … in a parched and weary land where there is no water. … I sing for joy in the shadow of your wings"* (Psalm 63:1, 7). The psalmist, David, knew what it was like to find sanctuary in places like Engedi. An oasis. But oases are located in the desert, places of refuge, just enough to rejuvenate you for the journey through the desert. Stepping-stones of refreshment and restoration.

The prophet Isaiah likened God to *"streams of water in the desert and the shadow of a great rock in a parched land"* (Isaiah 32:2). His presence is like cold spring water bubbling up under the shade of a broom tree or the shadow of an overhanging rock. You fill your water container and sit in the shade for just a few minutes' reprieve. The sun keeps moving so the shade keeps shifting. So you sit in the shade of God's presence and provision just long enough to fill your emotional and spiritual tank. The reality of life is that we don't live in the shade. Our course runs along desert paths against relentless winds of adversity and under the debilitating heat of harsh conditions. But along the way God provides places and people, spiritual disciplines, and reminders of His care for us. Just enough to inspire you to keep going to the next oasis. The next well. The next broom tree. The next shadow under a great rock. God is God of the desert. That's where He is most visible, observable, and evident.

The revivalist John Wesley, whom I introduced in the previous chapter, prepared and preached countless messages. He organized his followers into numerous groups or classes, each with leaders to teach and encourage holy living. He was a life-long scholar, wrote treatises, tracts, and letters. He established schools for England's underclass, intentionally helped the poor, opposed the slave trade and worked for social and political reform in Britain. And he did it all with relentless energy, passion, love, and deep serenity of being. How was this possible?

Wesley attributed this to hours of solitude on the road. An accurate image of Wesley is the silhouette of a man riding horseback through a wooded pathway, head down, book in hand, travelling from place to place. This became the trademark of preachers in the American colonies and Canada, mounted riders trotting along the trails following preaching circuits, to minister and preach to their scattered church communities. They became known as circuit riders. Wesley used those times of riding the circuit as a time of solitude. He was alone with God, a book … and his horse. That was his oasis. A stepping-stone to the next preaching engagement.

The oasis is a place where you become reacquainted with two persons. Two persons from whom you can begin to feel isolated in the midst of life's demands and responsibilities. But two persons who are essential to the quality of your existence. Let's talk about them for a moment.

GETTING REACQUAINTED WITH GOD

It is striking when you read the creation narrative, that God didn't create everything all at once with one word. He could have. Rather, He spread it out over six days. Then the narrative reads, *"On the seventh day God had finished his work of creation, so he rested"* (Genesis 2:2, emphasis added). Now that doesn't mean God was so tired that He had to lie down and take a break. It doesn't mean He was burnt out. It doesn't mean that He sighed, "Thank me, it's Friday!" No. He was Almighty God. So, what does it mean? What was God establishing so early on?

I believe God was establishing a pattern or a rhythm for people created in His image. The word *rested* means to "stop." God was finished His work, so He stopped. God then took the seventh day, a unit of time, and called it *holy* (Genesis 2:3). This unit of time was considered set apart from the rest of the week. Set apart for God. Meaning, we are to establish a rhythm in our lives when we stop what we are doing and refocus our thoughts on God. When we reorient our lives around the living God. Unlike God, we get tired. We overextend ourselves. We burn out. The stresses and the stuff of life have a way of dividing our attention, depleting our energy, and isolating us from the Source of our strength. We need to get reacquainted with our Source of life.

The Israelites had been slaves in Egypt for hundreds of years. Working and toiling was ingrained into them. They were addicted to tasks. I have heard them described as "doing machines." When God liberated them, He gave them Ten Commandments. Interestingly, the commandment God spent the most time addressing was Commandment #4. *"Remember to observe the Sabbath day by keeping it holy."* He explained that they had six days to work, but the seventh day was *"a Sabbath day of rest dedicated to the Lord your God."* The word *Sabbath* comes from the Hebrew word to "stop." He then rooted this command in creation and the rhythm that God had established in the beginning (Exodus 20:8–11). My purpose here is not to debate the particular day or what activities should be done or not done on that particular day. My purpose is to remind us that God established at creation and confirmed in His commandments at Sinai a rhythm of work and rest. We need to establish regular time-outs when we cease from our everyday activities, responsibilities, and demands, and get reacquainted with our Creator and our Source of strength.

Years ago, when I was a teenager working on the farm, the summer months were haying season. We woke before daybreak and worked until it was too dark to see. Baling hay was the order of the day. Every day. I grabbed each bale by the twine as it dropped from the baler, and learned to stack a hay wagon with a high, sturdy load of hay. No sooner had I thrown a bale into place when the next one dropped from the baler. Sometimes the baler seemed to spit out bales faster than I could swing them into place. The sweat rolled down my face and back while the dust in the air stuck to my skin. A gentle breeze blowing up through the valley sometimes brought a much-welcomed relief. We had just a few months to mow, rake, dry, bale, and get the hay in to the barns. Not to mention repairing machinery whenever it broke down. Most farmers worked seven days every week. But the farmer I worked for had a strong faith and believed that we should stop work for one day, give the time to God and rest. That day was Sunday. It looked foolish to some of the other farmers in the township, especially when the previous week had had lots of rain, and then the Sunday was warm and sunny. Wasn't it critical to get out and make hay while the sun shone?

This Christian farmer believed that if he set aside a day for God, God would not fail him. It was more important to be acquainted with the Father than with the fields. It was more imperative to be connected with the Provider than with the provisions. He often brought the subject up at day's end as we leaned up against a tractor tire chewing on the end of a blade of sweet grass. Every Sabbath reminds us to *"be still, and know that [he is] God"* (Psalm 46:10). We don't need to worry about tomorrow. If we put the Kingdom of God above everything else and live righteously, God will provide everything we need (Matthew 6:31–34). He believed that the Provider would provide and bless. And God always did. There was never a year when we failed to get all the hay into the barns. They were always full. These faithful men succeeded in all they put their hands to. And Monday morning, at daybreak, we always felt replenished and ready for another week of hard work. Receiving a day from God, for God, honours God, and is good for you.

Embedded into the rhythm of rest is the faith to believe that when I take a break from the wheel of my life, my life won't run off the road, because God is in the driver's seat. The Israelites had not been very long in the wilderness after leaving Egypt when they ran out of food and water. God responded to their prayers, or should I say complaining, by a miraculous provision. I've mentioned this story before, but it is worth briefly repeating. In the morning, when they awoke, there was

RUN! THE AMAZING RACE

something that looked like frost all over the ground. Everyone was asking, "What is it?" No one knew. So that's what they named it ... "Manna," the Hebrew word for "What is it?" It tasted sweet and proved great for mixing up honey-tasting pancakes or baking bread. Every night was a different manna casserole.

But as you know from earlier, there was a deal. They were to gather only enough to meet their needs for that one particular day. Any excess would turn from manna marvel to maggot meal. Except on Friday. There was an exception to the rule. On Friday, they were to gather enough for two days. Why? Because the next day was a day of complete rest, a holy Sabbath day set apart for God. Time off for God. They needed to gather manna on the Friday and trust God for the Saturday. There were two reasons for the Sabbath. It gave everyone, including the working animals, a chance to rest and be refreshed. Secondly it was recognition that when you stop taking care of busyness, God doesn't stop taking care of you. In fact, it is recognition that God is your Provider and the Source of your life, *every* day.

The principle of rest was particularly and remarkably demonstrated every seventh year when the Israelites were commanded by God to give the land a complete rest. No one was to work the fields. Now this would be good for the land and the people. This was wise management of the soil. But there would be no crops growing in the fields. Think about that. The economy of Israel depended upon agriculture. Can you imagine the government shutting down all the factories, oil refineries, and gas stations in our country for one year? Can you envision what that would mean? Yes, God was teaching Israel something about wise management of their natural resources and human welfare. But there was something even more significant being taught here. God promised that He would provide. Could they trust Him to provide through something that so jeopardized the entire economy? The reason for getting into the rhythm of work and rest is to remember that God is the Provider. The rhythm reorients your life around Him. Jesus said, *"Don't worry about these things, saying, 'What will we eat? What will we drink? What will we wear?' These things dominate the thoughts of unbelievers, but your heavenly Father already knows all your needs"* (Matthew 6:31–32).

218

The memory is "frozen" in my mind of waiting for the school bus on many cold winter mornings at the end of a long icy laneway. Some days, the wind bit into our faces, the snow swirled, and we stood stationary like one of the fence posts lining the road. Watching. Waiting. Hoping … that this was one of those days when the bus didn't show. Our only motion was periodically sneaking a glance at a wristwatch. After an hour of waiting, with no bus showing, we would run back up the lane. Our bones quickly thawed. Our minds grew alert. Our spirits revived. We had a snow day! A break. A stop in the school routine. A Sabbath. I like how Peter Scazzero puts it: "Sabbath is like receiving the gift of a heavy snow day every week. Stores are closed. Roads are impassable. Suddenly you have the gift of a day to do whatever you want. You don't have any obligations, pressures, or responsibilities. You have permission to play, be with friends, take a nap, read a good book. Few of us would give ourselves a 'no obligation day' very often."[3] God gives you 52 snow days every year. Wow! And I believe that if you would take those gift days, you would soon find yourself assimilating that same spirit into every day.

GETTING REACQUAINTED WITH YOURSELF

The other person you can lose in the treadmill of daily life is yourself. It is so easy to fill your time and empty your spirit. To be so occupied with *doing* that you fail to practice just *being*. As I noted in a previous chapter, you can be so occupied with yesterday and tomorrow that you forget to live today. This moment is your most important moment. Yesterday has gone and cannot be retrieved. Tomorrow does not yet exist. Time cannot be rushed. Wishing for the dawn will not bring it any faster. But you have this day. This moment. "This is the day the Lord has made … be glad in it" (Psalm 118:24). It is important to live this moment mindfully.

> The best solution seems to be reacquainting yourself with your own 'beingness'—that quiet part of yourself that exists independent of your busyness, goals, and responsibilities. This is the part of you that feels satisfied simply because it exists— rather than because it is accomplishing yet another task.[4]

I'm not talking about putting your mind into a state of emptiness. That is why I say we should live this moment *mindfully*. I'm not suggesting you withdraw to a monastic lifestyle of isolation from reality. I'm not suggesting you spend your days just sitting around. I'm not saying you should renege on your responsibilities and obligations. It is unrealistic to deny that demands, stress, concerns, and burdens are part of life. It is naïve to think you can totally separate yourself from the expectations of other people. But, in the midst of all of this, you need to intentionally and mindfully get reacquainted with yourself.

From time to time, experiment with doing *nothing*. Yes—nothing. Give yourself time to reflect upon what God fashioned when He formed you. Celebrate the miracle of being alive and breathing. I love the way that our little four-year-old granddaughter, Mackenzie, begins every prayer: "Dear God, thank you for my life." It's this kind of marvel many of us have lost in our adult busyness. It is a childlike enthusiasm for life that can be reclaimed, however, by allowing yourself to become more conscious of your "beingness."

Be intentional to loosen the bowstring of your mind. Any archer knows the string cannot remain tight for very long or else the bow will lose its rebounding quality. Relax the bowstring of your mind so that your being will have rebounding power when it needs it. Find a release from the daily routine and tension. Get in touch with yourself. You may need to take an extended vacation, go for a long walk, or just sit down alone for 10 minutes with a cup of coffee, and think about … nothing. Just "be."

In his book entitled *Leadership,* Rudolph Giuliani details extremely insightful principles for effective leadership he learned and demonstrated throughout his years as mayor of New York City and during the September 11 attacks on the World Trade Center. It is a resource worth reading by any person in a leadership role. One's interest is quickly captivated by his narration of personal stories that take you through the days of a crisis that changed the face of America.

I was particularly moved by a story he told of the days immediately following the catastrophic attack. One can barely imagine the pressure weighing upon a leader of a city that had just endured such a disaster and been shattered to its core. September 12. Giuliani appeared on the *Today* show to reassure the country that New York City was still here. Every minute of the day filled with coordinating rescue efforts, phone calls, interviews, and meetings. He moved from meeting to meeting with deputy mayors, commissioners, city administrators, military spokespersons, police and fire officials, federal and state government officials, business executives, and the media. Decisions had to be made. Immediate decisions that had high impact on peoples' lives, while still in the fog of what had really happened and whether or not there was more to come. Just the day before, Giuliani had coordinated the evacuation of 25,000 people from the Trade Center, one of the greatest rescue operations in history. Now he faced the task of rescuing any people from the rubble that might still be alive. Recovering the bodies of dead victims. Providing emotional support to the rescue workers who were digging up body parts everywhere. Coordinating the dispersion of information, assistance, and comfort to thousands of families. Funerals. Providing hope and security to a large city that was living in absolute shock.

After 48 hours with little sleep, Giuliani sat down, took off his glasses, rubbed his eyes and cried, "The pain is just immense. The pain is unbelievable. And the worst part of this is that these people are going to live with this for the rest of their lives."[5] Everyone had been touched by this disaster. Giuliani felt their pain. The emotional pain was excruciating. And so was the physical pain. Giuliani was experiencing severe pains in his shoulder and back. His first thought was heart attack. But this must not happen. There was no time to get sick right now. He could get sick later, but not now. His wife, Judith, suggested a simple remedy. A walk. By himself. He followed her advice.

He grabbed his FDNY ball cap and, with his security detail following at a discreet distance, walked toward the East River. Thick clouds of smoke hung over the city. And a thick cloud of anguish hung over him as he thought about the challenges the city faced and the despair many families were feeling right at that moment. The river had a potent effect on him. He stared out into the water. A simple but profound thought struck him. Despite the deadly destruction that an enemy had inflicted, the river was still flowing. He stood for a moment and looked around.

221

It was as though he stepped out of himself to catch a glimpse of the big picture. And he could see his place in that picture. The water current was still moving. The city was still standing. The people were still here. Life was still going on. And he was present, in this moment of time, to be their leader. His mind began to settle. His perspective was becoming clearer. His strength was beginning to rebound.

All it took was a long walk. But that is what I mean by relaxing the bowstring so that you have rebounding power. Stepping out of the *doing* and becoming aware of your "beingness." Reacquainting yourself with who you are and why you are, in this moment of time. Being able to pray with heartfelt gratitude, "Thank you, God, for my life." Giuliani said to himself, "'I can handle this. I am handling this. This is what I know how to do. This is what I was trained to do—to take charge, to make sound, sensible decisions.' This brief half-hour of solitary meditation gave me an abiding feeling that I'd get through it. I then returned to make sure the rest of the city would as well."[6]

SOLITUDE

May I close this chapter with a word on *solitude?* Solitude is the discipline of withdrawing from people, noise, conversation, distractions, and any external stimulus for the express purpose of connecting with God, yourself, and replenishing your spirit. The length of time can vary from a few minutes every day to longer periods of time at regular intervals every year. It can be given to an activity such as prayer, or to *nothing.* It is finding a place of simplicity and ease. I specifically use the word *ease* because the lack of such is *dis-ease.* And we all know that's not good for anyone.

Jesus practiced the discipline of solitude numerous times. Sometimes the crowds and demands grew so great that there was no time to eat. After a full day of healing the sick right up until sundown, Luke recorded that, *"Early the next morning Jesus went out to an isolated place"* (Luke 4:42). Luke wrote, *"Vast crowds came to hear [Jesus] preach and to be healed of their diseases. But Jesus often withdrew to the wilderness for prayer"* (Luke 5:15–16). After Jesus' disciples returned from a busy ministry tour, He said to them, *"Let's go off by ourselves to a quiet place and rest awhile"* (Mark

6:31). After feeding 5,000-plus people, *"[Jesus] went up into the hills by himself to pray. Night fell while he was there alone"* (Matthew 14:23).

I believe this was one of the primary reasons that, despite the busyness and noise in Jesus' life, He kept loving and caring for people. Usually, busyness reduces one's capacity to love deeply and meaningfully. The two are usually essentially irreconcilable. Loving requires time, and a busy person has no time. Busyness usually breeds resentment and frustration with people because they are in our way. Jesus was able to keep loving and caring deeply because He was careful to maintain the rhythm God established in the beginning. A rhythm of work and rest. Engagement and withdrawal. He made certain that His life stayed oriented around His Father in heaven. He stayed close to His Father's heart.

I love the words of the 72-year-old black woman from Montgomery, Alabama, who, during the civil rights movement in the '60s, refused to ride segregated buses. She responded to someone who expressed amazement at her vigour in the midst of the tiring struggle: "My feet is tired, but my soul is rested." She got it! So did Jesus. And so can you.

FIFTEEN

MORE FIRE

THIS YEAR I DID SOMETHING I HAVE NEVER DONE BEFORE. I WATCHED the Boston Marathon on television. I watched because a friend of mine was participating. For most of the race, Kenyans led the way, never fading, with little discernible effort, like leopards in relentless pursuit of their prey. At the finish line, Kenyan Geoffrey Mutai shattered the course record for the Boston Marathon with a blazing 2:03:01. It was his first time running this race. Amazingly, the same thing happened in the women's race. Another Kenyan first-timer, Caroline Kilel, crossed the finish line in first place. With runners from 67 countries, Kenyans took top spots for both men and women. When asked how she felt about her win, Kilel replied, "I just came to do my best."

Her response embodies the Kenyan spirit. In his book, *More Fire,* Toby Tanser inserts a quote on the inside introductory page. It is addressed to the Runner: "Begin with having a compelling dream, burn with desire to succeed. Your watchword is discipline and your password is perseverance. More painful than stumbling, as we all must, is to have never strode out. At the end of the run, at the close of the day, you will remember not the results of a position or stopwatch, but how intensely you tried, and at what velocity you lived in your life. Run, and live, with More Fire."[1] Again, the long-distance footrace holds many parallels with the race of life. Living with More Fire embraces having a compelling dream and doing everything you can to see that dream succeed. It is staying disciplined in the quest for that dream. It means accepting the risk of striding into the unknown, experiencing the difficulty of the course, falling down and getting hurt, but getting back up and persevering forward. It means running with passion and doing the best you can with what you've been given in the pursuit of excellence.

Earlier in this book I told the story of Pheidippides, the Athenian messenger, who ran 240 kilometres (150 miles) in two days to Sparta and back to request help against the invading Persians. After a hard-fought battle on the Plains of Marathon, which became known as the Battle of Marathon, he then ran another 40K (25 miles) from the battlefield to Athens to announce the Greek victory over the Persians. After delivering the victorious message, he collapsed from exhaustion and died. Robert Browning gave his version of the story in his 1879 poem *Pheidippides*.

So, when Persia was dust, all cried, 'To Akropolis!
Run, Pheidippides, one race more! The meed is thy due!
Athens is saved, thank Pan, go shout!' He flung down his shield,
Ran like fire once more: and the space 'twixt the fennel-field
And Athens was stubble again, a field which a fire runs through,
Till in he broke: 'Rejoice, we conquer!' Like wine thro' clay,
Joy in his blood bursting his heart, he died, the bliss![2]

It was this poem that inspired the founders of the modern Olympic Games to create a footrace of 42.2 kilometres called the Marathon. But what I noted in the poem was the description of Pheidippides running from the battlefield to the city of Athens. He ran like a blazing fire, leaving only a trail of burnt stubble in his path. It is the depiction of someone running with passion and the pursuit of excellence for a cause. He ran with More Fire.

The success of the Tarahumara is due to their passion for running. They run for the pure joy of it. But what is the key to Kenyan success in the field of distance running? How does a country suffering from so much poverty and desperation turn out so many great long-distance runners? Is it their physical structure? Are their thin legs, narrow hips, and strong ankles the perfect frame for long distance running? Is it in the genes? Do they have superior cardiovascular systems? Is it that they train in high altitudes? Not really. There are other countries with high altitudes that do not produce great runners. It may be a little of everything above combined. But the master key that seems to unlock the secret is their intense drive for excellence. What they call *More Fire*.

So where does this intensity originate? Kenyans begin their lives with very little. They live in a culture of poverty and desperation. They literally run their way out of poverty. Their success in running determines their success in life. They run to survive. They run like hunters on a hunt for survival. Tanser quotes a Kenyan professor who once told him, "When Kenyans run they are hunters, they are fighting, as they did from the first day that they realized life is a fight. That is the Kenyan secret."[3] This *hunt* for survival is what drives them to the pursuit of excellence. Runners willingly leave family and home to live in a training camp in Spartan conditions, in a small hut with no comforts, electricity, or running water. They do it to become the best they can be.

Sylvia Kibet is a typical multitasking African woman, combining motherhood and home responsibilities with a profession. She is a policewoman. And an athlete. When Sylvia runs, she is described as "a leopard padding through the jungle." She has been extremely successful in her running career, especially with the shorter-distance indoor races, focusing on speed. She set national records for both the indoor 1,500-metre and 3,000-metre races. She is from a family with rich distance-running pedigree. But, despite her success, she has always lived in the shadow of her sister, Hilda Kibet, and her famous distance-running cousin, Lornah Kiplagat. Race after race, Sylvia fails to get the attention and acclamation that many of her countrywomen receive. Her response to all of this is that she will *talk with her legs*.

Sylvia Kibet continues to silence her doubters and skeptics with the speed of her legs. After qualifying for the 2008 Summer Olympics, she said, "I ran with More Fire! I was thinking, More Fire!"[4] Sylvia embraces the heart and spirit of Kenyan runners. It is all about the hunt for survival and the pursuit of excellence. Tanser writes, "Nothing comes easy is another slogan of Kenyan running, but what is achieved by pushing your own limits is life's richest reward. To collapse out on the roads with blood in your shoes knowing you gave it your best shot is reward beyond words."[5]

Right after the 1924 Paris Olympics, Eric Liddell returned home to Britain a national hero. Eric had stunned the world by his refusal to run the favoured 100-metre race on a Sunday. But he stunned the world even more later that week when he ran the 400-metre race, setting a new world record. Now, everyone's attention was focused on him. Eric stood on the front steps of St. Giles Cathedral in Edinburgh, cognizant of his success but also mindful of his many fellow athletes who had tried their hardest for Great Britain but had not returned as Olympic champions. He began by saying, "In the dust of defeat as well as the laurels of victory there is glory to be found if one has done his best."[6] He then went on for several minutes to expound on living your life that way. It's not whether you won or lost; it's whether or not you did your best. Eric lived the way he ran. Years later, confined in a Japanese prison camp as a Christian missionary, he died living that way.

The spirit of More Fire burned within Dean Karnazes in his *Run Across America*. He arrived in New York City on May 10, 2011, after running 75 days from sea to sea. He had run 3,000 miles, averaging 40 to 50 miles per day, running through all types of weather conditions. He wore out 50 pairs of shoes. When he was asked to identify the worst moment of the run, he answered instantly:

> The end of the first day. ... I was destroyed. I thought, "How am I going to do this for 74 more days?" It had been so easy to talk about it, but after that first day it hit me: the enormity of what we were about to undertake. Then I told myself, "Get up in the morning and try your best. You may or may not make it, but your commitment is to try your very hardest."[7]

That's the way to live your life. To wake up every morning and make a commitment to yourself and to God to try your very hardest and give your very best. If you live every day that way, one day you will enjoy the fulfillment of knowing you lived your life that way. You will have seized one of life's richest rewards.

MEDIOCRITY

The apostle Paul was in prison or under house arrest when he wrote, *"I press on to possess that perfection for which Christ Jesus first possessed me"* (Philippians 3:12). His legs may have been chained, but, in his imagination, every muscle strained as his feet pounded the track. He was in full stride as he turned into the last lap of the race. The race was not over. The course ran down through the prison corridors and up into Caesar's palace. It would spiral downward again onto death row and out along the Ostian Road to the place of execution. His last lap was run the way he had run his entire Christian race. With excellence. Paul was intent on possessing everything for which Christ Jesus had first possessed him.

In Latin, the word *mediocrity* means, literally, "halfway up the rock or mountain." Excellence is striving for the summit. Mediocrity is becoming satisfied with the halfway mark. Contented with a decent run but not a great run. Settling for something less than your best. Mediocrity is the enemy of excellence. There was no mediocrity about the runner, Paul. He lifted his clenched fist with the chain dangling from his wrist and avowed, *"I press on to reach the end of the race"* (Philippians 3:14).

His goal was perfection. Spiritual and moral perfection. No, he had not excelled to this point yet. One day he would reach final perfection when he crossed the finish line and arrived in heaven. Presently, he pressed on to possess it. And he seemed happy with what he had attained at this stage in the race. Let's call it *stage perfection*. Let's say that you want to run a marathon in three hours. So you place coaches with stopwatches at various distances along the course. The three-kilometre mark. The six-kilometre mark. The nine-kilometre mark. And so on. When you reach that particular point, if you are on time to complete the race in three hours, the coach yells, "Perfect!" Now, the race is not over. That is not final perfection. But for where you are in the race, you are running perfectly. That's *stage perfection*.

In Matthew 5:48, Jesus said, *"You are to be perfect, even as your Father in heaven is perfect."* Well, how can you be as perfect as God? You can't. God does not expect you to be as perfect as He is, but He does expect stage perfection. To set your goal as perfection at this stage in your race. Therefore, there can be no lingering, loitering, or lagging. Perfection demands excellence. The Christian life is to be one of stage-by-stage progress toward Christ-like perfection.

Paul admitted that there were some who disagreed with him on this (Philippians 3:15). I don't know what they were saying. Perhaps it went something like this: "I'm a Christian. I'm in the race. I'll get to heaven someday. Heaven is in the bag. What's the stress? Why overdo it?" It's an attitude that says running with mediocrity is acceptable. Good enough is good enough. Well, not according to the apostle Paul, or Jesus, or the rest of the Bible. Mediocrity is not acceptable on the Kenyan team. Neither is it acceptable on God's team. Paul exhorted, *"We must hold on to the progress we have already made"* (Philippians 3:16). Don't slacken. Don't fall back. Don't lose the ground you've taken. Press forward. With excellence. More Fire.

BEST OR BUST

Mediocrity is contempt for God's name. God told His people that they showed Him no honour or respect because they brought Him defiled sacrifices for His altar (Malachi 1:6–14). They were supposed to bring God the best of the flock to sacrifice to Him. But they brought lambs that were crippled, blind, and diseased. The animals they couldn't sell or trade at market. The leftovers. How often do we give to God our leftover time, spent energy, heartless worship, or spare change? Things that reflect our mediocre attitude toward God.

God said, *"Try giving gifts like that to your governor"* (Malachi 1:8). Try sending the government a card of sincere appreciation instead of the money to pay your taxes. Try giving your wife a box of chocolates that were on sale because the date had expired. Or a dozen roses you bought for 70 percent off because they were dying. What does that reflect about the value you place on her? And when you give to God your second best rather than your best, the leftovers rather than the first fruits, mediocrity

229

rather than excellence, you show contempt for His name. You also shoot yourself in the foot, because God refuses to accept what you give and shuts off His favour in your life (verse 9). He added, *"How I wish one of you would shut the Temple doors so that these worthless sacrifices could not be offered! I am not pleased with you"* (verse 10). God desires your best, or nothing at all. Give your best, or don't give at all. Run your best, or don't run at all. Live with More Fire, or extinguish the flame all together. He continued, *"Cursed is the cheat who promises to give a fine ram from his flock but then sacrifices a defective one to the Lord. For I am a great king"* (verse 14). God is King, and, as I noted earlier, when we run and live, we do so to declare that Jesus is King. Therefore, give Him the honour He deserves. Run! Give your all for the One who gave His all for you. And, if you won't? Quit! You dishonour His name.

My daughter, Sarah, spent some time in Zambia working with young orphans. These children lived in dire poverty in contrast to our North American standards. One day, she had the joy of passing out shoeboxes from Samaritan's Purse to the orphans. Each shoebox contained a toy, some clothing, trinkets, a toothbrush, and a bar of soap. Hundreds of children lined up, without shoving or pushing, and waited for the box that contained the only gifts they would receive all year. As each child received his or her box, Sarah witnessed something incredible. They sat down in circles and opened their boxes. Then they began to share the contents with each other. For instance, if someone lacked a toy, another would share or give away their toy to the one who lacked. If someone had two toothbrushes and someone else had none, the child with two would give to the one who had none.

This spirit of generosity became very personal the next morning when Sarah awoke and went to the door to get her pail of warm water. There was no running water in her humble abode, and so each morning a young girl would place a bucket of warm water outside her door for washing her face. This particular morning when Sarah opened the door and bent down to pick up the bucket, her eyes filled with tears. There on the ground, lying beside the bucket, was a bar of soap. Her young friend had given her the one bar of soap that she had received in her shoebox. The only bar of soap that she would personally own all year. Sarah had five or six bars stored away in her suitcase. But this young girl had given her best, even out of her poverty, to show her love and appreciation. She was a visible and poignant example of excellence.

THE BATTLE WITH COMPROMISE

Do you remember the nursery rhyme about the cat that went to London to visit the Queen?

Pussy cat, pussy cat, where have you been?
I've been to London to visit the Queen.
Pussy cat, pussy cat, what did you there?
I frightened a little mouse under her chair.

Stupid cat! He had the chance of a lifetime. He went to see London. Westminster Abbey. Big Ben. Buckingham Palace. Trafalgar Square. The Marble Arch. The Tower of London. St. Paul's Cathedral. Her Majesty the Queen. He went to see it all. Did he see it? Not this feline. He was a mouseaholic. He couldn't stop chasing mice. Even in the presence of the Queen, his mind was on mice.

I remember visiting London. If you were to ask me what I did in London and I replied, "I stayed in my hotel room, slept, and watched television. London is a great place to sleep and watch television," your jaw would drop. I'm sure you would search everywhere in your brain bank to withdraw something to say in response. But you would be found wanting. Why? Because what I had done makes no rational sense.

And yet that is precisely what many people do with their lives. God has given them the opportunity to run the most amazing race. Along canyon trails. Over mountain passes. To experience the sun setting behind the red desert buttes. Life is an amazing experience. But they are snoozing or frittering their lives away. Squandering their time. Not necessarily with bad things, but with many good things. It would be easier if it were a choice between the bad and the good. But this is a choice between the good and the best. It's a battle with compromise. It's a subtle battle because there are so many good things we can do. And we can even rationalize that they are necessary. I mean, cats eat mice. It's in the genes. And people need sleep and relaxation. It's a matter of discerning the necessary and best things I can be doing with my life at this particular time and in this particular place.

The battle with compromise is one of the reasons why the biblical character Daniel is such an important example for us. Daniel had been taken from his homeland as a Jewish captive to the foreign land of Babylon. He was strong, healthy, good-looking, and smart, and was chosen to be included in a group of young men to be re-educated and trained for three years to become elite advisors to the most powerful ruler in the world, Nebuchadnezzar. It involved rigorous training, but it came with some attractive fringe benefits. The finest food and wine available in the king's court. Now the food was good, but Daniel *"determined not to defile himself"* by eating the king's provision. Daniel made a stand. We're not told why Daniel believed the food and wine would defile him. Perhaps it wasn't kosher. It may have been offered to idols as part of pagan religious rites and Daniel wanted no part of it. It is quite probable that eating the king's food was, in that culture, a sign of friendship, allegiance, and loyalty. Perhaps Daniel didn't want to compromise his allegiance and loyalty to God. We don't know whether it was a decision between bad and good, or good and best. We do know that Daniel, for whatever reason, made up his mind that he would not compromise himself, even if it cost him his career or life.

The rule of non-compromise became a guiding principle for his life. He went on to become an influential and successful politician and prime minister in the most powerful nation of his day. His milieu was one of paganism, corruption, and sleaze. But he had determined he would never compromise his convictions even if it meant risking everything. There is no evidence in the biblical record that Daniel ever negotiated with evil or mediocrity. He lived a life of excellence in the midst of decadence. Excellence in the midst of political compromise. Intellectual excellence. Moral excellence. His entire life was characterized by excellence. When a law was decreed that no one should pray to any god except the king, Daniel knew that the decree had been treacherously premeditated to throw him under the bus, or should I say, the chariot. What would he do? Would he risk execution? What would you do? Well, he really didn't need to even think about it. He opened his window and prayed in full view as he had always done, knowing it could mean a one-way ticket to the lions' den.

There are times when compromise is needed to maintain healthy relationships. Times when a couple need to find middle ground in their marriage in order to restore a broken bond. Or adversaries must concede ground to negotiate a peace. But you must never negotiate with sin and evil. These must be defeated. You must never compromise convictions, morality, or excellence.

One day, a hunter aimed his gun at a big bear and was ready to pull the trigger. Suddenly the bear turned and spoke to him in a soft, soothing voice, saying, "Isn't it better to talk than to shoot? Why don't we negotiate the matter? What is it you want?" The hunter lowered his rifle and answered, "I would like a fur coat." "That's good," said the bear. "That's something we can talk about. All I want is a full stomach. Maybe we can reach a compromise." So the hunter lowered his rifle and sat down with the bear to talk it over. A little while later the bear walked away alone. The negotiations had been successful—the bear had a full stomach, and the hunter had a fur coat!

When it comes to running the race God has set before you, you must not negotiate with mediocrity. This is the race of your life. And you run to win. Never compromise the best for the good. If you are going to thrive in life, you must reach for the best and settle only for excellence. Run with More Fire. Anything less … you lose!

SIXTEEN

THE WIND AT YOUR BACK

IF YOU HAVE EVER RUN AGAINST THE WIND, YOU KNOW HOW DIFFICULT IT is. Your arms and legs begin to feel as heavy as lead. Your heart beats faster and faster. The intense strain saps your energy as rapidly as running up a long, steep hill or through water up to your knees. It can add hours to your race. It is excruciatingly painful and debilitating. On the other hand, what a difference it makes to have a wind blowing at your back. To feel the lift of a tailwind. You feel like you are being carried along. It increases your speed and reduces the time required to complete the race. You run with an advantage.

Long-distance runners testify repeatedly to the crucial advantage and necessity of other people around them to successfully run a race. I have listened to them confirm over and over again the value of support from family and friends, the supervision of a support crew to manage their progress, the encouragement of good pacers to run alongside them and the comradeship of fellow-runners. I would liken the impact of support people to a tailwind blowing at one's back. They lift you. They carry you.

Several chapters ago, I recounted the incredible story of three ultrarunners who successfully ran across the Sahara Desert. The grueling trek was documented in the 2007 film, *Running the Sahara*. One of those runners was Kevin Lin. At one point in the race, Kevin came to within a hair of quitting. His two companions sat with him for hours challenging his commitment and speaking encouragement into his life. He decided to continue. At the completion of this remarkable achievement, Kevin spoke into the camera and condensed the critical value of the team with these words:

> The three of us used all our efforts, all of our energy, and people may think that we were able to do it because we are tough. No. It took the three of us together to achieve it. We took steps forward together, we took steps backward together and we got angry together. There may have been unpleasant moments from the experience, but reaching the Red Sea made all the bad memories disappear.[1]

This clearly illustrates what the biblical writer meant when he wrote these words: *"Two people are better off than one, for they can help each other succeed. If one person falls, the other can reach out and help. ... Three are even better, for a triple-braided cord is not easily broken"* (Ecclesiastes 4:9–12).

Interestingly, exactly four years later in February 2011, one of those same runners, Ray Zahab, ran 1,200 kilometres through the Atacama Desert along the Pacific coast in Chile. National Geographic considers the Atacama the driest place on the earth. He ran 60 kilometres a day for 20 punishing consecutive days, carrying his own gear. I spoke with Ray soon after he completed the Atacama Expedition and he told me that the run was much more difficult than he had anticipated. I asked him, of all the races that he had run to this point, which one was the most demanding. He answered, the Atacama. I wondered, why? Was it the dryness? The intense heat? The harsh terrain? The physical strain? Ray's foot had become so bloated by an infected abscess that he had to cut his shoe open to fit his foot into it. It was none of the above. His answer was unexpected but thought-provoking. He answered that it was the most difficult because he had run it *alone*.

There is a moving story of two Mexican runners who competed in the 2010 Badwater Race. One of them, Jorge Pacheco, had won the punishing race in 2008. Now, two years later, he had returned to compete again. But things unfolded very differently this time. Pacheco faded as the event progressed into the night, and retired to the crew's van to wait out the race. The small forehead light of fellow-runner, Oswaldo Lopez, spotted Pacheco resting just inside the open door of the van. Lopez approached the vehicle and spoke yearningly to his friend. "We can walk; we can run. Come on! Come on!"

Pacheco answered, "Really, really, I can't. I just can't … You keep going … Get back in the race."

Lopez looked his friend in the eye and pleaded with him to persevere. Pacheco shook his head. The disappointment and regret was obvious in the faces of both runners. Lopez turned away and continued to run into the darkness. Suddenly and unexpectedly, Pacheco broke the uneasiness of the moment and called after his friend. "Give me a minute."

Lopez, who would go on to finish the race in 2nd place, gave a quick affirmative glance back at Pacheco. "Thank you. Give it your all!"

Pacheco held his legs with his hands and lifted them out of the van. He slowly slipped his runners back on. Stood up to get his bearings. He then moved gradually forward, hobbling badly at first. His tense muscles and stiff body began to loosen up as he shuffled his feet along the road. His limp improved to a walk. His walk progressed to a slow jog. But he continued on to finish the race. And who was waiting for him at the finish line? His friend, Oswaldo Lopez.[2]

When Marshall Ulrich ran across America, he affirmed his absolute dependence on others and his need of connection. His existence subsisted of the space between a white line and the shoulder of the road, and, at times, he felt an intense loneliness. His wife, Heather, was the only one who knew how fragile he really was. His primary motivation was the knowledge that she was waiting for him at the end of the day, when he would fall into her arms and feel at home. "I knew that I'd come to a state of mind where I wouldn't be able to go on without her, and to lose her would be to lose myself."[3]

Then there were those who came unexpectedly out of nowhere. Good Samaritans. Like the trucker who stopped his rig because he wanted to chat. It was a hot day and Ulrich was running down a dusty, barren back road. Not the kind of place you would expect to meet up with a big rig. Gerald seemed a friendly trucker and good-naturedly ordered him to bend over. Ulrich looked at him. That came across like a strange command. Was Gerald harmless? He smiled and gave the impression that he was an okay guy. So Marshall bent over. That was when Marshall felt a splash of cold water from a big jug soaking his clothes and refreshing his body. Both men howled with laughter. Another great connection. He ran on with the wind at his back.

Then there is the crew. Marshall writes that when a runner is trying to sustain over 400 miles a week,

> it takes the right amount of food and water, reliable gear, a few choice pieces of medical equipment, and key people to make sure all of it is available and ready as needed. It also requires a good deal of moral support and sufficient emotional resources to keep a runner in good emotional health. Everything hinges on the crew.[4]

These are the people who ensure that you are drinking enough fluids. Maintaining a right balance of electrolytes. Eating a proper diet with sufficient calories. The crew administers medications as needed. Pays attention to the runner's physical condition and provides medical care as required. Gives good objective advice. Provides massage, stretching, and physical therapy. The members of the crew are your cheerleaders. They plan the daily schedule and look after all the details. These are the people who laugh with you and cry with you. They experience the highs and the lows. Good crewmembers are people who are committed to the runner and to the accomplishment of the expedition.

THE TEAM

The writer of Hebrews says that since discipline and pain are necessary and inevitable, we must strengthen ourselves. *"So take a new grip with your tired hands and strengthen your weak knees"* (Hebrews 12:12). Stay strong yourself. Look after yourself. You can't help others if you fall out of the race yourself. There are times when you will feel the weight of discouragement, despondency, and even depression. Your arms will feel like lead and your hands will hang down exhausted. Your knees will buckle. You will feel you can do no more than drag your feet.

So brace your flagging limbs and press on. But you will need to pull together a good crew. You can't go on without the assistance of others and to lose others is to lose yourself.

In an earlier chapter, we studied the huge crowd of witnesses of Hebrews 11 who ran their race, handed the baton to us, and now sit in the stadium cheering us on. Read their biographies of struggle, failure, success, faith, and endurance. Their stories will be wind at your back. Read the biographies of people whose faith has endured since those days. Personally, I find few things more inspiring than the biographies of people whose faith struggled and persevered.

Then there are those people along the way who have impacted our lives. My grade 5 teacher inspired my life in more ways than she ever knew. Her love of history was imparted to me. She made it come alive and made me live it. I paddled the canoe with the early voyageurs. I surveyed the wilderness with David Thompson. I explored the Zambezi with David Livingstone. I walked into Sitting Bull's tepee with James Walsh. This teacher gave me a strong appreciation for where we have come from in understanding who we are and where we are going. But then there was my Grade 4 teacher. She attended my church. She intimidated, embarrassed, discouraged, and ruled with sharp finger and thumb nails that would clamp like vice grips into your ear. Then she would tell my parents at church what a lovely boy I was. I learned from her what not to be. You need to be careful not to allow people who have influenced you negatively to become a headwind that exhausts you in the race. Rather, embrace the people in your life who have lifted you forward. Just add them up, and you will be amazed at how many people have inspired you along the way. Some in just small ways; others in significant ways. But all together, they have helped to make you who you are and get you to where you are today.

When Dean Karnazes was running the 100-Mile Western States Endurance Run, he was nearing the end with just 10 kilometres to go. But at the very end of the course was a wicked 900-foot ascent. He climbed the hellacious slope, but not without nearing a complete breakdown. He was dehydrated. His hands were cut. His legs and feet were scraped and bleeding. He was covered in dirt, and the drool running down from the corners of his mouth and onto his chest made him look like some pre-historic creature that had fallen into a muck puddle. His eyes were almost shut and he could see no further than a few feet in front of him. Fading in and out, he fell into the arms of the man at the last aid station. About two kilometres to go and he couldn't go on. Imagine making it this far only to fall short by a few kilometres.

Then he saw a familiar face looking down at him. It was his dad. He was crying. Through the tears his dad said resolutely, "Son, if you can't run, then walk. And if you can't walk, then crawl. Do what you have to do. Just keep moving forward and never, ever give up."

"I will, Dad," he muttered. "I won't give up."[5]

Karnazes rolled over and began to crawl on his hands and knees up the road. Darkness fell. A couple stopped their car to ask if he was all right. He was flat on his stomach but slanted his face sideways at them and muttered, "Yes, never felt better." He was only a short distance from the finish line, but it might as well have been on another planet. The couple watched him as he rested his head back on the warm asphalt. Then something strange happened. His mind began to replay all the good memories of people who had helped him along the path. Everyone … from the people along the course who massaged his feet, provided water, and handed him delicious brownies … to his sister whose life and death had so deeply inspired him … to his parents who had supported him all along. Everyone who had helped to get him to this point. Suddenly, he jumped to his feet, shook his arms and legs wildly, and, to the total stunned surprise of the couple who had been standing over him and observing him the entire time, yelled out with an animal-like screech, "I can … Yes, I can!" And with that he charged down the road straight toward the finish line.

Karnazes writes,

> Running is a solo sport, but it was no longer about me anymore; I became almost irrelevant. My struggles were not about a single runner trying to finish this unfathomable challenge but about the greater ability of a human being to persevere against insurmountable odds. The many supporters who'd provided

encouragement and strength along the way. … Upholding my
end of the commitment meant crossing the finish line.[6]

Yes, you need to renew your commitment to go the distance, and
then assemble a team of encouragers and supporters who will help you
get there. There are many who have given you the moral support and
emotional resources to get where you are. Appreciate them. Value their
contribution. Celebrate them.

It is a common pitfall to begin to think that we get to where we
are because of our own personal skills and resources. Especially when
we get a taste of success. Success is a double-edged sword. It can be a
step toward greater achievement in your life. Or it can be a recipe for
disaster. It can foster that independent spirit that declares, "I got here on
my own." "I did it my way." "I can go from here on my own." Success
should humble you. It is an illusion to think you got to where you are
on your own. Or that you can go from here on your own. We are all
deeply indebted to others. Both divine and human. I have made the
point before that sometimes God has to allow us to come to the end of
our own resources to reveal the reality of our need.

One of the most-remembered moments in Olympic history occurred
at the 1992 Summer Olympics in Barcelona. Derek Redmond was
favoured to win the 400-metre race. About 250 metres from the finish
line, Derek heard a pop and felt a sharp searing pain like a bullet tearing
into his leg. His head flung back and he hobbled to a halt, falling to the
ground. He had torn his right hamstring. He gripped his leg with one
hand and held his head with the other. His face paled. His leg quivered.
He looked up in sheer disappointment and despair and rolled onto his
back. The medical personnel unit ran toward him with a stretcher. Just
as they got to him, Derek lifted himself to his feet and began to shuffle
with extreme difficulty along the track.

Few noticed that Steve Lewis of the USA had won the race in 44:50.
All eyes were on the drama unfolding 200 metres back. Derek Redmond
was attempting to finish his race, one agonizing step at a time. His face
grimaced with pain as the tears rolled down his cheeks. Suddenly, a large
man wearing a Nike T-shirt that read, "HAVE YOU HUGGED YOUR

FOOT TODAY?" and a cap that said, "JUST DO IT!" shoved his way through the crowd. He pushed past the security, leaped over the railing and down onto the track. He hurried toward the lone runner with two security people chasing right behind him. When he reached Derek, he grasped his arm. Derek resisted. Then looked. It was his father. His father embraced his waist with his arm. He said, "Derek, you don't have to do this."

"Yes, I do," replied Derek.

"Well then, we're going to finish this together!" declared his dad.

The father tightened his grip on the son. Derek seemed to be weakening, limping more and more painfully. His father wrapped Derek's arm around his neck, sustaining the weight of Derek's body. The crowd of 65,000 began to rise to its feet. The roar grew louder and louder. Derek rested his head on his father's shoulder. His hand covered his eyes as he sobbed. The father held his son tighter and closer. At one point the security personnel tried to separate father and son. The crowd cheered them on. A few steps before the finish line, Derek's father released his grip on his son and let him go. He had helped him to the finish line. Derek would cross it alone. The crowd remained on its feet, giving the two a standing ovation as they hugged and wept together. Derek had not finished in first place, but he had finished his race. An example of the perseverance of the human spirit and the faithfulness of a father's love.

God, your Father, knows when you falter and fall. He sees your pain and hurt. And He responds. He comes alongside. The Holy Spirit is called the *paraclete* in Scripture. *Paraclete* means "one called alongside to help." He holds you up. Helps you out. Sustains you. Carries you. He supplies the grace to help you when you need it most (see Hebrews 4:15–16). His love will never let you go. Sometimes God alone comes alongside. Mostly, He uses people. At times, He will even use angels.

You may or may not believe in angels, but the Bible speaks often of their existence. The psalmist penned, *"For he will order his angels to protect you wherever you go"* (Psalm 91:11). The Bible describes angels as *"servants—spirits sent to care for people who will inherit salvation"* (Hebrews 1:14). When Elijah retreated to the desert and wanted to die, God sent an angel to prepare some food and strengthen him. After Jesus had been through the grueling temptation from the devil, we read, *"angels came and took care of Jesus"* (Matthew 4:11). In the Garden of Gethsemane, Jesus endured a battle in His soul more agonizing than He had ever encountered before. It is not surprising that *"an angel from heaven appeared and strengthened him"* (Luke 22:43). Angels are God's servants sent to protect, care, strengthen, and support us.

I believe I have had several encounters with angels. One that stands out in my mind was during my years on the farm. It was the last day of haying for the summer. My friend and I set off to pick up the last wagonload from the field. I stacked the flat bed of the wagon higher than usual. On the return trip, I scrambled up onto the top of the hay load and stretched out on a bale at the front of the wagon to enjoy the breeze. The road wound down a small, steep hill with a short bend at the bottom. As we crested the hill and began our decline, the weight of the heavy load of hay suddenly set in motion a whole chain of events. The tractor began to slowly accelerate while its engine strained to resist the thrust of the wagon. The driver jammed the clutch down to shift the tractor into a lower gear and thus restrain the momentum. The timing was wrong. Suddenly the gravitational force of the heavy load began to push the tractor uncontrollably. The driver panicked. He pressed his foot down hard on the brake. The tractor began to slide sideways as the large wheels dug into the dirt. The load of hay began to shift frontward. I felt it going and reached out my hand to grasp the limb of a tree that hung out over the road. All of a sudden everything gave way beneath me. My feet swung up into the air. I felt myself falling. I remember clearly my back hitting the iron tongue of the wagon. In that split second I anticipated I would be dragged underneath the wagon and killed under several tons of hay.

God had other plans. Unexpectedly and swiftly, I felt a hand lift me from the iron tongue. I sprang like I had fallen on a heavy elastic band, and was catapulted to the side of the road where I landed safely away from the carnage. What had happened made no sense! One doesn't fall on one's back on an inflexible iron tongue attached to a moving tractor pulling a full load of hay that is avalanching upon you ... and walk away unscathed. It was as if I had been flung by an unseen hand like a stone from a sling out of harm's way. All in a split second.

The driver came running up the hill, shaking, and shocked to see me sitting on a bale of hay alive. Debris lay scattered all up the hill. But I was in one piece, and trying to process what had just happened. I looked at my friend and said, "I think that I was just rescued by … an angel." I wonder how many times this happens without our awareness. Angels guarding, protecting, caring, strengthening and supporting us in our weakness. The remembrance of these kinds of episodes inspires and enthuses me in my race. They are wind at my back. They remind me that God knows, sees, cares, helps and holds control over my life. These kinds of experiences make me jump to my feet, shake my hands and legs, and cry out, "I can … Yes, I can!" Whether I crawl, hobble, walk or run, I will keep going.

PACE BUNNIES

Joy had never been a runner, but she now found herself running in the Paris Marathon, one of the most popular long-distance annual running events in Europe. She was running in memory of her beloved mother who had passed away with cancer. Her goal was to run the distance in 5 hours and 30 minutes. So she was on the lookout for her *pace bunny*. Her what? Yes, you heard it right! *Pace Bunny*. Pace Bunnies are experienced runners who wear big pink rabbit ears and carry signs with their predicted finishing times pasted on their backs. They are confident that they will finish the race within a minute of the time on their sign. So, if their sign carries the time that you want to complete your race, then that is the person to keep your eyes fixed on. Joy kept her eyes on the 5:30 pace bunny and completed her race in 5:22.

Pacers are extremely important people to an ultrarunner. Their job is grueling and thankless. Christopher McDougall describes pacing as:

> so grueling and thankless, usually only family, fools, and … good friends let themselves get talked into it. The job means shivering in the middle of nowhere for hours until your runner shows up, then setting off at sunset for an all-night run through

wind-whistling mountains. You'll get blood on your shins, vomit on your shoes, and not even a T-shirt for completing two marathons in a single night.[7]

Pacers run a nice, even pace. They are encouragers. They are companions. They engage the ultrarunner and help keep the mind from becoming disoriented by the heat and elements. After 20 or more hours of nonstop running, the mind can become too numb to replace flashlight batteries and can easily wander away from the marked trail to follow some unfamiliar path over a precipice. McDougall discusses the peril of hallucinations. For example, the runner who leaped into the woods every time he saw a flashlight, certain there was an oncoming train. Or the runner who saw rotting corpses all along the side of the road. The runner who stared into space and spoke to the empty air, "I know you're not real." Pacers deal with this kind of thing. "A tough pacer … can save your race; a sharp one can save your life."[8]

It is amazing how many significant runners in the Bible had either a crew of people or an individual who came alongside to encourage or hold them accountable. Elijah had Elisha. David had Jonathan. Naomi had Ruth. Esther had Mordecai. Jesus had His disciples. Paul had Barnabas. Paul had Timothy. Paul often had a whole crew surrounding him.

Sometimes we need others to help us combat discouragement. At other times, we need someone to go deeper. We need the accountability and sheer help to climb a perpendicular rock face. Think of addiction, for instance. Let's consider pornography. You don't need to look for pornography; it will find you. It begins with a curiosity or someone introducing it to you. Your mind is imprinted with images that cannot be erased. You quickly move on to the experimental stage. You find yourself needing to act out. You are addicted. This process can take place in just a few days. You think that you can stop, but you can't. Like every addiction, you need more and more to get you to the same kind of experience. Things become more graphic, more intense, more frequent.

Addiction is the kind of bondage that incapacitates. You need to take a new grip on yourself. But you can't do it alone. This is not a self-correcting problem. This is something that is stronger than you and will drag you progressively downward. Your will is important, but will not suffice. You need a support crew. You need a tough pacer whom you trust and who is not overly impressed by you. A mentor. Someone in whom you can confide. Someone to watch out for you. Someone to keep you accountable. Someone to help you maintain a good pace and encourage you to keep going. These are the people who can save your life. They are the wind at your back.

WEARING RABBIT EARS

We are exhorted to reinforce our tired hands and shaky legs *so that* we can assist other runners to persevere and run a strong race. *"Mark out a straight path for your feet so that those who are weak and lame will not fall but become strong"* (Hebrews 12:13). You are to become a strong runner so that you can become a pacer for someone else who is weak and struggling.

Weaker runners are easily tripped up. God forbid those who are following your example end up bewildered or misled. God forbid that they end up bruised and bleeding with a dislocated shoulder or sprained ankle down over some embankment. Rather, remove anything that would cause them to stumble and fall. And when they get injured, bind the sprained ankle and bandage the wound so the whole team can complete the race without loss. The Bible warns against anything in our lives that has potential of making another person stumble and fall. *"We should help others do what is right and build them up in the Lord"* (Romans 15:2).

In one sense, life's race is a solo venture. You run to improve your personal best. You work to overcome the challenges in your own life. You are responsible for yourself. The Bible says, *"We are each responsible for our own conduct"* (Galatians 6:5). But life's race is also very much a corporate venture. We run as a team. In this same chapter, the apostle Paul wrote, *"If another believer is overcome by some sin, you who are godly should gently and humbly help that person back onto the right path. ... Share each other's burdens, and in this way obey the law of Christ"* (6:1–2). This means that if you know of a fellow runner who has wandered from the path or fallen down over an embankment, you should stop and help. Reorient their thinking. Treat their injuries. Take the time to put a splint on a broken bone. There were times when you needed others to assist you along the path. Now, you must watch out for others. When someone is carrying a burden that is too heavy, help to shoulder the load. In this way, you will be obeying Christ's command to love one another. Love is an action word. The greatest fulfillment you will ever experience is stopping on the path of life to help another runner. Step forward and be the encourager. Be a support. Become the pacer for someone else. Put on the rabbit ears and lead another person to becoming a stronger runner. Be the wind at someone else's back.

THE POWER OF A TEAM

God created us in community and wired us for community. We need the support of community to reach our greatest potential and effectiveness. Stephen Covey refers to what he calls life's *maturity continuum*, a three-step progression from *dependence* to *independence* to *interdependence*.[9] *Dependence* is the state of totally needing others to nurture and sustain us. "I need you to take care of me." But quickly we grow and develop to become increasingly *independent*, able and wanting to take care of ourselves. I see this clearly in my grandchildren. For months I fed them, spoonful by spoonful. Then, one day, as I approached the mouth like an airplane coming in for a landing, the lips clamped shut, the plane crashed, and mush splattered all over the face. A small but confident voice assured me, "*I* can do it." The "terrible twos" arrive and the spirit of independence is daily stimulated as the shackles of dependence are thrown off. Independence is a normal and healthy stage in development. But it is not the highest level of development. True, it is proclaimed by many individuals as paramount, but there is something much more powerful and effective.

Covey writes,

> *Interdependence* is the paradigm of *we*—*we* can do it; *we* can cooperate; *we* can combine our talents and abilities and create something greater together. ... Interdependent people combine their own efforts with the efforts of others to achieve their greater success.[10]

It is the power of the team. The team has synergy. The team will propel you further than you can go on your own. You may be very capable on your own, but you can still accomplish more with others than you can alone. You may hold a very strong and healthy sense of self-worth and self-confidence. But you need to love and *be* loved to truly feel emotionally secure and to function most effectively. You may be an intelligent thinker, but you will never reach the level of understanding on your own that you will by combining what you know with the finest thinking of others. An interdependent person is capable of using his or her physical, emotional, and intellectual resources to share meaningfully with others. But they also appreciate and enjoy the benefit of having "access to the vast resources and potential of other human beings."[11]

The power of interdependence is illustrated in the world of running most noticeably in Kenya. As previously noted, Kenyans are known for being great runners. Kenyan women are great athletes, but, historically, have not achieved the same fame or success as the men. Why is this? Is it that women have smaller hearts? Less hemoglobin? A higher percentage of body fat? Apparently, the answer is not found in physiology, but in sociological and cultural dynamics.

Traditionally, Kenya has been a predominantly male-centred culture. Women are mostly responsible for raising the children, tending the crops, doing the household chores and anything else that needs to be done. There is little time for training. A Kenyan boy has a much better chance of graduating from school and proceeding to one of the athletic camps to train as a runner. Girls, typically, leave school to remain at home to help with the everyday chores or settle into a prearranged marriage. Thus the talent pool for girls is very low. There is little equal opportunity. If a girl does have the opportunity to attend an athletic camp, she finds herself in a man's world. She is an object of ridicule and contempt. It has been a long-held belief and tradition that success in running is an opportunity that belongs to men, by right, not women.

Things are slowly changing. The community is beginning to appreciate the reality that women, given the same opportunity as men, can be as successful as men. More and more women are entering the world of running and their acceptance into that world is having great results.

They are getting faster at a faster rate. But it is significant to note that the girls who have succeeded in the running world are those who received the support of their parents. Women who have become great runners testify to enjoying sound and supportive relationships with husbands who are not threatened by the successes of their wives. Kenyan women like Catherine Ndereba, Lornah Kiplagat, Esther Kiplagat, and Leah Malot are world champions and have pursued long careers in athletics. They are extremely skilled athletes. But they attribute their success to parental, spousal, and community support. Their successes are changing attitudes and freeing growing numbers of young girls to pursue the same goals. As they move along the continuum from dependence to independence to interdependence, they have more and more access to the resources and potential of others. Soon women will be as competitive as men.

Kenyan men have appreciated the power of the team for generations. They train together. They live together. They run together. There is a general unwritten code that one can be better as an individual if one trains and runs with a team. Runners push each other to be better than the other. Kenyan runner Daniel Komen said, "When you are tired there is always another man pushing and not letting you rest. Even if you think you are at full speed, you can always be pushed a little faster."[12]

Kenyans are very aware of their status in the running world and often take a pre-race jog together for the purpose of intimidating other competitors.

Like a pride of lions they prowl the course reminding the opposition of their united force. ... [R]unners jog to the line with a flag bearer leading them as they chant in unison to remind their opposition—"Together we shall win." True to their word, win they do![13]

Kenyans hold 75 percent of the world records in long-distance running. Many times in a race, the team will choose a particular runner and propel him forward to win. They act like the wind at his back and thrust him toward the finish line. They believe that if one of the team wins, the whole team wins. William Mutwol said, "If you run and train as a team, you can defeat anyone."[14]

I love the Bible's imagery of running the race of life. I envisage a group of runners keeping pace with each other along a rugged path. Each carries one's own backpack containing everything one needs for the run. Sweat pours from their brows and down between the shoulder blades. The strain is imprinted on their faces. The stronger runners set the pace for the weaker. They run as a team, a united whole, intent on finishing the race without loss of anyone. One runner stops to assist another who is falling back. It is not unusual to witness the whole team circle around an injured runner and take the time to tend to his wounds. Sometimes you will observe someone carrying the added burden of another runner's pack until the weaker runner is able to carry it. From time to time you'll even see one runner struggling to carry another. They encourage and motivate one another. They propel each other forward, pushing each other to running a little faster. Each runner combines his or her efforts with the efforts of the team to achieve synergy and the greatest success. They believe they are individually stronger when they run as a team, together. If they run as a team, they can defeat anything.

SEVENTEEN

GOING THE DISTANCE

FOR THE FOURTH TIME IN FOUR YEARS, AT THE 2011 TORONTO Waterfront Marathon, a Kenyan runner crossed the finish line in first place. His name was Kenneth Mungara. But attention was focused on another runner at the back of the pack. Six hours back. Fauja Singh, dubbed the *Turbaned Tornado,* crossed the line in 8:25:16 in 3,850th place. Last place. The media pressed in upon him as he crossed the finish line. Why? Singh had made history. He was 100 years old. The oldest person ever to go the distance and complete a marathon. It was a remarkable achievement. The Guinness World Records refused to include him in their records because he could not produce a birth certificate confirming his age. Birth certificates were not kept in India in 1911. Singh said that God helped him to achieve this accomplishment, but that even God must be tiring of helping him. *The Turbaned Tornado* is the title of a biography recently published about his life. Singh has not read the book himself because he is illiterate.

Near the beginning of this book, I told you about a runner who has become a friend of mine. Jim Willett. Jim was 37 years old, a healthy athlete, a fitness advocate and personal trainer. In January 2010, he was diagnosed with colon cancer. After major surgery to remove part of his intestine, tests showed that the cancer had spread to the lymph nodes. He had stage-three cancer. His life became centred around a lengthy chemotherapy treatment plan. During this time, he made a decision to endure the chemotherapy, but to centre his life around other plans. He decided to boost his physical and mental health by focusing on something new. Something big. He had read about it. He had spoken to people who had done it. He began to train for the monumental 250-kilometre Gobi March in China. The Gobi March is a self-supporting race, meaning each runner must carry his or her own gear in a 20-pound backpack over some of the most unsympathetic landscape in the world. First aid, sunscreen, sleeping bag, clothing, multi-tool, compass, electrolyte pills, and at least 14,000 calories of food. He trained, researched gear, and raised support.

By March 2011, he was training in earnest. He trained in an infrared sauna to customize his body to extreme heat. His main concern was his feet. Chemotherapy had caused numbness in his extremities, and Jim was worried about injury to his feet. Lack of pain sensation means one has no warning system to alert to occurring damage. He borrowed a trick boxers use to toughen their hands. He ground his feet in a box of uncooked rice to toughen the soles and help prevent blistering and injury.

The race began with 152 runners following the Old Silk Road that Marco Polo had travelled more than 700 years earlier. The first 40 kilometres consisted of steep uphill climbs of altitudes up to 2,150 metres, and extreme heat. On day 4, the course led them through the Turpan Basin where temperatures soared to 60 degrees Celsius. The heat emanated from the sand and salt surface, melting the glue in Jim's running shoes. The Turpan Basin is the second-lowest point on the face of the earth and the furthest point in the world from any ocean. The pain and heat was excruciating. At times, Jim keeled over heaving and vomiting. His run eased to alternating between a slow walk and a shuffle.

The distance race is a microcosm of life. There is the adversity. For Jim, day 5 was another wall of heat. The running was particularly difficult. His shoes sank into the flowing sand up to his ankles. Every step was an effort. He had to watch out for scorpions and camel spiders. Ah yes, camel spiders. Aggressive creatures that expose their fangs and run toward you prepared to execute a painful bite that can make you very sick.

But, as with life, there are times of refreshment and blessing. Jim experienced the beauty of the landscape. The enchanting splendour of the desert. The colours. Herds of wild animals. Wild horses. And the people. He entered a region called the "Vineyard," with lush, green fields of watermelon and cantaloupe. A group of Uyghur farmers stood around a wagon loaded with melons and cantaloupe ready for market. They stared at Jim. They were not used to seeing westerners dressed up in running gear jogging along their roads. They seemed amused at this grubby, mysteriously dressed desert runner. They made gestures he did not understand. Jim hesitated, unsure of what they were saying or what the local customs dictated. Should he stop? Should he keep going? Were they upset with him? Were they welcoming him? He smiled and waved. Then decided to approach them. They seemed friendly. In fact, they were very friendly, hospitable and generous. They drew him in with their arms and offered him a large cantaloupe. He gave a nod of appreciation. One of the Uyghurs held the cantaloupe in his hand and, with a few swift swipes with a machete, cut the juicy fruit into manageable chunks and gave them to Jim. Never had he enjoyed such cool thirst-quenching refreshment. The succulent melon. The Uyghur farmers. The chance encounter. It was the highlight of the run. It invigorated him.

That evening, a few kilometres from camp, Jim conducted a little simple but memorable ceremony. He buried his chemo port in a sand dune. A chemo port is a little device inserted into the chest to assist health care professionals with administering chemo treatments. When the doctors removed it, Jim had asked to keep it. Why? He wasn't sure at the time. But now he knew. The little mechanism weighed only a few ounces, but as he walked away, his pack felt lighter than air. It was an act of defiance. A resolve to triumph over the worst that life can send you.

The night before the final stage of the run, Jim lay on his back with his hands behind his head, staring up at the stars. He was nursing thoughts about his battle with cancer, and thinking about the finish line only 14 kilometres away. The midnight air seemed eerily calm. Suddenly, without warning, the wind whipped up, lifting the canopy of the tent about 30 feet into the air. The sand blasted against his face, stinging the skin. He quickly pulled his T-shirt up over his face to act as a mask. He and a fellow bunkmate struggled to anchor the tent down and secure the sides. They finally succeeded and took refuge inside their shelter. The storm raged outside for the next five hours and the sand swirled inside the tent.

Jim burrowed down into his sleeping bag. He was soon revisiting his earlier reflections. The storm reminded him of his cancer diagnosis. Sudden. Unexpected. But it only strengthened his resolve to persevere. His mind drifted back to all the preparations he had made for this race and then on to everything that had been compressed into the past week. At some hour of the night, his thoughts led him down a tunnel into a sound sleep. When morning broke, everything was covered with a thick layer of sand. Jim opened his eyes, jumped up, shook the sand out of his sleeping bag and smiled. This was the day he had prepared for. He was ready to go!

We have no choice in terms of how we begin our lives. We have no choice regarding many things that happen to us. We do have choices, however, as to how we live our lives and run our race. Difficulties, failures, and discouragement can lead us to quit or make us all the more determined to go the distance. After a tough run, there is the thrill of finishing well. These thoughts filled Jim's mind as he ran the final 14 kilometres down through the narrow V-shaped slot canyons. He felt light-hearted. Exhilarated. He could taste the finish, and he was already savouring the accomplishment.

He finished in a little Buddhist village. The drums were beating as he ran along the village road. Some runners crossed the finish line waving flags. Others carried signs in memory of loved ones attached to their packs. Jim carried a note he had written to cancer. It read, "Cancer. You attacked me because that is what you do. And I know, given the opportunity, you'll do it again and again. But you should know who you're up against. Today's finish line is just the starting line for so many other things. The war may not be over, but I will fight you every step of the way. I'm stronger than you ever thought possible. And I will never, ever quit." I have a photo of Jim high-stepping across the finish line, 24th out of 152 competitors. The grim determination that had been sketched into the lines of his face for a week was replaced by a smile that stretched from ear to ear. He was high-stepping for the benefit of the medical staff. Jim had been *red flagged* at the beginning of the race because of his medical condition. The medical team had observed him closely at every checkpoint, and now they watched him making a strong finish. They cheered him in.

The finish line is an exciting place. Runners crawl across. Limp across. High-step across. They are greeted by family members, friends, and fellow runners. They greet each other with tears. Arms lifted. High-fives. Draped in flags. They pose for photos in front of the victory banner. There is an overwhelming sense of fulfillment and joy. An overwhelming sense that this is not the end, but just the beginning of something new. Jim told me, "Crossing the finish line didn't feel like the ending of something significant; it felt like I was crossing into the beginning of something monumental."

THE FINISH LINE

Hebrews 11 is the Hall of Faith and records the names of many of the greats. Record-breaking runners. Abraham. Moses. Samuel. David. It also records the lives of many others whose names have been lost to us, but who ran incredibly difficult runs. They all finished their race. Hebrews 12 tells us we are surrounded by these runners from the past and exhorts us to now run our race from start to finish. We are to keep our eyes fixed on Jesus, who began and finished His race.

The apostle Paul wrote, *"I press on to reach the end of the race"* (Philippians 3:14). He strained to reach the finish line. Paul ran a magnificent race. The physical distances he travelled are staggering.

> The New Testament registers the equivalent of about 13,450 miles that the great apostle journeyed. … When one takes into account the winding, circuitous roadways and tracks he necessarily had to employ, the total distance would exceed that figure by a sizeable margin.[1]

These paths wound through rugged, mountainous terrain where bandits laid in wait to attack unsuspecting travellers. One can only imagine the exertion of physical energy. Paul wrote a personal account of his journey.

> *I have worked harder, been put in prison more often, been whipped times without number, and faced death again and again. Five different times the Jewish leaders gave me thirty-nine lashes. Three times I was beaten with rods. Once I was stoned. Three times I was shipwrecked. Once I spent a whole night and a day adrift at sea. I have traveled on many long journeys. I have faced danger from rivers and from robbers. ... I have worked hard and long, enduring many sleepless nights. I have been hungry and thirsty, and have often gone without food. I have shivered in the cold, without enough clothing to keep me warm. Then, besides all this, I have the daily burden of my concern for all the churches* (2 Corinthians 11:23–28).

The physical, emotional, mental, and spiritual strain is inscrutable. But every race comes to an end. Paul entered the last lap. The finish line came into sight. He faced it squarely. *"The time of my death is near"* (2 Timothy 4:6). There was no illusion of any more laps. It is healthy to face the time of one's death realistically. As a Christian, you can face it with hope and certainty. For Paul, it didn't feel like the end; it felt like he was crossing into the beginning of something monumental. *"I have fought a good fight, I have finished the race, and I have remained faithful. And now the prize awaits me"* (verses 7 and 8). It had been a tough race, but the taste of victory was sweet. It's the last lap when the crowd stands and cheers. It's the last lap when the energy level peaks and the runner makes that final push. It may be painful getting there, but the runner who runs the race of faith knows that when he or she pushes through the finish line, the course leads right into eternity. The best is yet to be. Whether one crawls, limps, leaps, or high-steps over the finish line, the taste is one of exhilaration and glory.

When Paul wrote his epistle to the Philippians, he shared his heart regarding his desire to bring honour to Christ, whether he lived or died. Both life and death were so wonderful that he vacillated between which was better. Running the race of life meant to run for Christ. It meant loving and serving God and people with purpose and passion. Despite its struggles, it was rewarding and fruitful. The other option was death. He described dying as even better than living. *"I long to go and be with Christ, which would be far better for me"* (Philippians 1:23). He decided he should opt for life since it was better for them. But, nonetheless, dying was something to be looked forward to.

For the believer in Jesus, death means to enter into the eternal realm of heaven. The body is buried in the ground, but the soul goes immediately to be with Jesus. Heaven is where Jesus lives. Heaven means to live with Jesus. Jesus told His followers He was going to return to heaven to prepare a place for everyone who believed in Him. When everything was ready, He said, *"I will come and get you, so that you will always be with me where I am"* (John 14:3). Heaven is home. Home is where you are loved for who you are, not for what you do. It is the place where you can take your shoes off and put your feet up. Home is where you can unpack your suitcase for the last time. Home is where you feel most comfortable. Home is where you can rest. Heaven is where you will know God and everything completely, just as God knows you completely (see 1 Corinthians 13:12). The apostle John recorded that heaven is a place where God will wipe away every tear from your eyes. There will be no more sorrow, crying, pain, or death (see Revelation 21:4). Heaven will be an incredible place.

A little while ago, I was hunkered down in a room taking some time to put my thoughts together for this book and doing some writing. Every day, Ruth, a jovial black lady, showed up to clean my room. She arrived each morning by bus with many other women from the black communities in the city. They vacuumed, made beds, and replenished the rooms with towels and soap. Then at day's end, they got back on the bus and returned home. I told her I could clean my own room, but she insisted. It soon became apparent to me that she was in love with Jesus. I could hear her talking away as she worked. I thought she was conversing with someone on her earphone. But she was talking to Jesus. And singing. She radiated the joy of the Lord. I told her I was writing a book about running life's most amazing race. She smiled and nodded, "I knows lot 'bout runnin' dat race." I gave her a copy of my previous book, *Hitting the Wall*. She thanked me and promised to begin reading it that evening.

The next morning, I was strolling along the hall just outside my room. As I walked past an open door, I heard a voice call out. "Mista David!" It was Ruth. She came running to the doorway, gave me a big hug, and thanked me again for the book I had given to her. Immediately she went into *preaching* mode. She preached in such a melodious tone that you would think she had been rehearsing all night. The words came straight from her heart. She told me that life is like a rose. You will either be hurt by it or you will see its beauty. "It 'pends on how you hold it," she said. She warned me to watch out for the devil and not give him a pinhole. "Mista David, he can git through a pinhole," she cautioned, wagging her finger at me. I was afraid she was going to break out into song. Then what would I do? Was I supposed to chime into a refrain? I could see her grabbing this white guy by the hand and the two of us dancing down the halls and singing, "Watch out for dat ol' devil, he will git you if you don't!" I actually looked forward to the experience. It didn't get that far. But it was one of those moments when God speaks directly *at you*.

She shared from her own life story. I was captivated by it. It was a story of struggle and hard times. But it was a story of God's grace to supply her daily needs. She had little of this world's material goods, but she was wealthy beyond compare with the joy of the Lord. She was a mother of 12 children. Tragically, she had lost two sons. Her eldest son, 17 years old, had perished in a house fire. She recalled the night she was called to the burning house. By the time she arrived, the house was reduced to a pile of ashes. She was informed that everyone had escaped the flames, except one. Her heart sank. She knew which one. Her heart was racked with deep pain. But she felt a stream of grace from God flowing into her inner being. It filled her with a peace that exceeded anything she had ever felt. She dropped to her knees and prayed, "Lawd, hep me let go. He's wid You now. Hep me! Hep me!" She looked into my eyes and said, "Mista David, you is writin' a book 'bout runnin' duh race of life. It ain't no easy race. But I know dat whilst my baby no longer runs in dis life, he is runnin' bedda than ever on duh udda side." Her words resonated with me as I considered writing this chapter.

257

I asked her what had happened to her other son. He had been ill for a long time. She knew the illness would shorten his life, but she had promised him she would be with him when he left this world. When she arrived home from work one evening, she was met by someone who told her that her boy was not responding and may be gone. She could not accept that he was gone. She had promised him she would be at his side when that moment came. She ran to his bedside. She knelt down beside him. He lay motionless, his eyes shut. She touched his arm gently, softly pressed her lips against his ear, and spoke. "It's your mamma. I dun jes like I told yuh. I'd be here when the time came." He responded. His head moved slightly. His eyes stirred. Just a little. Just enough to let her know he knew she was there. "It's your mamma. I'm here. It's okay. You can sleep now." Tears rolled down over her big smile, like rain over a rainbow. Our eyes locked as she spoke in a loud whisper, "Mista David, I has two babies runnin' on duh udda side. I miss ma chirren so much. But it's goin' to be all right. I'm gonna leave 'em een duh han' o duh Lawd. I'm a lookin' beyan de grabe. I'm a lookin' down duh road. One day when I lay een de grabe, or when Gabriel blow dat trumpet, I'm going to see 'em and run wid 'em."

What a perspective! The finish line is not the end. It's the beginning of something monumental. The cemetery is not your final resting place. It is where your body will rest for a time. It symbolically marks the finish line on this earth. But the soul of the person is not there. It lives on. The course broadens into terrain no human mind can imagine or language express.

WHEN THE CLOCK RUNS OUT!

The Hall of Faith records the names of honourees that ran their race of faith and completed it. The writer, however, enters a surprising conclusion. *"All these people earned a good reputation because of their faith, yet none of them received all that God had promised. For God had something better in mind for us, so that they would not reach perfection without us"* (Hebrews 11:39–40). These exemplary runners did not receive all that God had promised. They would be rewarded for their faith together with the Christian runners who are still running. The rewards will not be given out until the last runner is in and the clock of time runs out.

The Athens Classic Marathon is not as well-known as many marathons, but no marathon can match its history. The course follows the same route as that run by Pheidippides in 490 BC to announce to Athens the victory over the Persians. It is a tough course that begins by the sea near the ancient battlefield, climbs the base of Mount Penteli, and ends on the plains of Attika, today the centre of Athens. It is a run through history.

The race usually draws about 3,000 competitors on a good year. Although I read of the 2003 race that drew 4,000 runners and there were only four portapotties for everyone. (Think of it this way... one toilet for every thousand people). To make matters worse, at the end of the race 4,000 plastic bags of clothing belonging to the runners were dumped on the pavement at the finish line and everyone had to find their own bag. It was worse than trying to retrieve your luggage on the carousel of an old, crowded Middle-Eastern airport.

That year, the first 10 runners into the stadium were a Tanzanian, seven Kenyans and two Greeks. After them, everyone else straggled and hobbled in. Average people with normal bodies. Young people. People in their seventies and eighties. Runners with leg-braces. Runners with disabilities. They all crossed the line in assorted physical conditions and over a wide range of running times. Every person who ran, walked, hobbled, shuffled, or crawled across the finish line received an excited applause from the eager crowd of spectators. The ovation continued until the last runner crossed the line and the clock ran out at the six-hour mark.

One day, the clock of time will run out for all of us. That time will arrive in one of two ways. There is a personal clock running on each of us. None of us knows the time of the end of our race. But it will come. It's called death. At that point, the path you have run will be fixed for eternity. Jesus said, *"The highway to hell is broad, and its gate is wide for the many who choose that way. But the gateway to life is very narrow and the road is difficult, and only a few ever find it"* (Matthew 7:13–14).

But there is another clock that is running down. We could call it God's universal clock. The clock by which the ages run. This clock will run out of time when Jesus comes again. That single event will bring time to an end and introduce the state of the eternal. The apostle Peter called it the day of the Lord.

The heavens will pass away with a terrible noise, and the very elements themselves will disappear in fire, and the earth and everything on it will be found to deserve punishment. ... [God] will set the heavens on fire, and the elements will melt away in the flames (2 Peter 3:10, 12).

When Jesus returns in judgment, His first priority will be to rapture all who belong to Him out of this world. One can only imagine the earth-shattering impact of such a heaven-imposing assault.

When Jesus returns, God will bring back with him the believers who have died. ... For the Lord himself will come down from heaven with a commanding shout, with the voice of the archangel, and with the trumpet call of God. First, the Christians who have died will rise from their graves. Then, together with them, we who are still alive and remain on the earth will be caught up in the clouds to meet the Lord in the air. Then we will be with the Lord forever. So encourage each other with these words (1 Thessalonians 4:14–18).

Jesus will suddenly, unexpectedly appear. He will bring with Him the souls of all who have died in the ages past up to the present who are in heaven with Him. He will then miraculously resurrect their bodies from the graves. He will, along with the resurrected dead, lift all believers still living on the earth to meet Him in the air. He will wonderfully transform their earthly bodies that were fashioned for earth into spiritual bodies fashioned for heaven and reunite them with their souls. You can read about this cataclysmic event in 1 Corinthians 15.

What kind of bodies will these be? What will they be like? While we are not told specifically, we are given some clues. Paul expands on the heavenly body in 1 Corinthians 15:42–53. He tells us our earthly bodies are broken and weak. They often let us down with illness, limitations, weakness, aging, and finally death. They are limited by mortality. They just stop working. By contrast, the heavenly bodies are described as glorious and strong. They are called spiritual bodies. Bodies under the control of the limitless spirit. They are immortal and will never die. They are equipped for eternity. Paul makes an amazing statement that our heavenly bodies will be like Jesus' body. *"We will someday be like the heavenly man"* (verse 49). Just look at Jesus' resurrection body. He travelled at the speed of thought. He could go through walls and closed doors.

Let's use a little imagination. Think about the new heavens and new earth that God is going to fashion (see Revelation 21:1, 5). Peter wrote that after God has destroyed the old heavens and earth, He will re-fashion a new world. *"We are looking forward to the new heavens and new earth he has promised, a world filled with God's righteousness"* (2 Peter 3:13). Why will God create a new heavens and earth? We're not told. But we can guess. We will have a universe to discover. The frontiers of infinite space. And bodies fitted for eternity to do it all in. Travelling at the speed of thought. Without limits or borders. And I would suggest that there will be a new earth for our enjoyment, pleasure, and exploration. And we will be at liberty to discover all of this with new minds that operate with full capacity. Learning and growing in our knowledge of the magnitude and glory of God. Whatever we dream, it will be a million times better.

The imagery of Hebrews 12 is complete. The last runner will enter the stadium and cross the finish line. The clock will run out. The race on earth will be finished. The bodies of those who cheered in the stadium bleachers will be resurrected and go up to meet the Lord in the air. The ones crossing the finish line down on the track will be lifted up. Everyone will be raised together. Everyone will shout the victory cry: *"Death is swallowed up in victory"* (1 Corinthians 15:54). Everyone who has run the race of faith will stand before God to give account of the race each has run. We will stand together. We will bow together. We will be rewarded together.

Many have tried to foretell the hour of the finish time. All have been wrong. No one knows the time that the clock will run out. Peter said that *"the day of the Lord will come as unexpectedly as a thief"* (2 Peter 3:10). The thief does not warn you of his arrival to break into your house. He shows up when you least expect it. Paul warned the Thessalonian Christians that we don't know when all of this will happen. *"The day of the Lord's return will come unexpectedly, like a thief in the night"* (1 Thessalonians 5:2). He then added that, while we may not know the precise time, we should be ready. *"Stay alert and be clearheaded. Night is the time when people sleep. … But let us who live in the light be clearheaded, protected by the armor of faith and love, and wearing as our helmet the confidence of our salvation"* (verses 6–8).

What does it mean to be ready for this event? If you are a Christian, it means to keep your life pure and clean for Him. The apostle John said everyone who belongs to Christ and is living in ready anticipation of Jesus' return will live in a way that honours and pleases Him. *"All who have this eager expectation will keep themselves pure, just as he is pure"* (1 John 3:3). If you are not a Christian, it means to believe that Jesus died for your sin, and then turn away from your sin and surrender your life to Him. In fact, the primary reason that the clock has not run out yet is that God has extended the time to allow for more people to join His race of faith. Peter cautioned that God is not being negligent about His promise to come again; He is being patient and merciful. *"He is being patient for your sake. He does not want anyone to be destroyed, but wants everyone to repent"* (2 Peter 3:9).

FAILURE, NO EXCUSE FOR QUITTING

The book of Hebrews was written to people who were ready to give up the race. The trail was tough. Struggles were severe. Risks were numerous. The failure rate was high. The writer exhorted them as a coach would his runners: "Run! Don't quit! You might trip up, but keep your eyes, heart, and mind on Jesus. He went the distance for you. Now you go the distance for Him." The second half of the race divides the finishers from the starters. The course becomes littered with runners who are flagging. They started well, but are faltering near the finish line.

Brother Colm O'Connell is a priest who came to Kenya from Ireland in 1976. He knew almost nothing about athletics, but over the years has become a successful coach who has trained some of Kenya's best Olympic runners. O'Connell emphasizes a philosophy of winning and losing with his runners. They must learn to run the way they need to live, and live the way they need to run. He educates them to the reality that accepting defeat is a fundamental step to becoming a great athlete. Coach O'Connell says, "I talk more about losing than winning. … They know it is only one race; another will follow. … When the race is over, it's over—until next time."[2] His philosophy underscores that a true winner must first learn how to lose. One must understand that you will never prevail if you do not discipline yourself to get back up after a fall. You will never triumph if you lie on your back and allow self-pity to overwhelm you. You will never overcome if you do not choose to rise above. Success is the fruit of perseverance.

The apostle Paul's final words were about some of his fellow runners. *"Demas has deserted me because he loves the things of this life"* (2 Timothy 4:10). Demas had been a faithful co-worker with Paul. When Paul had been imprisoned the first time, Demas stood by him. So what happened? It could have been the earthly pursuit of anything that compromised his desire to persevere. His affection for Christ and loyalty to Christ was compromised with the secular, hedonistic, materialistic, narcissistic world around him. Whatever it was, he quit. The Bible is filled with runners who failed to go the distance.

But then there was Mark. Paul asked Timothy to bring Mark with him when he came to Rome. Mark was a runner who had stumbled coming out of the blocks. He had accompanied Paul and Barnabas on their first missionary journey, but before the journey had hardly begun, Mark turned back. He quit. We aren't told why. Discouragement? Disillusionment? Fear? Whatever the reason, he returned home. He was rejected by Paul and must have felt a deep sense of shame upon returning to his church, friends, and family. But that is not the last we hear of Mark. Thanks to his friend, Barnabas, he learned that accepting defeat is a fundamental step to becoming a great runner. You prevail by getting back up. You overcome by choosing to rise above. God is a God of second chances. And third chances. And by the end of Paul's life, he writes, *"Bring Mark with you when you come, for he will be helpful to me in my ministry"* (2 Timothy 4:11). Mark also went on to write a beautiful record of the life of Jesus, the Gospel of Mark. He became a strong, proven runner. And we benefit greatly from his life even today.

When you read the names of the people in the Hebrews Hall of Faith, something stands out. Most of them experienced serious personal failure. Abraham. Jacob. David. Moses. And yet, despite their failures, we are told: *"All these people earned a good reputation because of their faith"* (Hebrews 11:39). You'll recall that Moses disobeyed God and struck the rock with his rod rather than speaking to it as God had commanded him. For that reason, God disqualified him from entering the Promised Land. After 40 long, difficult, challenging years, he was not allowed into Canaan. He had failed, and there were consequences. But was he a failure? No. God wrote on his epitaph: *"There has never been another prophet in Israel like Moses, whom the Lord knew face to face"* (Deuteronomy 34:10). God looked at his whole race of faith. After considering everything, He inducted Moses as an honouree into the Hall of Faith. His portrait hangs on the wall of fame as an example to all that you can fail and still honour God by going the distance. We are flawed. But God sees the bigger picture of our lives. He sees the whole race before His eyes. If you have lost your spiritual balance through a sinful choice, fallen or been injured, repent, get back up and keep running. There are second chances in life, but no second chance with life. So make the commitment to go the distance.

THE CALL TO FINISH

There are many portraits hanging on the Runners Wall of Fame. There are the portraits of men and women who ran fast and broke records. There are also the portraits of men and women who did not win or break records, but who endured against adversity and symbolize the courage and tenacity of the human spirit. These are the ones who inspire all of us to endure in our race.

I stand and stare at the portrait of John Steven Akhwari. A Tanzanian runner. The number 36 is pinned on his vest. There is a look of anguish sketched into the lines on his face. A tattered bandage is wrapped around his right leg. He is scraped and bleeding. His story takes us back to the 1968 Mexico City Marathon. Three men stood on the podium to receive their medals. Akhwari was not one of them. Early in the race, he had taken a severe fall, knocked his head, damaged his knee and been trampled before he was able to get back up. A voice from deep within called him to get up and keep going. He obeyed. One hour after the first three had crossed the finish line, number 36 limped into the stadium. He was the last runner still remaining on his feet. He stopped under the arched entrance as though to ponder the sight before him and reflect upon the distance behind him. His spirit surged. He took a step. And then another. He began to run. The crowd stood and cheered. They cheered because this was a runner who symbolized the finest of the human spirit.

This celebrated race was best summed up in the words of John Steven Akhwari himself. When asked why he kept running, he answered, "My country did not send me 5,000 miles to start the race; it sent me 5,000 miles to finish the race." His example and words rouse the spirit of each of us to endure to the end, however long and hard the road.

The closer you get to the finish line, the more empowered you should be to run strong. You have proven experience. You have learned to embrace pain. The distance behind you has cultivated endurance, faith, wisdom, discernment, knowledge, relationships, and character. The trials of life and the despair of personal failures have broken, humbled and strengthened you. You are equipped with everything you need for the distance ahead of you. There is a simple test to find out whether or not your race is finished. If you are still breathing, and you are reading this book, it's not. So run! Press on.

EIGHTEEN

MOUNTING THE PODIUM

WE HAVE ALL FELT NATIONAL PRIDE SWELLING UP IN OUR HEARTS UPON witnessing one of our own country's Olympic athletes mount the podium to receive a gold medal. The medal is draped around the athlete's neck. A gold medal may as well have been draped around all of our necks. The whole country has been decorated. The flag is raised. The national anthem is played. And the whole world acknowledges that we are the best. A seismic tremour of pride and gratification pulsates along the spine of the entire nation. The chill of triumph runs up and down our backs.

The most notable award ceremonies in history may have been conducted at the Berlin Summer Olympics in 1936. The buildup to the Games was filled with intrigue. These were pre-war days and Adolph Hitler was establishing his power and control over Germany. The Olympics were a perfect venue for him to showcase his success and influence and to impress the world with Nazi Germany's glory. This was the opportune occasion to demonstrate white Aryan supremacy. There was much discussion about whether or not countries such as the USA and Canada should participate due to Hitler's anti-Semitic and racist policies. Athletes were asked to boycott the Games as a protest against the German government. The boycott fizzled.

In July 1936, a ship left New York for Berlin. On the ship was a young black athlete who would stand between Hitler and his self-aggrandizing and egotistic goals. His name was Jesse Owens. Jesse was favoured to do well at the Games. He was well aware of the tensions that existed. He was also very aware of the attention and expectation placed upon him to be a testimony against everything Hitler represented. He sensed that he had boarded a ship to do battle with Adolph Hitler.

When the Berlin Games opened, there was no notice of anti-Semitic sentiment. The opening ceremonies were elaborate and intentional as to their purpose. All eyes were on Hitler as he drove into Berlin's massive new stadium in a train of limousines. He positioned himself with his entourage in a box overlooking everything. He stood admiring the scene. Banners with swastikas waved in the breeze. Thousands of people cheered. It was more like a religious event. Hitler spoke and officially opened the Games. A runner carrying the Olympic torch entered the tunnel that led into the stadium. This was the first time the Olympic torch had been incorporated into the opening ceremonies. The Nazis had originated the idea of a torch run from Greece to the host stadium to light the Olympic flame. Everything was dramatic and staged to impress.

The atmosphere was electric as preparations were made for the running of the 100-metre, the highlight of the Olympic Games. Owens stood at the starting line waiting for the crack of the starting pistol. When the gun went off, the sprinters leapt out of the starting blocks. Owens ran like a gazelle, pulling out ahead of the other competitors. He broke across the finish line first, breaking the world record with 10.3 seconds. Hitler was furious. The leader of the host country was supposed to congratulate the winner, but Hitler refused and simply snubbed him. "Do you think that I will allow myself to be photographed with a Negro?" he retorted. It was a humiliating moment for Hitler. The young black runner had stuck his finger in the eye of the Nazi regime.

The embarrassment was only beginning. A tall, blonde German, Carl Luz Long, was favoured to win the long jump competition. Owens was a sloppy jumper and often stepped over the board. To everyone's amazement, Owens jumped a distance of 26 feet, winning a second gold medal. It was even more shocking when Owens and Luz Long walked around the stadium together, arm in arm. Owens continued on to win gold in the 200-metre race, shattering the Olympic record. And again, in the 4x100-metre relay. Four gold medals. The first black man ever to win four gold medals.

The German crowds had fallen in love with Jesse Owens. He had won international fame. He was the most famous athlete on the planet. And he had done it all on the stage Hitler had set to showcase himself and Aryan supremacy. The Nazis were infuriated. Joseph Goebbels, one of Hitler's closest associates and a principal influencer in the Nazi party, was enraged. "White humanity should be ashamed of itself," he snarled.

Jesse Owens returned home a hero. But alas, reward and honour here on earth is short-lived. Success on the track did not translate into respect off the track. This was the '30s. And there was not much acceptance of a black man in white American culture until the '60s. He was never invited to the White House. There were no honours bestowed, not even a telegram sent, by President Franklin D. Roosevelt. The greatest athlete in America was relegated to the back of the bus. But this quintessential hero competed and lived with grace. He died of lung cancer in 1980 at the age of 66.

An Unfading Wreath

The unfolding of Owens' story is the unfolding of every athlete's story. Success is soon ignored. Glory is short-lived. The winners of one year's Stanley Cup are forgotten by the time the next season begins. The praise showered upon the winners of this year's World Cup quickly turns to scorn and vilification after next year's dismal loss. The trophies on the shelf are relegated to the attic within a few generations. The acclaimed and rewarded heroes of today are soon eclipsed by the heroes of tomorrow.

The apostle Paul contrasted the awards of this world with the awards of the next. *"They do it to win a prize that will fade away, but we do it for an eternal prize"* (1 Corinthians 9:25). The winning athletes in Paul's day mounted the podium and received a laurel wreath made of wild olive, ivy, or parsley leaves. It represented the glory of the present. But the glory lasted about as long as the leaves. By contrast, the wreath with which God will award His runners will last forever. It is eternal. This truth alone should help us to prioritize our lives. It should assist us in deciding where we should be putting our time, energies, and efforts. We have one life to live. One race to run. And everything we do with our lives should have something of the eternal embedded into it. We should run with purpose in every step.

When Eric Liddell returned home from the 1924 Paris Olympics, he was a hero. He had not only won a gold medal for winning the 400-metre sprint, he had set a new world record of 47.6 seconds. His race did not end there, however. It was only beginning. God had called him to be a missionary teacher in China. He announced his intentions to an audience: "It has been a wonderful experience to compete in the Olympic games and to bring home a gold medal. But since I have been a young lad, I have had my eyes on a different prize. You see, each one of us is in a greater race than any I have run in Paris, and this race ends when God gives out the medals."[1] Eric did not know it at the time, but he would spend the rest of his life serving God in China. And he would die there in a Japanese prison camp, still running the race God had set for him. His greatest race finished, and now he awaits the medal that will never fade away.

ANTICIPATING THE PRIZE

After the apostle Paul acknowledged the end of his race, he set his pen down for a moment and lifted his eyes and thoughts heavenward. A smile crossed his face that caused the guard to look over at him quizzically. He picked up the pen again and returned to the letter he was writing to Timothy. *"And now the prize awaits me—the crown of righteousness, which the Lord, the righteous Judge, will give me on the day of his return. And the prize is not just for me but for all who eagerly look forward to his appearing"* (2 Timothy 4:8). He didn't focus on his death. He didn't concentrate his thoughts on what it would be like to be beheaded. He didn't worry about being led down the Ostian Road outside Rome to his place of execution. Rather, he anticipated the reward that one day the Lord Jesus would give to him. And he added that we can all look forward to this.

Anticipating tomorrow's prize brings fresh perspective to today's struggles. When you are struggling through school and knee-deep in homework, late hours, tired eyes, expectations, and exams, focus on the day when you will walk across the platform and receive your diploma. The hard-earned prize. When you are cleaning up after a household of small children with messy faces and dirty diapers, look forward to the day when they will be mature adults who love God and serve Him. Anticipate handing the baton of faith on to your children. Envision those little sticky-fingered, runny-nosed kids as adults running their race for Christ. Look forward to the day when they will hand on the baton of faith to the next generation of grandchildren. Focus on the prize. Focus on the glory to come. That's how Paul lived his life and approached the finish line.

EXTRINSIC REWARD

There are both extrinsic rewards and intrinsic rewards. It's not that one is good and one is bad. They are just different. An extrinsic reward is something more material or physical, such as the belt buckle and medal a runner receives at Badwater for finishing the race in under 45 hours. On the other hand, an intrinsic reward is the sheer internal satisfaction one feels for just completing the race.

The primary motivation for Kenyans is extrinsic. They run for dollars. There is no money for running at the Olympics or World Championships. Western athletes who win at the Olympics receive sizeable amounts of sponsorship money. But few Kenyans receive anything of the sort. That is why the Olympics are not a priority for Kenyans. They focus on the major city marathons. That is where the money is to be won. So one chooses which races to run with finances in mind. Why is this?

Most Kenyans live in poverty. But they are good runners. And running is the best way to become financially autonomous. A successful runner can buy a house for the family. Provide an education for one's children. The lure for prize money is very powerful. Whereas a teacher in rural Kenya might earn an annual salary of approximately $580, winning one marathon might award a runner $750. Imagine for a moment two runners competing against each other near the end of a marathon. One is a Western runner; the other is a Kenyan. They have run neck and neck for 40 kilometres and there are 2 kilometres to go. For the one, a win will mean an upgrade to a nicer car. For the other, it will mean a house for the family, an education for the children, and health care for a sick child. Who do you think is going to win?

There is wonderful extrinsic reward for running the Christian race. Heaven, and everything that will entail. No more sorrow, tears, or death. A sinless world. Magnificent beauty. Living forever with Jesus. Jesus delighted to promise us heaven. He has gone to heaven to prepare a place for us. The apostle Paul encouraged us to never give up. Why not? Because our present troubles are small compared to the glory to come. *"Fix our gaze on things that cannot be seen. For the things we see now will soon be gone, but the things we cannot see will last forever"* (2 Corinthians 4:18).

INTRINSIC REWARD

Then there are intrinsic rewards. Such rewards are basic and essential to internal fulfillment. An intrinsic reward is to appreciate and enjoy the thrill of the race as it unfolds. Valuing more and more the gift of life. Appreciating small things. Tasting chocolate. Feeling a gentle breeze against your face. Welcoming sleep as a blessing, not just as a necessity. Giving a bicycle to a needy child, bringing more joy to you than to the child. Making a positive difference in someone's life. An intrinsic reward is more than a medal. The real prize is the sweat and blood, courage, determination, perseverance, generosity, and joy that go into running. It is knowing you gave it your best. After Dean Karnazes completed the Western States 100-Mile Endurance Run, he stated,

> There was a certain spring in my stride, a newfound levity in my disposition. Even if most people I interacted with had no idea of what I'd done, I knew. That was all that mattered. The greatest rewards of high achievement, I had come to believe, were intrinsic.[2]

When Jim Willett ran the Gobi, he was not interested in being first to the finish line. It was about far more than that. He wanted to run well.

He wanted to experience the run. He wanted to be a difference-maker in people's lives. As a survivor of cancer, he had learned to embrace every day, and he wanted to help others embrace the joy and privilege of living every day to its fullest. One evening, the runners ended up at a Uyghur village called Peach Village. There were no peaches growing there. Peach Village got its name from the peach-coloured mud huts that lined the one side of the beaten path running through the centre of the community. Each door opened into a small inner court. The court enclosed a very basic kitchen with a fire pit that accommodated four families. Four cloth-covered doorways opened into each court. Each doorway led to one room lit only by a flickering light bulb that hung from the centre of the ceiling. This room was the sleeping quarters for a family. These rooms would be the runners' lodgings for the night. The toilets were located on the other side of the path in the animal pens. The villagers had warmly and hospitably opened their homes.

When most runners stopped for the night, they gathered with each other quite apart from the villagers. Jim came into the village about the middle of the pack. He unloaded his backpack and retraced his steps to the finish line on the edge of the village. Jim made it a practice at the end of each day's run to wait at the finish line and greet every runner until the last one crossed the line. The same elderly man always finished last, but knew Jim would be waiting there to greet him.

Jim sat on a small hill and took a few photos of the villagers with his camera and showed them the pictures. A small group began to gather around him. More and more assembled to get their picture taken and to see what they looked like in a photo. Soon Jim had the whole village congregating around him. He took photos. People posed, laughed, and giggled. Jim did not understand a word of Uyghur and the villagers did not understand a word of English, but a strong connection was established. They understood his care, compassion, interest, and gratitude. They understood Jim was about more than using their humble abodes to get a good sleep for himself. He was about entering into their lives and sharing some joy, even if just for a brief moment of time. He was about making a difference. He was experiencing the reward of the run.

When Jim Willett completed the Gobi run, he sat down at the post-race Awards Banquet. The last award of the evening to be presented was the *Cable-French Award*. The name of the award originates from the names of three missionary women … Mildred Cable and Eva and Francesca French … who served with China Inland Mission in eastern China at the turn of the past century. In the 1920s, they travelled northwest across the Gobi Desert. It was a wild wasteland inhabited by brigands and criminals. Someone wrote with reference to the three women that there are no fools like old fools. Mildred Cable replied that only a fool would cross the great Gobi without misgivings. They were convinced God had called them and they set out with determination to obey His call even if they looked like fools, and to leave the outcome with Him. They spent the rest of their lives visiting the lonely and rejected, giving to the poorest of the poor, feeding orphans, administering medicine to the sick and providing education for girls. The three missionaries shared the good news of Jesus and demonstrated His love and compassion in countless ways. They were attacked by bandits, endured local wars and suffered great hardship. Mildred Cable best described their focused resolve and undeterred passion to run God's race in these words:

In this trackless waste, where every restriction is removed and where you are beckoned and lured in all directions … one narrow way is the only road for you. … In the great and terrible wilderness, push on with eyes blinded to the deluding mirage, your ears deaf to the call of the seducer, and your mind un-diverted from the goal.[3]

Jesus called it faithfulness.

The Cable-French Award is presented to the competitor who best embraces what these three women embodied. A congenial spirit. A friendly attitude. An encouraging presence. The person who inspired and strengthened others. The person who embraced the culture of the desert inhabitants and took time out of his or her race to stop and eat a cantaloupe with local farmers. Or took the time to enrich and supplement the lives of isolated villagers. The Cable-French Award represented an intrinsic reward. And yes, it was presented to Jim Willett. Congratulations, Jim!

No one has run a perfect race. Jesus is the only One who did. But your life has profound intrinsic value to God. God looks at your whole life from beginning to finish. You have kept your eyes fixed on Jesus. You have run to please Him. You have run with caution lest you be deluded by mirages. You kept your ears tuned to Jesus' voice. Your mind was not diverted from the goal. When you strayed from the true path, you admitted your error and returned to the right path. You encouraged, inspired, and strengthened other runners. You found deep joy in stopping to share some water from your canteen with a thirsty runner. There are things you would do differently if you had the race to run all over again, but you can say that you experienced the thrill of the run. And the further you ran, the more fulfilling it became.

THE PODIUM

The apostle Paul wrote, *"We will all stand before the judgment seat of God. … Yes, each of us will give a personal account to God"* (Romans 14:10, 12). *"We must all stand before Christ to be judged. We will each receive whatever we deserve for the good or evil we have done in this earthly body"* (2 Corinthians 5:10). The word Paul used is *bema*. The bema was a raised platform or podium that one mounted by steps. On the bema sat a judge. This was the seat from which the judge listened to charges, presided over court proceedings and handed down decisions. It was also the raised platform at the Grecian games where the judge carefully watched the contests. When a winner was determined, the athlete would ascend the bema to stand before the judge. The judge would congratulate him and place the wreath, his award, upon his head.

As believers in Christ, we will ascend the steps of the bema to receive our awards. We will not be judged on our guilt or innocence. That question was settled long ago at the cross of Jesus when He died for our sins and we believed. We will be judged on our performance running the race in the arena of faith. The Bible is not absolutely clear on what that day will be like or just how it is all going to play out. But what is clear is the image of the Grecian games. Runners crossing the finish line. The

274

race on earth coming to an end. The winners mounting the podium and standing before the judge to receive their awards.

The greatest award to be received will be the heartwarming words that will come from the lips of Jesus, Himself. *"Well done, my good and faithful servant. ... Let's celebrate together!"* (Matthew 25:21, 23). Congratulations! You used the resources God gave you and invested them for His glory and His Kingdom. You sacrificed and gave your best, according to your ability. You endured testing and temptation. *"God blesses those who patiently endure testing and temptation. Afterward they will receive the crown of life"* (James 1:12). You remained faithful even when you faced death for your faith. Jesus said to the church in Smyrna, *"If you remain faithful even when facing death, I will give you the crown of life"* (Revelation 2:10). Jesus encouraged the church in Philadelphia, *"You have little strength, yet you obeyed my word and did not deny me. ... Hold on to what you have, so that no one will take away your crown"* (Revelation 3:8, 11). There is reward for being faithful to endure the race God has called you to run. We don't all have the same resources, skills, abilities, or opportunities, but we can all be faithful with what we've been given. One day, you will know it was worth it all. You will hear Jesus speak words of commendation to you for your faithfulness. Whatever is worth attaining is worth sacrificing for.

I find it noteworthy that Jesus will say to each faithful runner on the podium, *"You have been faithful in handling this small amount, so now I will give you many more responsibilities."* That would seem to suggest that, based on how you handled the smaller responsibilities on earth, you will be rewarded with greater authority and responsibility in heaven. How you managed the resources you were entrusted with for running the race on earth will determine the resources you are entrusted with for running the race into eternity. How you served Christ during your time on earth will ascertain how you will serve Him forever in heaven. It will establish your position of service in heaven.

LOOKING FOR THE PRIZE ON THE OTHER SIDE

This week, I watched Nik Wallenda walk a tightrope across Niagara Falls. This was the first time anyone had actually crossed directly over the falls. The Wallendas are a family that goes back two centuries with a reputation for amazing daredevil stunts. In the '40s, they were named *The Flying Wallendas,* and became known as aerialists who performed the seven-person chair pyramid. They are recognized for their skill and, particularly, their daring performance of high wire acts without safety nets. Nik Wallenda is extremely aware of the history and reputation of the Wallenda family. He believes it is not good enough to merely be known as a Wallenda. One must not merely rest back on the laurels of what was; one must be what one is today. It is not good enough to talk the talk; one must walk the walk. He is a Wallenda. That means he is one who inspires people to follow their dreams. To go beyond the limits of what is the norm. He wants to inspire people to have the courage to take the risks and follow their dreams. For him, as a Wallenda, that means walking the high wire.

Nik told reporters he had been preparing for this day for his whole life. When it was time, he got up from where he was sitting and said confidently, "Let's do it!" With that he jumped up onto the platform, gripped the pole with his hands, placed a foot on the wire and took a step. He wore a red waterproof jumpsuit and elk-skin shoes his mother had made. He walked calmly, slowly, painstakingly, step by step along the five-centimetre diameter wire, dripping wet from the mist, holding the 40-pound horizontal pole for balance. It was a spectacular scene to see him step out over the roaring falls and begin to move across the gorge of churning water and treacherous rocks 60 metres below. There was no turning back with 550 metres of cable stretched out before him. The fast-moving water below and the rising mist spiraling around him would have distracted and dizzied any other person. But Wallenda stayed composed and focused. His greatest threats were the swirling gusts of wind that blew in haphazard, random directions, and the heavy mist that made it difficult to see. It was like battling one's way through driving rain. At times, he looked like a tiny lone figure walking on nothing but the white mist.

At the halfway point, he began the long, steady climb up toward the Canadian side. During the walk, reporters were able to speak with Wallenda and asked him what was going through his mind. He said he was just staying focused on the other side. At the 22-minute mark, he was asked again how he was feeling. He replied that he felt strained, drained, and increasingly weak both mentally and physically. His hands were growing numb. And then he said something that, I think, stirred the spirit of every person listening in on the conversation. Nik Wallenda is a strong believer in Christ, and must have had the journey of life in mind when he answered: "I'm just looking at the prize on the other side, and that anticipation is building … I want to get through that homestretch and hit the finish line."

"Nik, what is it that will carry you to that finish line?" asked the reporter.

"Pure endurance," answered Nik. "Endurance … and this audience that is here that I'm hearing at this point." The crowds on the Canadian side were cheering wildly. "I'm just starting to hear them, believe it or not," he said. "Those falls are so loud that, until now, I haven't been able to hear them. … But I'm hearing them, and that's what will get me across to the other side."

He reached the other side in 25 minutes, 17 seconds. The spectators were yelling, "Welcome to Canada, Nik! Welcome to Canada!" A big smile crossed his face. To everyone's surprise, he ran the last few metres. He fell into the arms of his uncle, who was waiting for him at the finish line and the two embraced. He was then met by two grinning customs agents who asked him for his passport. Nik joked with them as he searched for the folded piece of wet plastic with his passport tucked inside. "And, no," he bantered, "I'm not carrying anything over. I promise." When questioned by the customs official regarding the purpose for his trip, he responded, "To inspire people around the world."

"You have," she replied.

The name *Christian* is more than a name. It represents a family with a history that goes back 21 centuries to the God-man, Jesus, Who gave His life on a cross and promised eternal life to everyone who would believe in Him. The family has had its challenges. It has been misunderstood, misrepresented and misjudged. It has been ravaged, broken, and violated by frauds and deceivers. It has been held hostage by religion and politics. But the true members of the family have stood true to their faith in Christ, even to death. Despite tremendous hostility against them, they have carried the good news and the compassion of Christ into the entire world. And today, it is important that we represent Christ and His family well. It is not good enough to just talk the talk; we must walk the walk.

The Christian life is filled with churning waters, treacherous rocks, winds of adversity that blow one way and then unexpectedly the other, distractions, danger and risk. Be faithful. Keep going. Don't look back. Don't look down. Keep looking forward. As you approach the other side, there is a long steady climb that will strain and weaken you mentally and physically. But you have been preparing for this day your entire life. Stay focused on the other side. Anticipate the prize on the other side. As you move through the homestretch and close in on the finish line, feel the anticipation building. It is now pure endurance that will carry you to the finish line. And the crowds. Do you hear them cheering? They've been difficult to hear up to now due to the thunderous roar and commotion of everything else in life. But as you get closer to the finish line, you begin to hear them. The believers of all the ages are cheering you in. "Welcome to heaven! Welcome to heaven!" they cry. You're almost there. You sprint the last few metres to the finish line and collapse into the arms of Jesus.

You present your passport. Issuing country: heaven. There are two dates of birth … your date of natural birth and your date of spiritual birth. Date of expiry: eternity. It is stamped with the blood of Jesus. You are not carrying anything else with you. You carry nothing with you to the other side except your passport and your record of what you have done for Christ. You are questioned regarding the purpose for your journey. Your answer: to glorify God and inspire other people in their journey of faith. Your heart is full. You can barely contain yourself. You have arrived. And you know that one day you will mount the podium and receive the award for faithfulness. It will be an award that will empower you to serve and glorify Christ more fully and completely with greater magnitude, capacity, and extent as you continue your run into eternity. Your spirit pounds with anticipation as did Paul's when he approached the other side. *"And now the prize awaits me—the crown of righteousness, which the Lord, the righteous Judge, will give me on the day of his return. And the prize is not just for me, but for all who eagerly look forward to his appearing"* (2 Timothy 4:8).

NINETEEN

LEAVING A FOOTPRINT

THE WRITER OF HEBREWS REMINDS US THAT THERE ARE RUNNERS coming up behind us who are weaker and less experienced on the path of faith. Run your race with them in mind. *"Mark out a straight path for your feet so that those who are weak and lame will not fall but become strong"* (Hebrews 12:13). Walk the path and prepare the way for them. Walk the path and leave it in a little better condition for the next generation.

The Bedouin are desert-dwelling tribespeople. I have learned much from them regarding biblical customs by watching the way they survive in the desert, relate to each other, practice their cultural traditions, dress for harsh conditions, lead their sheep and walk the desert paths. A quoted Bedouin saying is, "You keep a path clear for the next generation by walking it." When a Bedouin walks along a path, he or she picks up stones or obstacles so the person who travels along the same path next will not trip and fall. The principle applies to life and the next generation following along the same path in your footsteps.

It begins with you walking or running the path of this earth. When you tread upon a rock or stick that could cause another runner to trip and fall, pick it up. Throw it off to the side. Clear the trail for others. When you endure adversity or failure, walk the path with faith, power, patience, love, and grace. When you achieve success, walk the path with humility and faithfulness. There are weaker runners following in your footsteps. They are listening to your words. Interpreting your actions.

Picking up your attitudes. Adopting your values. Investigating your faith. Exploring the path you run. They are watching how you run your race, so show them how to run it.

The challenge for parents and grandparents is that kids are the world's best tape recorders and the world's poorest interpreters. For example, a child grows up believing dad could never be pleased. That may be an accurate recording. But then the child construes that to mean that one's heavenly Father can never be pleased. That is a wrong interpretation. Yet it is one that has serious implications for the way the child will run his or her own race of faith. Or, a child grows up listening to mom and dad always fighting. The mind of the child records the hostility and angry words. Unfortunately, he or she interprets this to mean that marriage is a battleground and not worth the risk. Or a poor interpretation may lead them to believe that this is what marriage is and to fall into the same kind of marriage for themselves. Everything a child records is subject to an interpretation. And every interpretation has emotional and spiritual implications for the life they will live and the race they will run. Your legacy deposited in the child usually embraces the interpretation deduced by the child.

How common it is to look at a photo of a young person and say, "Oh, I can see his father in him." Or, "She's looking more and more like her mother." The same eyes. The same forehead. The identical smile. But heredity extends to more than biological traits and physical appearance. You are passing along attitudes, behavioural traits, character, beliefs, perceptions, and worldview. Things that have huge impact for generations.

STANDING WHERE YOU STAND

I love to tell stories to our grandkids. One evening during a family vacation, we were sitting around a campfire beside a lake. All the kids were asking for the story of the night. They wanted the story even before popcorn or S'mores. All week I had been telling stories from the life of Elijah, God's prophet. I can be quite animated if I have to be. I had eaten from the beaks of ravens. Raised the dead. Called up the wicked King Ahab for his sin. Called down fire from heaven. You can read all about it in 1 and 2 Kings. This was the last night of our time together.

This night's story was about Elijah's exit from earth into heaven. Elijah's departure from earth was unique. He never died. He knew he had finished his course down here and that the time of his departure was near. So he asked his friend and disciple, Elisha, to join him for a portion of his last earthly journey. At various places along the way, Elijah encouraged Elisha to stay back while he went on alone. Elisha refused to stay behind. Elisha knew his master and mentor was about to leave this earth, and he was determined to be in attendance when that moment arrived. Elijah tried again and again to persuade Elisha to stay back, but he could not shake the younger man loose. Finally they came to the Jordan River. Elijah folded his cloak and struck the water of the Jordan. Miraculously, the waters divided and the two walked across on dry ground.

When they arrived on the other side of the Jordan, Elijah turned to Elisha and asked him if there was anything he could do for him before he was taken up. Elisha did not miss a beat and asked for a double share of Elijah's spirit. He was asking that he might be the one chosen to be Elijah's successor. He desired to be the next in line of God's prophets. The one to speak for God, work miracles through God's power and represent God to the people of Israel. His request was also an imploration that God give him a double share of blessing and use him beyond how He had blessed and used Elijah. Elijah told him his request would be granted if he witnessed him being taken up. Elisha nodded his head and assured the older man that when that time arrived, he would be present.

As they were walking along, suddenly an angelic chariot of fire drawn by horses of fire swooped down between the two men and swept up Elijah. In the confusion, Elisha cried out, "I see it! I see it!"

At this point in the story, I pointed toward the sky and cried out, "Look up! Look up!" All eyes looked straight up. "Do you see it?" I shouted. "Do you see it?" As all eyes gazed heavenward, I did one of those "don't do as I do" things. I threw a rag doused in gasoline into the campfire. There was a giant *ka-boom*. Immediately, all eyes returned to earth. The kids' eyes grew as big as saucers as they stared in astonishment at the sensational wonder that had just occurred before them.

"I saw it!" cried one of the kids.

"So did I!" exclaimed another.

Even the adults got caught up in the moment. The grandkids looked at me like I was some astounding wonder-worker. It felt good. "How did you do that, Grandpa?" one of them asked. I would not say. The secret has remained with me until now.

But the story didn't stop there. Elijah's cloak drifted down out of the sky. Elisha ran over and picked it up. The same cloak that had separated the Jordan River was now in his hands. Elijah's cloak would be worn and used from here on by Elisha. This was God's way of saying that indeed, Elisha was now God's prophet. Elisha wrapped the coat around him and strolled back toward the Jordan. When he reached the river, he took the cloak and struck the water with it just as Elijah had done. And it happened again. The waters divided. Elisha walked across on dry ground. He held the cloak close to his chest. The cloak was like a baton. It had been passed from Elijah to Elisha. Elijah had run his race. Elisha had received and learned much from his mentor. Now it was Elisha's turn to run. The power of God was in his hands. And God was about to bless and use Elisha in exponentially greater ways.

My attempt to mesmerize the kids with my life lesson was not over. I had their attention. To illustrate Elijah's cloak falling from the sky, I had pre-arranged someone from behind the heads of my captivated audience to throw my old camping coat into the air. I reached up, caught the coat out of the air and held it high. "I have it!" I shouted. "I have it!" Their eyes opened even wider as they looked around to see where the coat had come from.

"Do you see what this means?" I asked them. I wasn't sure they understood. So I lined everyone up in a semi-circle around the campfire from the oldest to the youngest. The procession led from me right down to baby Malakye, who, though it was far past his bedtime, was sitting wide-eyed in his car seat. I then held out the old coat and said it represented everything about me. Everything I stood for. It represented everything they learned and would receive from me. And then I began to pass it along the line. As it moved from hand to hand and person to person, I explained that one day I would be gone to heaven. They were next in line. Just as I had worn the coat, they were to wear the coat. The coat was like a baton being passed to them. Just as I had run my race, they were to run their race.

After the coat had passed through everyone's hands, it was laid over young Malakye who decided that it made a warm blanket, and fell asleep. I still wasn't sure they grasped what I wanted them to understand. So I asked again, "What am I saying here?"

Immediately, seven-year-old Austin piped up, "Grandpa, it means that one day I'm going to be standing where you are." He got it! I assured him that what he said was true. I addressed all of my attentive listeners and affirmed, "One day, you will be where I am. One day, you will tell the story of God. One day, you will pass the story of faith by your life and words to the next generation."

I don't want my kids and grandkids to keep pace with me. I want them to exceed me. I don't want them to "measure up" to me. I want them to grow beyond me. I want God to bless and use them, not in the same ways, but in greater ways. One day the next generation will stand where you stand. Where will they be standing?

MARATHON OF HOPE

I was returning home from a canoe trip in Northern Ontario. We were descending a long grade on the Trans-Canada Highway just outside Sudbury. We could see flashing red lights and a lot of commotion at the foot of the hill and wondered what we were coming upon. It soon became apparent. A runner. An unusual but recognizable gait. Step-hop, step … step-hop, step … step-hop, step. The extra short quick hop on the one leg allowed time for the springs on a prosthetic leg to reset after each step. The gait was unmistakable. Terry Fox! The Marathon of Hope! Terry had set off from St. John's, Newfoundland, and was running west across Canada to raise awareness and money for cancer research. He had begun his trans-Canada Marathon of Hope in relative obscurity, but was quickly becoming a national icon. The media was covering his story. Everyone was talking about him. We came quite unexpectedly upon him. Cars were pulled over to the side of the road. People were outside their vehicles with cameras in hand. We slowed down to get a good look. I rolled down the window to get a clearer view. I waved. Terry gave a rapid glance my way. I couldn't find my camera and regretted not getting a good up-close photo as we passed by. In just a few seconds, I had been a witness to history.

When Terry Fox was only 18 years old, he was diagnosed with osteosarcoma. He had a malignant cancerous tumour in his right leg. Four days later, his leg was amputated. Terry had been very active in sports both in his high school in Port Coquitlam, British Columbia, and his first year at Simon Fraser University. The night before his surgery, his high school basketball coach gave him an article about an amputee, Dick Traum, who had recently completed the New York City Marathon. Traum was the first runner to complete such an event with a prosthetic leg. That night, Terry read the story and was so inspired by it that he fell asleep with a dream … a dream of running across Canada.

The following 16 months of recovery made a mark on Terry. He saw incredible suffering. He watched young, strong bodies waste away. He witnessed kids his own age die in nearby beds. When he was released from the cancer clinic, he left with a new, burning purpose. He believed that, as a survivor, he carried a great responsibility to do something to help defeat this dreaded disease. Terry said:

> I was rudely awakened by the feelings that surrounded and coursed through the cancer clinic. There were faces with the brave smiles, and the ones who had given up smiling. There were feelings of hopeful denial, and the feelings of despair. My quest would not be a selfish one. I could not leave knowing these faces and feelings would still exist, even though I would be set free from mine. Somewhere the hurting must stop … and I was determined to take myself to the limit for this cause.[1]

As with everything Terry did, his dream of running across Canada was tackled with fervour. He pushed his wheelchair up steep mountains and along rugged logging roads until his hands bled. He began a running program and ran 101 days until he had worked himself up to 23 miles a day. By day's end, the stump of his leg was bruised, blistered, raw, and bleeding. But there was more than physical training. There was the tough task of raising financial support. Terry hoped to raise $1 million. The challenge of raising support was much more difficult than he had expected. The Canadian Cancer Society was skeptical and corporate sponsors were slow to respond. But it happened. On April 12, 1980, Terry Fox dipped his prosthetic foot in the Atlantic Ocean at St. John's harbour and set off for the adventure of his life. He filled two bottles with ocean water. He intended to keep one as a personal memory aid and empty the other into the Pacific Ocean upon the completion of his run. His plan was to run from St. John's, Newfoundland, to Victoria, British Columbia, 8,500 kilometres.

The Marathon of Hope was finally a reality. A dream unfolding. A supportive friend, Doug Alward, to drive the support van and cook meals. Terry, a curly-haired, good-looking, muscular young runner with a set, unflinching jaw and a determined, unbreakable spirit. A ribbon of highway that would lead him through small villages and big cities, but take him to something bigger than he had ever imagined. Terry had made a promise to himself that, should he live, he would prove himself deserving of life. He ran the way we should live our lives. With hope. With determination and courage to endure whatever life brings your way. With a belief that no matter how far your road takes you, life is a highway that stretches out before you, flourishing with opportunity, beauty, and challenge. A dream to pursue. A purpose to achieve. A desire to make a difference. A promise to prove yourself deserving of life. A readiness to go to the limit for a higher cause.

His fiberglass and steel artificial limb gave him that recognizable gait. He wore shorts and a T-shirt with a map of Canada and maple leaf printed across the front. He ran about a marathon a day through driving rain, bitter wind, ice storms, and burning sun. But the further he ran, the more people caught hold of his dream. By the time he reached Montreal on June 22, he had collected $200,000 in donations. About the same time, the Marathon of Hope caught the attention of Isadore Sharp, the founder and CEO of Four Seasons Hotels and Resorts. Sharp decided to get involved. He provided food and lodging at his hotels en route and pledged $2 per mile to the run. He convinced close to 1,000 other corporations to do the same. Donations began to pour in. Terry dreamed of $1 from every Canadian. Why not a goal of $23 million?

Terry was welcomed into Ontario by the cheers of thousands of people along the roads. The Ontario Provincial Police gave him an escort that would remain with him across the whole of the province. Crowds lined the streets in Ottawa as Canadians were becoming more and more deeply moved by Terry's efforts. He was welcomed by Governor General Edward Schreyer and Prime Minister Pierre Trudeau. As he made his way through the heart of Ontario, he was joined by NHL hockey star Darryl Sittler, who presented him with his 1980 All-Star jersey. He was also met by Hockey Hall of Famer Bobby Orr, who presented him with a cheque for $25,000.

His run across the north shore of Lake Huron and over the beautiful but rugged mountainous landscape north of Lake Superior took its toll on Terry's body. Shin splints. Inflamed knee. Cysts on his stump. Dizzy spells. It was a dull day just outside of Thunder Bay when Terry Fox experienced an intense coughing fit and chest pains. He could see the crowds of people ahead of him lining both sides of Highway 17 encouraging him to keep going. He did. At least for a few more miles. But he could go no further. Short of breath and with continuing chest pains, he was taken to the hospital. The diagnosis? The cancer had returned and spread to his lungs. The run was over after 143 days and 5,373 kilometres. The day before, he had run 43 kilometres and now he couldn't walk across the street without collapsing.

Terry was flown back to Vancouver. That week, the CTV television network organized a nationwide telethon that raised more than $10 million. Isadore Sharp sent a telegram to Terry that was pinned to his hospital bed. It said Terry had begun something that would continue. Every year a fundraising run would be held in his name to continue the fight against cancer until a cure was found. As Terry battled his disease through the winter, donations continued to pour in. By April, over $23 million had been raised. Terry Fox had become a household name. One could reach Terry by simply addressing a letter to "Terry Fox, Canada." He was the youngest person to ever receive the *Companion of the*

Order of Canada, the nation's top civilian honour. The *Ottawa Citizen* described the nation's response to Terry Fox as "one of the most powerful outpourings of emotion and generosity in Canada's history."[2]

Ten months after the end of Terry's run, on June 28, 1981, he fell into a coma and died. He was one month short of his 23rd birthday. There was a nationwide mourning. Canadian flags were lowered to half-mast, an honour usually reserved for statesmen. He was a true Canadian Pheidippides. Addressing the House of Commons, Prime Minister Trudeau said,

> It occurs very rarely in the life of a nation that the courageous spirit of one person unites all people in the celebration of his life and in the mourning of his death. ... We do not think of him as one who was defeated by misfortune but as one who inspired us with the example of the triumph of the human spirit over adversity.[3]

Terry's story didn't end with his death. His memory continues. The dream endures. His legacy of perseverance over adversity, courage, hope, being a difference-maker and going beyond the limits for a higher cause remains. The fundraising run Isadore Sharp had promised continues. Terry had agreed to Sharp's proposal on one condition, that the run be non-competitive. There were to be no winners and no losers. The first Terry Fox Run was held in September 1981. Over 300,000 people participated, raising $3.5 million. The Run raised more than $20 million in the first six years. The Terry Fox Run has grown into an international event with millions of participants. Since Terry's first run, over $600 million has been raised in his name for cancer research.

Terry left a footprint in people's hearts. He stands as a clear and unmistakable reminder that your life can keep giving long after you are physically gone. In fact, your impact upon people for good or bad never ends with your physical death. If you live your life right, the positive impact of your life can be exponential. It will influence and enthuse those who follow you for many years to come.

PASSING THE BATON

I like the image of running a relay race. You carry a baton in your hand that contains the DNA of your life. How you managed success. How you handled failure. How you made a difference in the lives of others. The love and compassion you showed to others. The grade you would receive for endurance, faithfulness, humility, meekness, integrity, servanthood, self-sacrifice, and obedience to God. It's the big picture of your life. The statement your life made. It's all contained in the small baton, and you place it in the hand of the next runner. The next generation. They grasp it. Your race ends. And now they run.

God wants you to live your life to the full so that when you pass the baton, you will do it with a profound sense of fulfillment and joy. In the words of George Bernard Shaw, the famed Irish playwright,

This is the true joy in life … being a force of nature, instead of a feverish, selfish little clod of ailments and grievances complaining that the world will not devote itself to making you happy. I am of the opinion that my life belongs to the whole community and as long as I live, it is my privilege to do for it whatever I can. I want to be thoroughly used up when I die. For the harder I work the more I live. I rejoice in life for its own sake. Life is no brief candle to me. It's a sort of splendid torch which I've got to hold up for the moment and I want to make it burn as brightly as possible before handing it on to future generations.[4]

In an earlier chapter, I talked about the art of passing the baton. The race is won or lost in how successfully each runner passes the baton to the next runner. This is possibly the most significant thing you will do in your entire life. What you hand off to the next generation will have a greater long-term impact than anything else you do. How you live your life and pass the baton of faith to the next generation will have a huge influence both in the kind of race they run and the outcome of their race of faith.

When the apostle Paul wrote his last letter to Timothy (2 Timothy), he was passing the baton. He recognized that he had finished his race and had remained faithful. Now it was Timothy's responsibility to grasp the baton and run. He reminded Timothy that he had been taught well by his mother and grandmother. He was well aware of what Paul had taught, how he had lived his life and what his life purpose was. Paul had lived very openly before him. Timothy had witnessed his faith, patience, love, and endurance. Now Paul urged him to remain faithful to follow his example and to the things he had been taught in the Scriptures. He urged Timothy to fully carry out the ministry God had given him in both favourable and adverse times. Throughout the letter, Paul was pressing the baton up into Timothy's hand. He cried, "This is what you have seen in me. Receive it! Take hold!" Then he released the baton and shouted, "Run, Timothy! Don't look back. Run! Run!"

Paul instructed Timothy to *"teach these truths to other trustworthy people who will be able to pass them on to others"* (2 Timothy 2:2). Just as Paul had passed the baton of faith to Timothy, he coached Timothy to be mindful that he must pass the baton on to others. And then they must pass the baton on to others after them. Paul's final letter is a reminder to all of us that when your race is over, the race is not over. Other runners will be running the course. Run with them in mind. Leave a good footprint.

ENDNOTES

Chapter One
1. Christopher McDougall, *Born to Run*, (New York: Alfred A. Knopf, 2010), 124.
2. Miles J. Stanford, *The Green Letters*, (Grand Rapids: Zondervan Publishing House, 1975), 81.
3. Christopher McDougall, *Born to Run*, 112.

Chapter Two
1. Dean Karnazes, *Ultramarathon Man*, (New York: Jeremy P. Tarcher/ Penguin, 2006), 82.
2. *Chariots of Fire*. Dir. Hugh Hudson. Perf. Ian Charleson. (Allied Stars Ltd., Enigma Productions, 1981).
3. Karnazes, *Ultramarathon Man*, 276.

Chapter Three
1. Dean Karnazes, *Ultramarathon Man*, (New York: Jeremy P. Tarcher/ Penguin, 2007), 220.
2. Ibid., 154.
3. Ibid., 21.
4. Ibid., 23.
5. Toby Tanser, *More Fire*, (Yardley: Westholme Publishing, 2008), x.
6. Rick Ball, http://rickballruns.com/home.html

Chapter Four
1. John C. Maxwell, *The 21 Irrefutable Laws of Leadership,* (Nashville: Thomas Nelson, Inc., 1998), 28.
2. http://runjimmirun.blogspot.com

Chapter Five
1. Jim Willett, *Taking it to the next level* (iRun magazine, Feb. 2011).
2. John Ortberg, *If You Want to Walk on Water, You've Got to Get Out of the Boat,* (Grand Rapids: Zondervan, 2001), 71,72.
3. Gordon MacDonald, *A Resilient Life,* (Nashville: Thomas Nelson, Inc., 2004), 73.
4. Ibid., 76.
5. Terry Wardle, *Draw Close to the Fire,* (Siloam Springs: Leafwood Publishers, 2004), 219.
6. Dean Karnazes, *Ultramarathon Man,* (New York: JeremyP. Tarcher/Penguin, 2007), 64.
7. Ibid., 64.
8. © Copyright Bible Prayer Fellowship. All rights reserved. Used by permission of Bible Prayer Fellowship.

Chapter Six
1. Toby Tanser, *More Fire,* 118.
2. Ibid., 115.
3. Ibid., 115.
4. Ibid., 116.
5. Ibid., 116.
6. Ibid., 116.
7. Ibid., 97.
8. Ibid., 263.
9. Ibid., 273.
10. Ibid., 90.
11. Jeff Galloway, *Marathon: You Can Do It,* (Bolinas: Shelter Publications Inc., 2001), 181,182.

12. Cited in Sherwood Eliot Wert and Kersten Beckstrom, eds., *Topical Encyclopedia of Living Questions*, (Minneapolis: Bethany House, 1982), 227.

13. Christopher McDougall, *Born to Run*, 212.

14. NAS

Chapter Seven

1. Toby Tanser, *More Fire*, 116.

2. Ibid., 126.

3. Stephen R. Covey, *The 7 Habits of Highly Effective People*, (New York: Free Press, 2004), 34.

4. Toby Tanser, *More Fire*, 282.

Chapter Eight

1. Toby Tanser, *More Fire*, 116.

2. Ibid., 249.

3. Ibid., 251.

4. Stephen R. Covey, *The 7 Habits of Highly Effective People*, 98.

Chapter Nine

1. Dean Karnazes, *Ultramarathon Man*, 143.

2. Ravi Zacharias, *The Grand Weaver*, (Grand Rapids: Zondervan, 2007), 183.

3. http://www.vancouversun.com/opinion/Legally+blind+skier+embodies+Olympic+ideal/2574986/story.html.

4. http://www.blindskiersedge.org/about.html.

Chapter Ten

1. http://www.famousquotes.com/show/1054332/.

2. Eric Metaxas, *Bonhoeffer: Pastor, Martyr, Prophet, Spy*, (Nashville: Thomas Nelson, 2010), 499.

3. Ann Spangler and Lois Tverberg, *Sitting at the Feet of Rabbi Jesus*, (Grand Rapids: Zondervan, 2009), 39.

4. Stephen R. Covey, *The 7 Habits of Highly Effective People*, 263.

Chapter Eleven

1. William Barkley, *The Letter to the Hebrews, rev. ed., The Daily Study Bible Series*, (Philadelphia: Westminster Press, 1976), 173.
2. http://www.marathonandbeyond.com/choices/ainsleig.htm.
3. Ibid.
4. Charles Wilkins, *The Wild Ride*, (Vancouver: Stanton Atkins & Dosil Publishers, 2010), 72.
5. Ibid., 66.
6. Ibid., 156.
7. Ibid., 159.
8. Redman, Matt; Ingram, Jason; Wanstall, Timothy. *Never Once.* Sony/ATV Timber Publishing, Chrysalis Music Limited, 2011.
9. Marshall Ulrich, *Running on Empty*, (New York: Penguin Group Inc., 2011), 207.
10. Ibid., 197.
11. *The Distance of Truth.* Executive Producer Roger Hendrix. (Pageturner Productions Inc., 2008).

Chapter Twelve

1. http://rayzahab.com/home.
2. Jeff Galloway, *Marathon: You Can Do It*, 78.
3. Ibid., 80.
4. Marshall Ulrich, *Running on Empty*, 68.
5. Ibid., 68,69.
6. Rick Warren, *The Purpose-Driven Life*, (Grand Rapids: Zondervan, 2002), 190.
7. Ibid., 190.

Chapter Thirteen

1. Christopher McDougall, *Born to Run*, 92.
2. Ibid., 95-98.
3. Ibid., 97.
4. Ibid., 98.
5. Dean Karnazes, *Ultramarathon Man*, 262.
6. Ibid., 33.

7. Paul L. Maier, *Eusebius—The Church History: A New Translation with Commentary*, (Grand Rapids: Kregel Publications, 1999), 293.

8. Ibid., 295.

9. Ibid., 298.

10. Dean Karnazes, *Ultramarathon Man,* 262.

Chapter Fourteen

1. www.workshopsforthehelpingprofessions.ca.

2. *Running the Sahara.* Executive Producers Matt Damon and Jim Van Eerden. (A LIVEPLANET and ALLENTOWN PRODUCTION, 2007).

3. Peter Scazzero, *Emotionally Healthy Spirituality*, (Nashville: Integrity Publishers, 2006), 171.

4. Kristine Carlson, *Don't Sweat the Small Stuff for Women*, (New York: Hyperion, 2001), 240.

5. Rudolph W. Giuliani, *Leadership*, (New York: Hyperion, 2002), 344.

6. Rudolph W. Giuliani, *Leadership*, 352.

Chapter Fifteen

1. Toby Tanser, *More Fire,* introductory page.

2. http://www.poets.net/2008/08/classic-poetry-pheidippides-robert.html.

3. Toby Tanser, *More Fire*, 93.

4. Ibid., 100.

5. Ibid., 283.

6. Janet Benge and Geoff Benge, *Eric Liddell: Something Greater Than Gold*, (Seattle: YWAM Publishing, 1998), 66.

7. http://www.npr.org/templates/story/story.php?storyId=136170965.

Chapter Sixteen

1. *Running the Sahara.* Executive Producers Matt Damon and Ji Van Eerden. (A LIVEPLANET and ALLENTOWN PRODUCTI 2007).

2. http://www.youtube.com/watch?v=XrXsaoR7vug&NR=1.

3. Marshall Ulrich, *Running on Empty*, 106.

4. Ibid., 166.

5. Dean Karnazes, *Ultramarathon Man*, 152.

6. Ibid., 155,156.

7. Christopher McDougall, *Born to Run*, 89.

8. Ibid., 88.

9. Stephen R. Covey, *The 7 Habits of Highly Effective People*, 48-52.

10. Ibid., 49.

11. Ibid., 50.

12. Toby Tanser, *More Fire*, 125.

13. Ibid., 125.

14. Ibid., 116.

Chapter Seventeen

1. Barry J. Beitzel, *The New Moody Atlas of the Bible*, (Chicago: Moody Publishers, 2009), 253.

2. Toby Tanser, *More Fire*, 157.

Chapter Eighteen

1. Janet Benge and Geoff Benge, *Eric Liddell: Something Greater Than Gold*, 69.

2. Dean Karnazes, *Ultramarathon Man*, 161.

3. http://www.4deserts.com/gobimarch/location_culture.

Chapter Nineteen

1. Frank Cosentino, *Not Bad, Eh?: Great Moments in Canadian Sports History*, (Burnstown: General Store Publishing House Inc., 1990),

een, "*Terry Fox: His run taught Canadians to hope,*" ember 29, 1980, 42.

ner, *Terry Fox: His Story*, (Toronto: McClelland &

ovey, *The 7 Habits of Highly Effective People*, 299.